E
181
P512

Palmer, Frederick
     John J. Pershing, General
of the Armies

DATE DUE

OCT 23 '74			
NOV 20 '74			
DEC 11 '74			
MAR 11 '8			

JOHN J. PERSHING

John J. Pershing

General of the Armies

A BIOGRAPHY

by

Frederick Palmer

GREENWOOD PRESS, PUBLISHERS
WESTPORT, CONNECTICUT

CONTENTS

	An Essential Foreword	vii
1.	The Approach	1
2.	Boyhood	4
3.	At West Point	14
4.	In the Old West	25
5.	He Was Ready	35
6.	Pacifying the Sultans	46
7.	"Invaluable"	55
8.	Reward and Test	64
9.	In Room 223	72
10.	On the Way	82
11.	Behind the Cheers	87
12.	Initialed "J.J.P."	100
13.	Plan and Goal	111
14.	Plan Ready—Goal Set	120
15.	At Chaumont	133
16.	Counted Minutes	140
17.	Mould of Discipline	148
18.	In Face of Disaster	154
19.	A Valley Forge in France	159
20.	"Out" or "In"	167
21.	Baker in France	175
22.	"All We Have"	183
23.	An Ordeal in Council	194
24.	No Gallery Play	208
25.	The Château-Thierry Crisis	223
26.	Not "Too Proud to Fight"	234

CONTENTS

27. Fifth and Last 239
28. Turning the Tide 244
29. A Crisis in the SOS 250
30. Closing the Marne Salient 265
31. Now for St. Mihiel 273
32. His Answer to Foch 281
33. St. Mihiel 288
34. Against Terrific Odds 298
35. Meuse-Argonne: Next Phases 313
36. Grim Mud Bound Fighting 320
37. Behind His Back 326
38. For Unconditional Surrender 333
39. On to "Cease Firing" 337
40. Reversing the Machine 344
41. Quiet Days 356
42. Over There in Spirit 365
43. Seeing It Through Again 373

An Essential Foreword

In arranging to write this biography of General John J. Pershing I stipulated that it should not be published until after his death. It was not to be submitted to him or to appear in the light of an official biography or one authorized by his heirs. I would write of him as I knew him, guided by his own terse remark of "There's the record," of which I have had opportunity to make a thorough study.

Another reason why a foreword is essential is that the manuscript was well under way before World War II began. In January, 1940, a few days before I started for Europe, it was delivered to the publisher who set it in type. At the time the people of the United States little more contemplated that we should send another crusading army to Europe than we had contemplated in 1914 that we should send the first one over there. Our faith, in the winter of 1939-40, that the Maginot Line would hold was heartened by Prime Minister Chamberlain's assurance that Hitler had missed the bus.

After the lapse of six years since the manuscript was set in type I have chosen to leave it unchanged. I have, however, written two additional closing chapters. These are mainly based on occasional talks with the General during the period before Pearl Harbor and the subsequent progress of the war. On this background the talks provide perspective on his role as commander of the first crusading army. They singularly reveal the character and spirit of the man. His reflections when old age precluded further action complete the account of his career.

He lived to have his wish fulfilled to see World War II through. Having held fast to his conviction from Armistice Day, 1918, that another world war could be avoided, if he had been allowed to compel the unconditional surrender of the enemy he fought in the first, he lived to see the unconditional surrender of that enemy in the second. His faint heartbeats would not permit the realization of his dream that he might see the second AEF in its hour of victory. In lieu of this in that hour he received this cable of tribute from the commander of the second AEF:

"8 May 1946

"Dear General Pershing:

"For the second time in less than thirty years American arms are celebrating with their Allies victory in Europe. As the commander of this second American Expeditionary Force, I should like to acknowledge to you, the leader of the first, our obligation for the part you have played in the present victory.

"In the Mediterranean campaign of '42-'43 and the European operation of '44 and '45 a very important factor in American success has been the tactical judgment and skill and the identical command and staff conceptions of our regimental, divisional, corps and army commanders. These abilities and common doctrines have facilitated smoothness and speed in handling large formations and permitted a crushing application of tactical power. They have resulted directly from our magnificent military educational system, a system that was completely reorganized and expanded under your wise leadership and with your unstinting support.

"The stamp of Benning, Sill, Riley and Leavenworth is on every American battle in Europe and Africa. The sons

of the men you led in battle in 1918 have much for which
to thank you.

Eisenhower"

A large proportion of the soldier host in the second
AEF were sons of men who served in the first AEF. From
their fathers they had learned what it meant to be "in the
Army now" and in the tradition of the Pershing school.
Among the leaders in World War II who had their train-
ing as youngsters in that tough exacting school were
General George C. Marshall, the Chief of Staff, and under
General Eisenhower in Europe there were Generals Omar
Bradley, George S. Patton, Courtney H. Hodges and
William H. Simpson, and in the Pacific General Douglas
MacArthur and Walter Krueger, as well as many of their
key subordinates. Among the Pershing disciples who
trained the army at home in World War II were Generals
Lesley McNair and Hugh Drum. We shall see how the
old master "J. J. P." watched the progress of all his dis-
ciples with both pride and discrimination.

Eisenhower missed combat experience under Pershing
in France. He was held at home in 1917-18 as a drill-
master along with more than half of our regular officers
who looked forward to being "over there" for the decisive
offensive in 1919, which was won in November, 1918. But
the Pershing stamp was upon him in the demanding cables
from GHQ in France for the firm training in the home
cantonments. It remained upon our little army in its low
period between the two wars when it lacked numbers and
equipment. As a star pupil in the "system that was completely reorganized and expanded under your wise leadership and with your unstinted support" Eisenhower singled
himself out for future high service.

Not only because, in World War II, I saw our army on
the new as well as the old battle fields in France, but
because I also had a view of our operations in the Pacific,

I was the more tempted to form certain comparisons between the army tasks of the two wars, without ever overlooking the fact that the second on two overseas fronts
was far the greater. The emphasis of the comparisons was
in the extent to which we had profited by the lessons of
World War I by taking leaves out of the book of past experience and where we learned afresh from present experience.

Consider the situation in 1941 if there had been no
pioneer AEF, if we had not sent a great army to the Rhine
in 1918. Suppose that in 1941 we had had no experience
in forming and handling large formations to apply "a
crushing application of power" to immense veteran European armies. Suppose that our last previous school of
battle had been that of the Spanish War which was the
background in 1918 upon our entry into World War I.

In this light we should measure the achievement of the
first AEF and its commander. In 1917 we started absolutely from scratch. Then we had only five thousand
regular officers, not as many reserve officers outside those
of the poorly equipped National Guard, not one squadron
of up to date planes, and only a shadowy liaison between
the Army and industry in procurement. Theory, not
practice, in the movement of imaginary armies in maneuver, was our guide, subject to conflicting advice from
our Allies and trial and error in raising immense armies
under the urgent call of a crisis in Allied fortunes. In
seventeen months after Pershing went abroad with his
pioneer staff we had two millions of men in France and
the war was won.

Home training in 1917-18 was much briefer, and bound
to be less thorough, if more intensive, than in the later
war. One year before Pearl Harbor we had more than a
million men in training, the draft act in operation, and
industry already processing for war production. It was two

years before the divisions in training in 1940 were to land in North Africa.

When the disaster of Pearl Harbor blasted us into the war, the more than a million had been increased to over two millions. Instead of officers rushed out after three months training in the officers training camps of 1917-18, we had available in 1940 those of the ROTC and, later, privates who were graduates of the officer candidate schools. Our war industrial production was well under way to meet the enormous demand for planes, tanks and the latest type of weapons. We had held the big Louisiana and Carolina maneuvers.

But unfortunately the training up to Pearl Harbor had been more for home defense than for the difficult problems of overseas warfare by which the war must be won. Therein was the supreme difference between the two wars. The second was an amphibious war for us. Our armies had first to gain a shore hold on the two fronts as a basis for decisive operations.

Pershing had ports in France, free from air attack, for the disembarkation of troops and supplies. He had the Allied trench wall, while it should last, behind which to school his army for offensive battle. But there came the crisis when he had as yet only four well trained divisions and it seemed that the trench wall was breaking. The Germans, in their March drive of 1918, had broken a gap between the British and French armies, and his little army, short of weapons and supplies, was in danger of being driven back to a last ditch defense of its ports of supply. It was touch and go, but the trench wall held to give him time to draw on the home cantonments for a big army.

Meanwhile he had to fight to save his little army from losing its independence under the Allied pressure for infiltration of our men into the Allied armies as replacements. But Eisenhower had at the start in France a greater number of troops than his allies, backed by greater air power, as cards on the Allied council table which insured his being chosen supreme Allied commander.

Either dealt with the task of his time in the way of his time, true to the emphasis Pershing always placed on the fundamental that the principles of war do not change, and their application is with the weapons which your country places in your hands.

Pershing, to hasten the end, pressed into ceaseless offensive battle, in the company of his veteran divisions, in the chill mud and rains of the Fall of 1918, fresh divisions from our home cantonments without previous trench experience. They had not the support of modern air power with mastery of the air, or adequate artillery, or always artillery with battle experience. Happily they had no such set-back as that of the second AEF in the Bulge in midwinter in fighting on until they won the victory.

In this the doughboy fathers of the GI's did not fail. It was not their fault if they did not succeed in the mission on which they were sent in the "war to end war" in saving their sons from serving in the second AEF.

In 1917-18 the one great task was victory in Europe under Pershing. In World War II, with its two fronts, victory in Europe, under Eisenhower, was set as the first task. Eisenhower's American army was one-third larger than Pershing's, which was incomparably larger than any we had ever previously sent overseas. But if the standing and quality of generals were to be measured by the size of their armies, then Washington, with an army half the size of a modern division, or Grant with his hundred thousand, or Lee with his sixty thousand, when they began their long final struggle in the Wilderness, would now appear relatively as platoon and company commanders.

At my command when I began this biography were my other books with their bibliographies of references on our part in World War I based on years of research and personal observation. In the General's conduct of operations in France I owe much to his own *My Experiences in the World War*. I draw on my close relations with him and staff and line in 1917-18 and with him in earlier days.

He was not given to phrases or promises. He was wholly aloof to any personal build-up by the now numerous experts in press agentry under the name of public relations. Others might not make phrases for the silent, canny soldier, the stern, incorruptible disciplinarian of himself and his army, who was subject to human impulses which he felt it his duty to repress.

Newton D. Baker, that great Secretary of War, with his gift of summing up a character in a single sentence, said once of Pershing that he was puzzled how a man who thought so much about buttons could have such great vision. The reference about buttons will be understood by veterans of the first AEF in memory of his inspections which missed no detail. The vision was in the strategic plan which he made in June, 1917. The plan was to strike the German army in flank on the Meuse. He carried the plan through, not in 1919 as he had anticipated, but in November, 1918. So never mind the public relations build-ups. "Leave it to the record."

1

The Approach

Usually We Have to wait on posterity to say
whether or not the fame of a man in his time will endure
or whether he will receive only a nod from the next
generation in passing him on to oblivion. The rare exception is one whose name will always be associated with a
mighty event or movement of undying memory as its
spearhead.

It was certain that Washington after Yorktown, Nelson
after Trafalgar, Wellington after Waterloo, and Grant and
Lee as well as Lincoln after Appomattox, would live in
history, each in his distinctive character. So, in his strength
and limitations, must the man on his headquarters railroad
car on a November afternoon, 1918, at the city of Treves,
which had been in Germany a fortnight ago and was now
in France.

Ahead of the car, which had the right of way in enemy
country, his troops were marching on to the occupation of
the Rhine. Color was back in his face, which had had a
stony pallor in his unrelenting determination in the crisis
of the fifty days of the Meuse-Argonne Battle, after the

strain of the preceding hundred days of continuous fighting.

Destiny had made him commander and ambassador, an American king in France, in an astounding crusade across the Atlantic ocean of two millions of American soldiers, to whom "J.J.P." on a piece of paper was the law for all.

When the signing of the Armistice set crowds surging in jubilant frenzy from the Vosges to San Francisco he had shown no outward emotion. His feelings were too deep for display. He had already discounted the last step in reaching the goal. The plan he had made eighteen months ago had been fulfilled, the victory won.

As he put it, "There's the record"—that of achievement. But the myriad dancing typewriter keys of modern administration do not include in their detail the oral councils in which policies are formed or a chief's reasoning which leads to a vital decision. General Pershing's own part in the achievement is not altogether revealed in the confidential cablegrams and letters between headquarters in France and Washington and the vast cordage of documents, to which I have had access.

This biography would enable us to know the living man, absorb the atmosphere in which he worked through his significant remarks and what those close to him were saying and thinking about him at the time and in later years of reflection. The general, whom I first knew as a captain, developed into a man of many parts.

There was the Pershing who seemed most cautious and then most daring; the Pershing of insistent deliberation in coming to a decision and then flashing the word for speedy action; the Pershing of the "thin-lipped" smile who exasperated Premier Clemenceau and of a variety of smiles and a hearty laugh when many of his soldiers wondered if he ever smiled; the Pershing of steel and stiff exactions and the Pershing of "If he were more human he would be happier" and "I do wish he had more sense of humor"; the Pershing who seemed to lack any form of words except an

explicit order and then could be most lucid in his expositions; the Pershing of brimstone bursts of indignation and
canny diplomacy against sieges of intrigue; and the Pershing of "That's politics, the statesman's business," and of
whom a British officer said, at first sight of him, "What a
soldier!"

What distances he had traveled in more than miles from
Laclede! Yet, in a sense, he was never far away from the
little Missouri town. His feet were always on the mother
soil from which his young roots had drawn their sap.

2

Boyhood

"But The Name Is Pfershing," as Alsatians reminded us; and so spelled and borne to America by the ancestor, Frederick Pfershing from that buffer land, neither truly French nor German, but inherently Alsatian.

The Alsace he knew was under French rule in the expansive reign of Louis XIV who held the Rhine as his eastern boundary by divine right. At the time young surveyor George Washington had yet to cross the eastern wall of the Shenandoah Valley on his first wilderness mission; a revolution in the American colonies was no more dreamed of than a revolution in France; Napoleon was not yet born.

There were nobility and gentry, peasants, craftsmen, tradesmen in class distinctions as rigidly set in Alsace as in France or in Germany. What the father was the son became almost inevitably in the social scale. Talk came over the Vosges from Paris about France's great holdings in hot Louisiana and snowy Canada and from over the Rhine about how some Germans had set up a community in a part of the new world which had a more temperate climate.

4

The sparse emigration to America from the continent of Europe went usually in groups promoted by some enterprising leader. That from France to French territory originally had been distinctively led by the French nobility under royal favor and regimentation. Young Frederick Pfershing was no leader of a group; he waited on the companionship of no group in collective, gregarious daring for the adventure which broke free of the provincial fold of inheritance.

The Rhine flowed to the sea, and across the sea was America where the tales had it—at least he would find if the tales were true—land did not descend from seigneur's son to seigneur's son, but a common man might earn the possession of a plot of virgin soil to hold as his own. Frederick lacked the passage money, but he had faith that he could work his way, which he did on the little ship *Jacob* in the fall of 1749.

His was not to be a case of "from immigrant to millionaire," which was quite rare even in later days when the much trumpeted phrase stirred the ambition of boys born in log cabins whose mothers did not look toward the Presidency for them but great wealth. In fact, there were no millionaires in America then. But Frederick got on well enough to enable him to be married within a year after his arrival to a Pennsylvania German girl. He owned and tilled his own land and supported a family. He had achieved in America what he sought in America.

It was not until the third generation, when the post-Revolution movement over the Alleghenies and the Cumberlands was spreading the pioneering march in a burst of speed, that the migrant spirit of Frederick reappeared in the Pershings. The f had been dropped from the name as many other immigrant names had undergone change, sometimes owing to the simplified spelling with which a clerk wrote a deed.

An American army had been to Mexico City, adding

Texas to the Louisiana Purchase and annexing California, which soon sent the electrifying summons to the gold rush of forty-nine. Steamboats plied the western rivers, the railroad was advancing behind the wheels of the covered wagons across the Mississippi. Horace Greeley's "Go west, young man" was no provocative phrase to awaken youth from lethargy but expressed the call of improved communications to the restless and ambitious.

John Fletcher Pershing, Frederick's grandson, worked his way down the Ohio as Frederick had worked his way across the Atlantic. He had become enough of a river man to get a job piloting a raft of lumber down the Mississippi to New Orleans. He was up and down the river in the fascinating days of racing steamboats and Mark Twain's tales, up and down and then ashore, wherever inquiring opportunism led him when individual freedom on the frontier or near frontier was unrestricted except by the laws against assault, arson and theft and personal attitude toward the Ten Commandments.

Men had not yet settled into occupational grooves. There was a desirable proficiency in being able to turn a hand at anything. A man might try many occupations in his search for one to his profit or liking and practice several at the same time. He scattered the investments of his energy and adaptability as a capitalist scatters his in money.

The girl John Fletcher married had her part in their settling in Linn County, northwestern Missouri, near the little town of Laclede. She came of the old Virginia stock which had migrated westward after the Revolution. Some had gone over the Alleghenian wall to the Ohio and beyond. Her ancestors were among those who crossed the Cumberland wall to the Mississippi.

Pennsylvania, by way of Pittsburgh and the Ohio River, and Virginia, by way of Tennessee, were united. On September 11, 1860, the first of nine children was born and named John Joseph. The Alsatian strain in the melting pot mixture of John Joseph's blood represented one-fourth.

He rarely went further than a pleasant acknowledgment in France of references to his Alsatian origin. His pride in that great grandfather's gallant adventure was that with it he ceased to be Alsatian and became American. At the time of his birth John Joseph's father was a section foreman on the Hannibal and St. Joseph Railroad.

The Presidential campaign of 1860 became warmer day by day. There was fuel to make it white hot in a region where northern and southern strains and the Germans who had come to Missouri after the Revolution of 1848 were neighbors.

With northern Missouri inclined toward the Federal side and southern Missouri toward the Confederate in the Civil War, communities and families were divided in their passionate sectional loyalties and traditions. John Fletcher Pershing became a sutler in a Federal regiment.

The son's first memories began in the atmosphere of war, with the news of Vicksburg and Gettysburg, with soldiers home on furlough, with the final battles and the return of soldiers who had been with Grant and Sherman in the western campaigns and under Sherman on his march to the sea.

Today communications and standardization have made American towns far more alike than in the eighteen-sixties and seventies. Then the Pershing's home town of Laclede was very different from a town in longer settled regions. It was not only western but distinctly Missourian. Today one who landed from a place in a neighboring field and walked down the main street of Laclede would not know, barring a telltale local sign, whether he was in a town in Missouri, Kansas, Nebraska, Illinois or Ohio. The same kind of stores, soda fountains, cars and filling stations and people in the same kind of clothes!

But fifty years after he had left Laclede to go out in the big world John J. Pershing was sure that he would know he was in Missouri anywhere in Missouri. Throughout his career he never missed a chance to return to Laclede.

In his boyhood the Pershings had their modest share of the post-Civil War good times in the late 'sixties which carried over into the first two years of the 'seventies. Riverman and railroadman, army sutler, the versatile father also farmed, contracted and kept a country store. More important than his occupations was the standing of the Pershing family in the community.

In the early settlements in America and on westward there were two types. These have been referred to as the God-fearing and the Godless, and also as those whose gathering place was the church and the saloon. It was the division—prevailing in old communities and sharpened in the new—between the self-respecting, self-reliant, stable and industrious and others whom they carried along in their progress. And the Pershings were of the first class which gave us the leadership and the direction that kept us on the high road. As the soldier son once remarked, "That is sufficient aristocracy of origin for anyone."

In the late sixties and seventies this division was very sharply drawn in northwestern Missouri, neighbor to "bleeding Kansas," to the outlawry on the borders of the then Indian territory, now Oklahoma, where the building of the railroads had brought a rough element, and the bandit James brothers and the guerrilla Quantrell flourished. Hold-ups and train robberies had a Robin Hood glamor in certain circles. Drinking bouts led to lawless sprees and shooting scrapes. One night in John Joseph's childhood a gang of bushwhackers sacked Laclede. His first teacher in the district school of the three R's was the daughter of a man who had been killed in a raid.

Neither the father nor mother brooked any compromises by the children with the basic moralities. The lesson of life was to stand on your feet and go straight. There was little danger of Jack becoming a spoiled child, and none, with

8

the rapid increase of the family, of his becoming a spoiled
only son. The makers of legends who like to dwell on incidents of boyhood forecasting the man will find little evidence of Jack's predestination for high command unless
they make a point that the boy had the same compact head,
without a bump on it, and close-set ears, as the man. He did
not play with toy soldiers or organize his fellows into a
rigidly saluting military company. The influences of his
boyhood which he never ceased to apply in his career were
those common to his environment.

Plentiful food he had—the Pershings grew their own
mostly—before we knew about vitamins and calories; and
no lack of fresh air and exercise in doing chores, in the
boyish games and the annual delight of roasting ears when
field corn was in the milk. He was just another sturdy
country boy in a comfortable, modest home—under the
spell of the father's irrepressible optimism in caring for his
growing family—keeping his pace well in front of his classes
at the district school. The parents planned that John should
go to college. The father foresaw that he could afford it.
John looked forward to going and planned to study law.

He heard the talk in his little world, reflecting that of
the big world at the turn of the 'seventies, about rising land
values; about how more railroads were building to bring
to the growing markets of our east and Europe more grain
and meat from the west. factories building in the growing
cities, immigration pouring in at Castle Garden, more
mouths to feed, more subdivisions everywhere into town
lots. Yesterday's high prices were still higher today and
bound to be higher tomorrow to continue the boom in our
continental breadth of endless room for expansion.

The father had caught the epidemic fever. He had
bought land at high prices in speculative anticipation they
would go higher. He was hit hard by the ensuing depression
after the panic of 1873, when John was fourteen, which
brought the same collapse of values as sunk that of western

9

farms, bought for two hundred dollars an acre and mortgaged for a hundred in the nineteen-twenties, down to fifty in the nineteen-thirties—if a purchaser could be found. Mortgages were foreclosed on the father's land. This was a lesson to be applied by young John who was never given to counting his chickens before they were hatched.

Any visions he had of going to college were out of the reckoning in the days before the largess of endowments held out a generously beckoning hand on an easy road. Big brother must help carry on until the return of good times which were to pass Laclede by in the prosperity of better located towns. That meant farmwork for John Joseph, and when he was a little older, a grip of the plow handles making a straight furrow.

A boy brought up in Laclede, where everybody rode, did not have to wait for coaching in the riding hall at West Point to learn how to ride. John had his initiation on a horse's bare back when his legs stuck out at right angles. He knew how to break a colt and mend a harness.

The remote figure to the soldiers of the AEF had the reputation in the community of being what is called a "good mixer." Everybody in the country around knew young Jack Pershing. He did not take himself too seriously. He was liked. It was good to see him approaching in anticipation of his happy greeting—his genuine and hearty "How are you?"—with a beaming friendly smile for all. This was the universal local view, strange as it may seem to some officers who served under him in France.

But he was more given to listening than talking after the greeting. Missourians of the soil with their drawl have been referred to as slow if sure moving. They like good horses but are fond of that famous stubborn, plodding, hardy Missouri mule. Jack might breeze down the main street with his happy greetings, but he was given to looking before he leapt.

We have the best proof of his excellence in his studies in

his receiving a certificate to teach school when he was eighteen. In rural regions before women had so largely monopolized the profession a term as district school teacher was considered to be excellent preparation for a young man for his future career. People enjoyed the prospect of the test of the assignment of a new man teacher to a tough school, which was decidedly not for a mistress but for a master who was of the sterner sex.

Prairie Mound had some rowdy male pupils, as old as John, who had kept faith with their established reputation that they preferred a riot to an education by forcing their previous teacher to throw up the sponge. John greeted the ringleaders with a prefatory disarming smile in token of friendships formed at first sight. Well, they would soon make him smile out of the other corner of his mouth.

But when the lips closed above the jaw and the well-knit figure some of them were disinclined to try him out. Those who did had a reforming second thought after the experience. Prairie Mound became a very orderly school. The previously recalcitrant bullies were getting an education whether they wanted it or not. John always welcomed them in the morning with the glad smile, while those who had ventured to try him out sometimes exchanged knowing grins with him.

His pay of thirty-five dollars a month for his first and second year at Prairie Mound—which was a good deal of real cash money when butter and eggs were exchanged at the local store for groceries—he invested in two Spring terms at the Kirksville Normal School. For dividends he received high marks in all of twenty-eight subjects, except vocal music, and a certificate to teach school anywhere in Missouri.

A third year at Prairie Mound, and now in his twenty-first year! Farm labor in the summer and doing his part in the big family as the big brother!

What of the future? The law still in mind, he read Blackstone in his spare time by way of preparation. His friends were not too sure about John in the law, which for the ambitious led to election as county prosecutor and rise in politics. He was not of the type of "smart youngster with the gift of gab" who got the plums in the political orchard. Oratory was the important asset before juries and on the stump. John had not improved as a speaker since he had stubbornly kept on reciting Mary's Little Lamb before the assembled parents as a primary pupil until, thank heaven, he could step down from the platform.

He had never thought of being a soldier, as he told me, and I remember his saying that he had been ploughing when he heard there was a vacancy for a cadetship at West Point in his Congressional district. West Point! Grant, who was then writing his memoirs against approaching death to pay his debts and provide for his family—the controversies over his Presidency forgotten in a wave of public devotion to the soldier, and Lee, Sherman, Jackson, Sheridan, Meade, Hancock, Thomas, MacPherson, and Reynolds had all been West Pointers linking the fame of the national military academy on the distant Hudson with their own records in the Civil War.

John had never been as far away from home as St. Louis. Here was an opening into a larger world, and education by the government, which made you an officer of the Army should you be able to survive the grind of the four years. If the appointment were to be personal by the Congressman, which still applied in many instances, friendship and political influence, which John lacked, would count. But he learned that an examination of all who wished to try was to be held. What chance had he against the competition of rivals who had had schooling superior to his own?

His mother was disturbed at the idea of his entering the Army, which would take him far from home, from post to post. Her heart had been torn by a conflict of loyalties in the Civil War. She had seen too much of the lawlessness of many of the returned soldiers around Laclede. And she had heard of the merciless drill at West Point, of cadets who had been dismissed because they could not endure it. For West Point had a more fearsome reputation then than in later days.

However, she would not stand in John's way after he had told her he might resign after his graduation, as many young officers did, and then he would return home to study law. In the company of seventeen other aspirants he bent over the examination questions. His was the highest rating.

Even so the Congressman might not necessarily choose the one of highest standing. This happened to young James G. Harbord of Kansas, later Pershing's right hand in France, who saw a rival with marks inferior to his favored and who then enlisted as a private, and thus won his commission from the ranks.

The Congressman from John's district followed the now established custom. John received the appointment. But the decisive test was yet to come, West Point's own, by her academic board in competition with boys from all over the land, before regional examinations under its auspices conferred admission.

3

At West Point

In Nothing Could West Point be more completely disinterested in the 'eighties than in more cadets for the sake of numbers. The prospect that our little Regular army, which was being reduced bit by bit, might be over officered at further national expense, reinforced maintenance of standards by rigorous elimination.

If John went to West Point, only to fail of admission, the door of opportunity which had been opened would be shut in his face. After his grand send-off at the railroad station he would return beaten, the Pershing family pride humbled. He must have any assistance available.

Just what was that sternly formidable West Point examination like? The Pershings were told that Colonel Huse knew. He had examples of past examinations for reference, and taught candidates how to pass. The family gathered enough money, in addition to John's savings, to pay the tuition the Colonel required. John was on his way east weeks before the examinations began.

Caleb Huse of the West Point class of 1851, with a truly

New England name, without a trace of Southern blood, had taken a strange attitude for one of his origin upon the outbreak of the War Between the States. In the conviction that the South had a right to set up in its own house he resigned from the Regular army and offered his services to the Confederacy, which sent him to England as an arms purchasing agent.

The cause lost, his career blasted, his dearest asset and consolation were his West Point training and memory. If he had forfeited the fellowship of his Northern friends he hoped he had not entirely lost that of Academy days. He was still a graduate of West Point. He would be close to West Point if he could not be of it.

West Pointers who served on opposite sides in 1861-65 had never shared personally toward each other the bitter animosity which endured into the 'eighties. They did not forget that Caleb Huse had once been a brother cadet.

He established a "prep" school for West Point at Highland Falls. Preparation was not only to pass written examinations. The school was so near West Point that his pupils could get the feel and atmosphere of it. After the day's grind to which he subjected them they might pass through the old South Gate to watch the cadet corps in corset muscled precision at evening parade.

Rarely had he more than a dozen pupils. He measured each applicant with a knowing eye; and might refuse him if he did not appear of the stuff of which soldiers are made, and very much in earnest.

The West Point academic board took care that no two of Caleb's store of past entrance examinations had duplicate questions. What pitfalls for the unwary would the next one have? This worried John who labored with deadly concentration. If he were equal to the written questions the West Point board was bound to see promising material in the well-set up Missourian in answer to the unwritten.

He was one of the 129 of the 183 appointees admitted to

the Academy in 1882, and at twenty-two, just within the age limit, six years older than the youngest. Could he hold out as one of the 77 who were to be graduated in 1886?

Will and physique did not assure the mental equipment or the temperament to survive the régime. Before he was far along in the "plebe" year he might wish to high heaven that he had never come. But to be plucked at West Point except for ill health—plucked though resignation was the form—carried a reflection for life particularly in rural communities where the neighbors all knew you.

So Sylvanus Thayer had planned. A boy of high education who became a volunteer in the War of 1812-14, Thayer's experience of the half mobs of soldiers, the lack of expert skill and discipline and supplies, the curse of permitted malingering and the profiteering in the sum of our military humiliation, sunk a lesson in him which gave him a mission. On his own, after the war, he spent two years abroad in the study of European military systems. Then Napoleon had just been exiled to St. Helena. At Vienna the victorious Allies had parcelled out Europe and much of the rest of the world for an enduring peace under the reigns of the monarchies which were "legitimate" by the "divine right" of their founders, who in their time had licked their rivals into submission.

As preceptor at West Point, which had been a child of politics and easy ways, he made the West Point we know in applying what he had learned abroad for the needs of the United States. He would form a human rock of discipline on the grey rocks overlooking the Hudson. In earning the right to become an officer you need not be born in the "officer class" as you must be then almost invariably in Europe.

Be the cadet the son of a general, a senator or a day laborer, clad in broadcloth or homespun when he arrived— one appointee for the class of 1886 from Texas appeared in a Prince Albert coat and a waistcoat which once had been white and another from Oregon walked a hundred miles to a railroad station—the past did not count when he was fitted in the cadet grey to be moulded in the pattern to make him worthy to be an army officer in war or peace. If it were not in his spirit or capacity to qualify then he should not be trusted with the command of men.

For doughty Sylvanus' aim was to make officers—just officers—not generals. Any cadet who became inflated with the idea that once graduated he was all set to be a general might not have been graduated under Sylvanus. Generals were made later out of the officers. The phrase about the cadets as "our future generals" overlooks how few ever become generals.

Between civil and military life Sylvanus drew a sharp line. His civil tradition was that of the New England town meeting. An officer was to have no say or part in politics; to profess no partisanship as the servant of the whole; to be true to his oath to the Constitution, which was his king; to go where he was sent and do what he was ordered to do by his superiors step by step up to the elective President of the United States, the supreme commander-in-chief. When his country sent him to war his part was to meet the soldiers of any king with hotter fire than they sent; to prevent a repetition of the disaster when the British regulars sacked and burned our capital in Sylvanus' own soldier days.

Every cadet passing from the parade ground could not fail to see on the face of the sally port of the oldest of the barracks this inscription on a bronze tablet from an address delivered by Major General John M. Schofield, then Superintendent of the Academy.

"The discipline which makes the soldiers of a free country reliable in battle is not to be gained by harsh and tyrannical treatment. On the contrary, such treatment is far more likely to destroy than to make an army. It is possible to impart instruction and give commands in such a manner and in such a tone of voice as to inspire in the soldier no feeling but an intense desire to obey, while the opposite manner and tone of voice cannot fail to excite strong resentment and a desire to disobey. The one mode or the other of dealing with subordinates springs from a corresponding spirit in the breast of the commander. He who feels the respect which is due to others cannot fail to inspire in them regard for himself. While he who feels and hence manifests disrespect towards others, especially his inferiors, cannot fail to inspire hatred against himself."

Major General James G. Harbord, who was not a West Pointer, wrote in his *The American Army in France:* "It is one of the principal advantages to a country of an institution such as West Point, for the training of officers, that through the years it acquired a group of men who, in addition to other benefits of military training, speak the same language."

By and large, after successfully conforming with the régime, it depended upon what cadet Pershing or any other cadet got out of the tradition, how capable and steadfast he should be in adhering to it through his army career. And the plebe year was the hardest. All the weight of the régime and tradition and the critical superiority of the upper classmen were upon him.

In the glow of reminiscence Pershing wrote in a letter when he was in the Philippines and could not be present for the twenty-fifth reunion of his class:

"What memories come rushing forward to be recorded! It was at Colonel Huse's school, now called 'The Rocks', I believe, with splendid old Caleb at its head, that several of us got the idea of what we were in for. Deshon, Frier, Winn, Andrews, Billy Wright, Stevens, Legare, and the rest of us at Caleb's used to wrestle with examinations of previous years and flyspeck page after page of stuff that we forgot completely before plebe camp was over.

"This brings us up to a period of West Point life whose vivid impressions will be the last to fade. Marching into

CADET JOHN J. PERSHING AT WEST POINT.

camp; piling bedding; policing company streets of logs of wood carelessly dropped by upper classmen; pillow fights at tattoo, with Marcus Miller, sabre drawn, marching up and down superintending the plebe class; policing up feathers from the general parade; light artillery drills; double timing around old Fort Clinton at morning squad drill; Wiley Bean and the sad fate of his old seersucker coat; midnight dragging; and the whole summer full of events that can only be mentioned in passing.

"No one can ever forget his first guard tour with all its preparation and perspiration. I got on all right by day, but at night on the color line my trouble began. Of course, I was scared beyond the point of applying any of my orders. A few minutes after taps, ghosts of all sorts began to appear from all directions.

"I selected a particularly bold one and challenged according to orders, 'Halt! Who comes there?' At that the ghost stood still in his tracks. I then said, 'Halt! Who stands there?' whereupon the ghost, who was carrying a chair, sat down, when I promptly said, 'Who sits there?'

"After plebe camp came Math and French. I never stood high in French and was prone to burn the midnight oil. One night Walcutt and Bentley Mott came in to join me. My roommate, Lucy Hunt, was in bed asleep. Suddenly we heard Flaxy, who was officer in charge, coming up the stairs several steps at a time. Mott sprang across the hall into his own room. I snatched the blanket from the window, turned out the light and leaped into bed, clothing and all. I paid the penalty by walking six hours of extra duty.

"The rest of it—yearling camp and its release from plebedom; the first appearance in the riding hall of the famous '86 New England cavalry; furlough and the return up the Hudson in the steamer Mary Powell; second class year, with its increasing responsibilities and dignity—must be passed over with slight notice."

At the outset of the plebe year, General O. O. Howard,

of the empty sleeve, who had lost an arm in the war, carried on the Thayer tradition as that mighty man, the Superintendent. He was soon succeeded by General Wesley Merritt, the dashing blade of youthful West Point ideals, graduate of the class of 1860, who had commanded a Federal cavalry division at the age of twenty-seven. Now only thirty-eight he had a glamor and a personal bearing which made his very strict rule the easier to bear.

Many graduates whose war fame was still fresh as commanders reviewed the cadet corps, but none who had been Confederates, although they were welcome privately and socially. To the northern public they were still "rebels." For one to have received any official attention in the 'eighties would have roused a "bloody shirt" protest from as yet unreconstructed fire-eaters who saw all Confederates as forever unreconstructed.

But after the Spanish War there was no official limitation on the welcome for Generals Fitz Hugh Lee and "Fighting Joe" Wheeler who had served in the United States uniform again. In 1902, at the West Point centennial, General E. P. Alexander, Lee's chief of artillery, made an address eloquent in its unconsciousness of an effort at eloquence and his deep feeling about the sincerity and sacrifice for the lost cause which he now realized was better lost.

Sheridan and Schofield came to West Point occasionally in Pershing's cadet days. Hancock "the superb"—unsurpassed corps commander—came frequently; and very often "War is hell" Sherman, with his lined face, his hair and beard still having a tinge of red in the white and still mixing pepper and salt in a sagely sententious or joking remark, which was never weakened by veteran prolixity.

And Grant was also among the commanders whose living presence cadet Pershing felt as a stimulus: Pershing's classmate, Major General Avery D. Andrews, relates how Grant —his strength fast ebbing as the shadow of death closed in upon him—would not take a seat on the slightly raised platform for a review, but had chairs for himself and Mrs. Grant placed near and just in front of the corps of cadets. Grant and Mark Twain! There was a contrast. Mark liked to go to West Point where he was accepted as an honorary brother in the school of arms.

But a call from the Almighty himself would not have influenced Wesley Merritt toward accepting excuses unwarranted in his military philosophy. Out of the 129 who entered in the Fall of 1882, only 88 survived as second classmen to have their turn in the riding academy. Then the cadets played baseball and some of them did kick a football about, but they had no football team, they knew no rah-rah's in stadiums with trips for the whole class to intercollegiate games. Except in the regular furlough for the class, no cadet might leave the grounds individually for any social purpose. He was fast held for his relaxation in "the shop."

Exercise was in military drill, in riding and fencing, and in dancing lessons which were included in the curriculum. Already a good horseman, Pershing became an equally good dancer, ever to be fond of dancing.

But, burning the midnight oil! West Point was showing up the different sides of Pershing which later appeared as inconsistencies to those who had not a personal knowledge of him. Whatever he came by as a student was by hard work. He used to go without his dinner to grind at his lessons.

It was a great day for him, as he relates in the letter quoted when he made "a cold Max in Philosophy at June examination, under dear old Pete (Colonel Peter Michie), with Arthur Murray as instructor. This was the only Max I ever made in anything. I fairly floated out of the library and back to barracks."

His classmate Walcutt tells how one recitation was heart-rending for him, "when he was required to discuss the subject of 'Pseudo-Metaphors' while in the English course in his Fourth Class year.

21

"The subject was treated in the book in an abstract and technical way and was not clearly understood by any member of the section. Pershing was in no hurry to recite, but when called upon made a great struggle to clarify the subject. It was evident he had not made even a beginning in understanding it; however, he struggled on, greatly embarrassed, almost hopeless—great beads of perspiration standing out on his forehead. The instructor showed no disposition to throw any light or suggestion that might help. Instead that dignitary finally said: 'Mr. Pershing, what is a Pseudo-Metaphor?' That was the final straw that produced the collapse."

"Mr. Pershing" was doing his best, and the remark about him that "he did his best in everything" carried its tribute.

He had started high in scholastic standing in his class, but began slipping. Records were read out at Saturday parade. Walcutt tells how, after a tumble was registered one Saturday, "I sought Pershing out after supper and found him in his room deeply immersed in his French books, with an expression of hopelessness and discouragement that indicated he felt he would sink unless he immediately started to work. Saturday evening was usually a time for recreation."

He was bent on surviving the "rigors of the institution by his own efforts. He never relied on anything else."

Promptness is most desirable in a soldier. But therein was a weakness Pershing could not overcome. Holding fast to his lessons like a dog to a bone, he was ever being reminded that he would be late for formations. Being late meant a matter of split seconds. His chief demerits were for tardiness. In spite of his tardiness and his fight to keep up with the middle of his class, Walcutt said he was accepted as its "leader in everything else" and that included the best record for markmanship among the plebes. He had shot squirrels with a rifle back in Missouri.

There was one merit about which his instructors had no

say. It was accorded by the members of his class. They elected their own class president. Their view as to soldierly quality might disagree with the official view. Any effort by an ambitious member to promote his candidacy was absolutely prejudicial. They were bound to choose a man they liked and respected in the fellowship of the corps.

Pershing had no close intimates. He was friendly with all. He had a kind of shyness which was an asset when any self sufficiency, any bumptiousness on the edge of being "too fresh," was brought into conformity by the methods well known to schoolboys, which the life at West Point favored.

Three years older than the average of his classmates, his age and his bearing had given him prestige. If he did not thrust himself forward, he was very much all there. His classmates turned to him for advice; he had become the arbiter of disputes among them.

No one else was proposed: he was not only chosen class president at the end of his first year, but in the succeeding years. He kept the class singularly free from cliques and personal feuds. It was "one for all and all for one."

In his instance his soldier instructors, overlooking his moderate scholarship and demerits for tardiness, agreed with his classmates' view that he was the most soldierly. Cadet corporals are appointed at the end of the first year from the plebe class; and so, in order, cadet sergeants from the second class, lieutenants from the third and captains from the fourth. In turn Pershing was named senior (highest ranking) corporal, sergeant, lieutenant and captain, although he finally stood No. 17 in discipline.

"The climax of days," he wrote in the letter quoted, "came when the makes (for the class of 1886) were read out on graduation day, June 1885. Little Eddy Gayle smiled when I reported five minutes later with a captain's chevrons pinned to my sleeves. No honor can ever come to equal that. I look upon it in the very same light today as I did then."

"Never morose, superior or priggish," said classmate Major General W. H. Hay of him. "Personal magnetism seemed to be lacking," classmate Lieutenant General Robert L. Bullard, who commanded the Second Army under him in France, wrote after the World War, "Pershing inspired confidence but not affection. He won followers, but not personal worshippers. Plain in word, sane and direct in action. His exercise of authority . . . of a nature peculiarly impersonal, dispassionate, hard and firm. The quality in him did not, as in many, give offense; the man was too impersonal, too given over to duty. His manner carried to those under him the suggestion, nay the conviction, of unquestioned right to obedience."

On the only occasion when the cadet corps of his time was allowed to leave West Point as a body they crossed the Hudson to Garrison. There senior cadet captain Pershing stood at the salute with the rigid ranks to pay their tribute to Grant as his funeral train passed. Pershing's class standing, upon graduation, number 30 out of 77, was to be relatively higher than Grant's which had been number 21 out of 39. Lee had been number 2 out of 40.

4

In the Old West

TONIGHT WAS THE NIGHT OF NIGHTS. Never would they all be together again. As the survivors of the West Point regime under Wesley Merritt theirs was more than the break in training of a college football team after the last game of the season.

Any disciplinary inclination on the part of Pershing, who presided at the graduation dinner of the class of 1886 at old Delmonico's in New York, would have been as out of keeping as stepping out of ranks to do a handspring on dress parade. Later Pershing referred to it as "a lurid scene" in which he joined.

Tomorrow they might rise as late as they chose for their holiday out of uniform in "cits" (citizen's clothes). They would be free agents until their graduation leaves were over and they took their places as second lieutenants at the bottom round of another ladder.

Second lieutenants of engineers, ordnance, artillery, cavalry and infantry in what seemed a hopelessly low period of the Regular army which saw no gleam of light ahead in the encompassing gloom! Most of them would report for service under first lieutenants whose hair was grey, and these were under captains and majors who had been colonels and generals in the Federal army in 1865. Promotion? You advanced another number in the line of lieutenants when some one ahead of you died, resigned or was retired for age.

In the West, where the regulars were mostly located, it was the army of the drawings of Frederic Remington, of the tough, lean, leather necked old sergeant, of long service privates who often had reached middle age; of the elders in command who lived over their Civil War and Indian campaigns, played poker most skillfully and cannily when nickels counted on their small army pay.

Many of the older commissioned officers were "rankers." Having risen from the ranks as volunteers in the Union cause and become habituated to army life they gained commissions in the Regulars after the war only to find that with the reduction of the regular force they were on a treadmill instead of an ascending stairway.

Wise old sergeants, who knew their post commanders, took the newcomers from West Point under their wings. Post commanders received them politely into the little family, but conscious of their own actual war experience were not oblivious of their obligation to take some of the academic stiffness out of the West Pointers in teaching them army practice as distinct from classroom and parade ground training.

And the elders wondered why any young man should want to become an army officer in face of the era's abundant opportunities in the civil world, which was given to seeing the Regular as a superfluous national policeman now that the redskins were apparently all "good Indians," content to accept the Great White Father's blankets and rations on the government reservations without the diversion of a single war whoop. Geronimo, the Apache chief, who appeared to be the final recalcitrant, had not been accommodating enough to wait until the class of 1886 was graduated before he surrendered.

With dictator Porfirio Diaz firmly seated on Chapultepec, welcoming, in an orderly régime, our leadership and capital in mining and railroad building, there was presently no more prospect of our having trouble with Mexico than with Canada. In the Far East, where little Japan was building a little navy and making an army in imitation of the German and British, our sidewheel naval relics of the Civil War could easily safeguard our trade and our missionaries.

Our press continued to carry war alarms from Europe in dull days for domestic news. Old Kaiser William I still ruled in Germany with Bismarck as Chancellor. The British navy, with its two-power standard, the Triple Alliance wedged between France and mighty Russia and the established Balance of Power served as a bulwark of world stability. Meanwhile Britain continued to have little wars with backward peoples in the course of her colonial expansion under the reign of Victoria, sometimes called "The Peaceful."

And what could we have actually to do with the affairs of Europe? In case it did have another war.this might enlarge the market for our meat and grain. We were sure no other nation could attack us although our coast defenses were twenty years out of date. With no Indians to fight and no one else to fight, never had the outlook been so peaceful.

Why not reduce the Regular army still farther? It was costing us forty million dollars a year. After the West Pointers had their education to be generals they could resign and enter civil life and be recalled to service in case we ever needed generals again. All of which is a reminder of the changes in the world between the day Pershing went to Arizona as a second lieutenant and the day his army reached the Rhine, not to mention the later changes in his lifetime.

Possibly the chance that there might still be more Indian fighting, but mainly the call of the horseman, the spell of cavalryman Merritt—horse and man in the open spaces—led second lieutenant Pershing to choose the cavalry as his branch of the service. Fortune and his rank as cadet captain favored him in his assignment to a six company post—one of the largest owing to its being in the Apache country—at Fort Bayard, New Mexico.

Before that, on his leave after graduation, he had visited Washington for the first time and "roamed about," as he put it in his home country around Laclede. The members of the class of 1886 had agreed to write letters about their experiences after graduation to be published in a class annual. The break-from-training spirit still reigned in a group of them, which included Pershing, on the train from Omaha.

"A jollier crowd than ours," he wrote, "never traveled over the A. T. & F. We told stories, sang class songs, cleaned out eating houses, fired at prairie dogs, hazed the peanut boy and practically ran the train. Our stories came to be such chestnuts that Bean bought an old-fashioned doorbell which was used as a chestnut bell, [a chestnut being in those days a stale story or joke] with which we had great fun until Bean rang it on a cowboy, and the bell was retired."

Maybe the tenderfoot could be fresh in the East but the cowboy evidently made it forcibly clear that this did not go out West. It would not have been pleasant for a fledgling second lieutenant to learn that his commanding officer had been informed of his altercation with a civilian. That would not be becoming in "an officer and gentleman."

"And remember," one hears the elder saying, "you're expected to be one even in 'cits.' You are out West now with the old army, and make sure you do not forget it, by God. Besides some Congressman may hear of it and tell the War Department which will be on my back with a lot more paper work." And that elder probably took his whiskey straight and likely without a chaser of water.

Pershing brought the prestige of having been cadet captain in his favor to Fort Bayard. He knew how to discipline others, and he had the further asset of adjusting himself to any group—amiable and friendly off duty and instantly the soldier on duty. His looks too were in his favor.

About five feet ten, he seemed taller, especially when he stood at the salute before a superior or when he entered a room. Beyond his scrupulous conformity to military forms it was clear that he was a practical man. The old Army looked on the cub and found him good.

Cavalryman Pershing did have some action in hard riding in desert stretches, over passes and through canyons in rounding up wily hold out renegade groups of young Apache braves who would not surrender with old chief Geronimo. He came under the eye of General Nelson A. Miles—youngest corps commander in the Civil War from civil life and now famous again as the captor of Geronimo —because Pershing's was the highest score in a series of anything but theoretical raiding games. And it is worthwhile for a second lieutenant to be remembered by a commanding general.

Pershing also "got on well" with the Indians. It was most important for the Army's standing in Washington to keep the Indians in a friendly mood and, therefore, off the war path. Suppression of an outbreak aroused a burst of outraged sentiment from the "Indian lovers" of the East and consequent irritation with army highhandedness instead of with the frequently venal Indian agents of the time who had the Indians at their grafting mercy.

The Army had to live down a widely heralded phrase, General Sheridan's "The only good Indian is a dead Indian," with which some of the elders of the Army, inclined to adipose, sympathized as they tightened their belts on short rations and their tongues felt like scorched leather in Indian campaigns.

One day, when Pershing's detachment rode into a friendly Indian camp, its old chief remarked, that the American horseman might ride as well as an Indian; but could he run as well? Pershing was dared to race the best runner in the camp and finally accepted the challenge.

The chief and an army lieutenant were chosen as judges. They drew the start and finish lines. Indians and soldiers lined up for the test. Bets were laid, the Indians having to give odds to our soldiers when Pershing, a paleface, said victory depended upon whether his ankle, which had been sprained at West Point and still troubled him at times, held out. The ankle held out until he dropped face downward, his feet short of the finish line.

But the chief agreed that Pershing's head was over the line before his rival's and he had won. The honor of the Army and the paleface had been sustained in telling fashion. The "white captain," as the chief called him, represented a promotion which the War Department was long in officially confirming for second lieutenant Pershing. From the Apache country he was sent to that of the Sioux where he served in the Black Hills in 1890-91 in the last campaign against them.

After his tough service in as varied an experience on the frontier as a young officer might have, he deserved the reward of a more restful tour. In the fall of 1891 he was assigned to what was generally regarded as a sinecure in those days.

Even then many of our colleges and universities had cadet corps for students who chose to take this elective. Few joined. Why should a student, when not even a wisp of a war cloud was visible on the distant horizon? Why learn something which marched you back and forth without ever being any use to you?

The training was frequently superficial and desultory,

the kind which experts are inclined to see as worse in any
specialty than none at all. The Regular officer in charge,
more or less on his own, might drift with sentiment and
have the rest of his time for leisure when his duties as instructor need not average two hours a day. This would have
been quite acceptable at the University of Nebraska where
Pershing would have the lengthy title of Professor of Military Science and Tactics and Commandant of Cadets for
four years.

Desire for military training was particularly low at
Nebraska. As Chancellor Canfield, the President of the
University, wrote, Pershing "found a few men, the interest
in the battalion weak, the discipline next to nothing, and
the instincts of the faculty and the President of the University against the Corps."

Pershing analyzed the situation. He had learned how to
get on with Indians. He must learn how to get on with a
college faculty. College faculties are not averse to discipline
among their students and this was not a negligible problem
with the sturdy western youth at Nebraska. To have square
shoulders and look another man straight in the eye had its
advantages although you never go to war.

Evidently the taunting phrase "Will you work, soldier?"
sometimes heard in the West did not apply to the new
commandant of cadets. Far from wanting a sinecure he was
not long in finding how to escape one. The university was
short of mathematics instructors. In addition to his military
classes Pershing said that he would consider it a privilege
to have a mathematics class. The professor of mathematics
found him qualified. And Pershing should like also the
privilege of taking the law course—a student at thirty-one.
This, too, was granted.

He mixed in university life. The professors liked him for
himself, not to mention that he had not the narrow outlook
they had anticipated in one sent bolt into the academic
shades from creeping through gullies on reconnaissances

with Indian scouts. Second Lieutenant Pershing as he walked across the campus—still having the smile of his youth in his greetings when he seemed to know everybody —was an example and an apostle of military training.

At co-educational Nebraska the co-eds soon learned that he was a good dancer. He was not given to dancing frequently with the same girl the same evening. Apparently a confirmed bachelor, he developed no particular attachments. After the party he might be burning the midnight oil over his law books.

More boys were joining the cadet corps. To be a cadet corporal became a distinction. Once you were in the corps there was thorough application of the tenet that anything worth doing was worth doing well. This meant discipline, and that of the West Point kind was not inductively neglected. Pershing made it acceptable to those who were at first averse to it. He developed competition and spirit of corps. He might be hard but the cadets learned that he was fair. He was strong for rifle practice. Shots that missed the target did not count.

In his critical moments all thought he had a poor opinion of the whole corps. But at the end of the second year his confidence in them was such that he sent one company into the Inter-State competitive drill. It had a triumph which stirred the exuberant pride of the faculty and student body. Against crack companies of older schools young Nebraska, "way out in the wild and woolly," won the silver cup and $1500 prize money.

Toward the close of Pershing's four year tour at Nebraska Chancellor Canfield wrote:

"I know something about the duties of his position, and I know something about officers of the army. I speak with both experience and observation, therefore, when I say without the slightest reserve that he is the most energetic, active and industrious, competent and successful I have ever known in a position of this kind.

"We have the second best corps of cadets in the United States according to the reports of the United States inspectors; the first being the corps at West Point. Lieutenant Pershing made the corps what it is today?"

The winning of the silver cup might not be, but the inspectors' reports would be on his official record following that in New Mexico and Dakota—ready for any future Secretary of War or army chief in Washington to turn to when considering any officer's qualifications for a given duty.

In that letter Chancellor Canfield also said Pershing "is thorough in everything he undertakes, a gentleman by instinct and breeding, clean, straightforward, with an unusually bright mind: and peculiarly just and true in his dealings." The Chancellor's praise was so fulsome that possibly he had in mind to make up for his previous inhospitable view of military instruction at the university.

His closing sentence about Pershing—"He is a man of broad outlook who sees things in their true relations, and who desires to know and be more than he is"—suggested the question of Pershing's future.

He was thirty-five now, still a second lieutenant, of whom it was said as it was of other proven officers lashed by linear promotion in the slow lock step, "Think of a man of his ability only a second lieutenant! Why does he remain in the army?"

Promotion was by branches then and slowest in the cavalry arm. Without any army expansion Pershing would be only a major when he reached retiring age at sixty-four. Youth's avidity had been served in such active service as he had had with no more in prospect. He had known the fellowship of the frontier posts, where expenses were small, and the glad days of release on leaves when young officers spent all their savings and returned broke to allow more savings to accrue for another leave.

Graduating high in the law school, he had been admitted

to the bar of Nebraska. He might recall the prospect he had held out to his mother, when she was loath to see him try for West Point, that he could resign after graduation and then turn back to teaching and study law.

Many young officers, including fellow classmates, had resigned after receiving their commissions. When they resigned young they had been usually successful in civil life, some highly so. Those who waited until they were in the thirties were often too late to learn other ways, although this would hardly apply to Pershing's live, receptive mind.

It was a case of resign now or never for him. His civil friends were certain of his success. The bar might be overcrowded, but there was always room for able men, they said, and good times were bound to return.

As a result of the panic of 1873 he had been unable to go to college and study law and had gone to West Point. Now that he had been admitted to the bar the ensuing depression after the panic of 1893 may have had an influence on him when he saw how many brilliant men had a youthful start on him. Certainly he did not hesitate long in his decision. He had been trained as a soldier. The army was the army to him. The plower would stick to his furrow.

Should one make a forecast of his future if he had turned to the law,—"fair," "impersonal," "untiring industry," "just and true in his dealings,"—it would be that he would have eventually become a Federal judge if the recommendation of bar associations had been followed by the appointing power.

5

He Was Ready

Now Came Another vital decision, which others made for him. If he had had enough influence of the kind that counted in this instance, and he had been disposed to use it, he might have been at the rear in the supply services in 1917-18. Restlessly taking account of the prospect, after his rejection of the practice of the law, that he would not be a captain in the cavalry branch under linear promotion until he was past fifty, he applied for a vacant captaincy in the Quartermaster's Department.

But compartment is a more applicable word than department. Such promotion as he asked for into a compartment of non-combat army administration was quite in order. Compartmental chiefs took it for granted in their secure position at their desks in Washington, and so impressed Congress, that any lieutenant of the line qualified to be a quartermaster was entitled to the rank of captain.

As they saw it he must have the executive ability to bundle up red tape which would hardly be expected of the average officer limited to the drilling of troops and keeping a watch out for balky Indians. Compartmental officers were responsible for property and line officers only for the lives of men. What a sacrifice of superior brains it would be for a compartmental expert to be transferred from Washington to a small western post!

The conclusion of the compartmental chiefs that no line officer was available for a vacancy frequently led to the appointment of the son, son-in-law or nephew of a Congressman, or of one of his useful supporters, who had been unable to get a job in civil life with equivalent pay. However, in case of war, a captain quartermaster's bars would be very inviting to the untrained from civil life who were shy about combat service, and a captain quartermaster with line experience might be reassigned to combat service with the volunteers or expanded Regulars.

As backing Pershing utilized such influence as he had within the bounds of professional ethics: his record and the tributes of Generals Miles and Merritt and his work at the University of Nebraska. But he lacked drag with the insiders of the bureaucracy who remained in Washington year after year without ever getting their feet dusty in a route march, not to mention that he was no expert in bundling up paper work. Second Lieutenant Pershing out in the wilds received the good old conventional answer that all the vacancies had been filled.

There was no further thought of the law. He would take what came. This was orders to Fort Assiniboin in Montana, with the Tenth Cavalry, colored, which was not unwelcome.

He had not been in Montana yet. It was an important if remote post. All the commissioned officers of a colored regular regiment were white. Commanders took care in choosing them. As a further education Pershing would learn how to get the best out of colored troopers, a hand-picked, stalwart lot out of a wealth of men eager to be in the army.

36

Who but Lieutenant Pershing who knew Indians and had won the disciplined devotion of his troopers should be useful in the touchy business of rounding up 600 renegade Kree Indians and returning them to their home country in Canada to the satisfaction of our own and the Canadian government?

From Assiniboin it was to his first service in Washington, which was also above his rank. For General Miles had not forgotten him since Apache days. Miles was now nominally Commanding General of the Army. This did not mean that he had much influence in its conduct. The real ruler, strangely enough—and not so strangely at the time—was the chief of the clerks, Adjutant General Henry C. Corbin.

If Corbin left it entirely to an old sergeant he probably could have marched a company of infantry from the barracks to a railroad station, and even put them in position for the advance, by rushes of the time, without getting them tangled up.

But Corbin did know that reveille was sounded in the morning and taps at night. He knew that Mexico was to the south, Canada to the north, Europe to the east and China to the west. What he most proficiently knew as an industrious specialist in geography was the location of the Capitol in Washington, and as a psychologist the ways of the Congressman of the time in their attitude toward the Army.

To them and to elderly Secretaries of War, taking it easy in the then least noticed of cabinet positions, he was the man "to get things done." If a Congressman, or anyone of influence, wished a favorite officer better cared for in his next assignment, just pass the word to Corbin, who was further intrenched by his resourcefulness in tying up any army rival for power in a strangle hold of red tape. If there were not enough existing red tape for his purpose he spun some more. He had a way of disposing of any critic of his methods by saying, "the g.d.s.o.b. has the bellyache."

However, Miles was still allowed to choose his own aide. He made Pershing, at last a first lieutenant at thirty-seven, his acting aide in the winter of 1897. By this time the prolonged Cuban rebellion at our doors commanded serious public attention. For ten years we had been building a modern navy, and now began showing some interest in our army by setting up some modern coast defense batteries and supplying the Regulars with the new long-range smokeless powder Krag rifles in place of the Civil War model. But the army field artillery was still thirty years out of date with its short range, slow firing, black powder guns. This would insure the needless loss of lives in case of war, as it did in Cuba and the Philippines, but without including the exposure to fire of those established in the Washington compartments.

Pershing was seeing the holy of holies, seeing the compartments zealously and jealously building higher walls around themselves as they made more paper work to encompass the line—and this was further education. It is quite comprehensible how the fattish bulk of Corbin should not see a "practical man" of his kind in the lean, mature, observant lieutenant of the line fresh from bushwhacking and that this lieutenant, favorite of commanders of the line, should have reservations about him which should be both reasoned and antipathetic.

But soon Pershing was to meet a man who was to have far more power over the future of the army than Corbin. General Miles sent him to New York to report on a military tournament at Madison Square Garden. There he was the guest in a box of classmate Avery D. Andrews who had resigned from the Army for the law. Another guest was Andrews' then fellow police commissioner, Theodore Roosevelt. Cowboys, cattlemen, Indians, plains, mountains and canyons! Roosevelt and Pershing both knew their west—Arizona, New Mexico, the Black Hills, Wyoming and Montana. They talked on and on. And Theodore was not to forget Pershing.

In the fall of 1897 it was West Point again for Pershing as instructor in tactics. The threat of a war with Spain grew apace. As March advanced into April the next year it appeared inevitable; and then the compartmental system faced it as a reality. Now we should see how Corbin, the great chief clerk, without the handicap of line experience, would conduct it. He made John Jacob Astor an inspector general in place of a trained officer. He had a stock of officers' commissions in the volunteers ready on his desk with names to be filled in to pass out to the sons of influence or those whose parents he liked socially, although the sons had never done a "right face."

One fulmination from the Washington bureaucracy, which restricted instructors at West Point from leaving West Point during the war, did not except the instructor in tactics when a knowledge of tactics had been invariably proven useful in war. Indignation flamed among the faculty of the Academy who held that older men, during the war, could take the place of the instructors who were in the prime of life.

Pershing was in no mood to rest under the order. He wrote to classmate Andrews, who now commanded the crack Squadron A of the New York National Guard, to please hold any vacancy for him. But he went further as his sense of outrage came to a climax in action.

What had his country trained him for? He had kept the faith by his application to duty in stagnant days to be ready for war—and war was here. The cadets under him had a saying that the instructor in tactics was "tough but fair." This order from Washington was both tough and unfair; and to that he would not submit without protest.

He received a leave of absence from the Superintendent, glad enough to grant to it a spokesman for justice, and went to Washington taking his plea to the Secretary of War himself. As he stood before the Secretary—we imagine steel determination in his eyes with his proper respect for his superior—he surely must have looked fit for line duty. Distinctly he was of the type of young officer, not universal, who considered it his duty to be always in fettle in physique as well as spirit to endure a long march on hard rations with the hardiest trooper under him.

As a pedagogue he had kept as fit as on the plains, ready whenever the leash should be slipped. If he were still held on the leash by that order evidently he was determined to slip it himself. There were other regulars in the First Volunteer Cavalry, then forming, than medical officer Leonard Wood who had been made its colonel. There might be room for still another who applied to Lieutenant Colonel Theodore Roosevelt who was rallying men who could shoot and ride for the regiment known as his Rough Riders.

Secretary Russell A. Alger had not himself given the order. It was not in this veteran of the Civil War to deny that it was unfair. And if the irrepressible "Teddy" heard that such a good fighting man and tactician as Lieutenant Pershing was to be shut up at West Point away from the front, he would have the ears of the press in an outburst, as he shouted the invitation, "Come on in with us. The water's fine." Pershing was sent to join his black troopers of the Tenth Cavalry at Tampa on the way to Cuba and to fight beside the Rough Riders.

If Sylvanus Thayer, West Point's great preceptor, could have witnessed the confusion in the Cuban jungle he would surely have exclaimed: "Eighteen-twelve-fourteen over again!" But he would have had consolation in the sight of the sons of West Point, and the officers of Regulars from civil life and the soldiers trained in his tradition, prepared to square the account for their maintenance in peace— prepared to pay back in full. And this was particularly true of the younger officers who were physically fit for the terrific trial in the tropical jungle in addition to having studied hard to be abreast with the progress of their profession.

The commanding general, William R. Shafter, weighing two hundred fifty pounds, the choice of Alger and Corbin, streamed with perspiration in the murderous heat in the necessity of a stationary position for his adiposity. He, too, was a victim of the compartmental system which tied itself into separate compartmental knots and wrapped the whole in one general knot.

Pershing was standing beside the road to allow a battery of artillery to pass forward into position. Wherever it should begin firing its first shot with the burst of black powder smoke would reveal its position to the enemy guns out of its range but within their range. A progressive young officer let out a hot stream of language of the old army style in his disgust over the waste of all his study and effort as he viewed the mess under that "fat old slob" of a Shafter and the barnacled incompetents in Washington.

But to Pershing, who might be learning how not to direct an army, he was criticizing his commander in a crisis. Shafter was there in command. Loyalty was due to him in the spirit of corps to keep up confidence. Whatever the handicaps there must be no let down. After listening a while to the outburst Pershing said:

"Why did you come to this war if you can't stand the gaff? War has always been this way. Did you expect to see the Old Man standing out here with a book in his hand, telling these mule-skinners how to handle their outfits? The fat Old Man you talk about is going to win this campaign. When he does these things will be forgotten. It's the objective which counts, not the incidents."

And the National Guardsmen with the old model Springfield rifles revealing their line with their black powder to the Spanish Mausers that had more than twice their range! Make way for the Regulars and the Rough

Riders with their new Krag-Jorgensen rifles which had the range of the Spanish rifles. There was the hill. Up the slope!

Cadet Pershing, who had been given to overlooking the flight of time in concentrating on the subject in hand, made up for his demerits for tardiness at West Point in the way he concentrated on the present one of leading his black troopers, fighting dismounted as was the rest of our cavalry. His elders of the old army, recovering the fire of their youth in Civil War charges, spurred their weary legs in keeping pace with the youth of a later generation.

Just as the people at home feared that our forces in Cuba were in trouble came the news flash that they had taken San Juan Hill. The heights commanding Santiago were ours. Now no one asked, "Will you work, soldier?" about the Regular. He had become a hero. Foreign military attachés joined in their glowing tributes to the achievement of the man and his rifle under the handicap of such disorganization when our civil industrial organization was already notably excellent.

Accompanying the national acclaim our national indignation rose to scandal over the lack of food and medical supplies, the cruel neglect of the wounded while the emaciated victors were dropping in sickness and exhaustion with an epidemic of yellow fever threatening. The inquiring finger for the cause soon closed in on the public's fist shaken in derision and condemnation on Washington. But Washington's explanations did not wash. The remark attributed to one sorely bewildered officer of a compartment may have been fictitious, but it expressed a fellow compartmental feeling in distress.

"We had a perfectly good organization, going on very smoothly and comfortably," he said, "until we had this d-d war which busted it."

Corbin, the super-bureaucratic expert in "getting things done," could not afford to tell the whole American people that they were "g.d.s.o.b's with the bellyache." Side stepping was in order for him. There must be a scapegoat. The lot fell to kindly old Secretary of War Alger who had accepted Corbin as his mentor.

And First Lieutenant Pershing had another item added to his official record. He received the Silver Star for "gallantry in action against the Spanish forces, July 1, 1898." More significant in a broader implication were a few words from Major General S. M. B. Young, a vigorous elder in command of the cavalry brigade in the Santiago campaign, who had seen men under hot fire many times in the Civil War before that in Cuba.

A soldier may think clearly in class-room exercises in tactics and on practice peace maneuvers, but although he is surcharged with will and ambition to do so he may not think clearly in battle action. Young said that Pershing was "the coolest man under fire I ever saw." This was professional tribute to more than gallantry and the glamor that goes with it. He had kept his head in the supreme test. Fortune had further favored him in that although his leanness had become skinniness he had not been on the sick list.

In easy times the sons of favoritism, the "gum shoe" artists, the good fellows with a pleasant front and little in their heads, may go their easy way undisturbed. The Washington administration had been acutely subjected to the old lesson that war consists of the unexpected. Wisdom and self-preservation under the public fire called for the disregard of personal friendships and in the search for remedial efficiency turned to those who had been under fire in Cuba. The fissures riven in the crust of the overlordism of the compartmental bureaucracy became openings of opportunity for the elders who had endured the strain with flying colors and for the progressive younger officers.

The War Department, groggy from the public flogging, had a rush of new and baffling problems dumped in its lap on top of its other miseries. As though the restoration of order in Cuba were not enough we had accepted destiny's challenge in our "new possessions" of Porto Rico and very much also, after the peace treaty was signed, the Philippine Islands on the other side of the earth.

Again it was "Pershing's the man for this job." He was a glutton for work and it would give him plenty. Where was he? With his exhausted regiment back from Cuba and fit for duty. The job was half military and half civil, requiring tact, balance, acumen and sagacity. A soldier who knew the law would be the better equipped, and Pershing had been admitted to the bar.

But the necessary rank? A captain might not be assigned to serve under a lieutenant. In that case the chief would be saluting a subordinate. As a temporary major of volunteers in the Ordnance Department Pershing reported to a desk in Washington laden with protests and questions from overseas. There was no predecessor to take over from. He initiated the future Bureau of Insular Affairs, which later ranked a brigadier general as its chief.

Information about the Philippines ran in the contrary channels of native appeals supported by the home "anti-Imperialists" and reports from the army holding only Manila and fast becoming besieged by the gathering insurgents. Rebellion flamed. Now we had to pacify the islands before the little red school house could spread the ideals and instruction for self-government among our "little brown brothers."

His superiors were satisfied with Pershing, but he was not satisfied with himself. He was unhappy at that desk in the War Department far from the scene of action, of army action, where the problem was being solved. He wanted to be out there; and his request for transfer was granted early in 1899 when it was clear that would enlarge his sphere of usefulness.

Soldier Pershing and lawyer Pershing was now under the

eye of the New York lawyer, Elihu Root, whom President McKinley had summoned as Alger's successor to bring order out of War Department chaos and develop a new régime for its expanded duties. He had already been under the eye of Theodore Roosevelt and was to be under the eye of William H. Taft. These were to be mighty men in our national affairs for the next decade.

6

Pacifying the Sultans

OCCASIONALLY WHEN he took time off between feudal wars an inland datto of Mindanao and some of his retainers would come down to the shore for a glimpse of the sea and on personal business. Datto and retainers wore turbans and clothes of brilliant colors made in Germany for the local market. Aside from knives in their belts they carried long two-handed *krises,* also usually made in Germany, the bright, sharp blades in thin wooden scabbards bound with string. The strings would be cut with the stroke which slashed off an enemy's head or arm or cleaved him to the midriff.

The Moros of Mindanao, second largest of the islands and nearest the equator, had the contempt of fighting men of the true faith for the effeminate infidels of the northern islands. Spanish priests, bearing the cross beside the conqueror's sword in Spain's great days, had converted the nomads of the northern islands and set them up in towns and pastoral villages around the plaza of the church, barracks and official palaces in the ways of a regimented paternalism; but the religion of the crescent had mastery in Mindanao. There all became Moros (Mohammedans). So they had remained through the centuries of Spain's decadence until we wrested the last of her distant dominions from her in 1898.

A perfectly peaceful Mindanao and Spanish Morocco would have left Spanish officers without any anticipatory military exploits to dream of in their siestas. Another Moro or Riff rebellion to suppress—another little Moro or Riff war—afforded youth the adventure to which it was entitled and captains-general glowing reports of victories.

But the Spanish punitive expeditions never went too uncomfortably far from the Mindanao coast. The Spanish never had attempted to pacify the interior. It was a forbidden, all but an unknown land. Around the great central lake of Lanao, set in walls of tropical verdure high above the coast in a cooler climate, a hundred little sultans, or dattos, ruled.

Brown hands parting the branches that made the jungle curtain, peering, ferret eyes gave the warning of a white man's approach for shots or the slashing of the knives from ambush. A sultan had the unanswerable reason, to him, that he could not prevent a subject brave from running amok and, for his own surer entry into Paradise, including an unbeliever in his swath of killings. So the Spaniard had better keep away from Lake Lanao. There was neither profit nor glory for old Spain in establishing its authority over the Lake Lanao region.

For the first two years of his Philippine service Lieutenant Pershing was adjutant of the department of the Moro provinces. In 1901, with the expansion of the Regular army to a size more adequate for its present demands, linear promotion made him a captain. Now, at forty-one, he could look forward to being a lieutenant colonel and possibly a colonel before retirement for age.

As adjutant, with so much information passing through

47

his hands, he knew the Moros and their ways and as much of the country as we occupied, which was already more than the Spaniard had ever held. His cavalry regiment, which he joined after his promotion, had a post on the edge of Lake Lanao, with all the rest of the shores and the interior in the hands of the defiant sultans who gave us continual trouble.

With the last of the armed opposition in the other islands suppressed, and under the civil rule of Governor General Taft, it was time we brought the Moro chiefs in line with our instructional policy. We had first to show them we were master after all forms of tactful appeasement had failed. The man in command of the initial armed missionary effort must make the lesson convincing with a minimum of fighting and of native bitterness which would lead to further uprisings.

It was quite possible for him to incur unnecessary fighting, even unwittingly stage a real Moro war in which victory would rebound to his soldier credit. Taft had the experience of such results in the inclination of some army officers, under the irritation of guerrilla sniping, to have too abundant faith in the efficacy of "civilize 'em with a Krag." And no news was the best news from the Philippines for our people at home when the taste of the oriental adventure with its climax in rebellion had long since become stale in our mouths.

Again Pershing was seen as the man for the job. Again appeared the question of rank for what was certainly a colonel's command at least. Not only many officers of his own years ranked him, but, in the slow promotion of the cavalry branch before the Spanish War, many infantry officers who had received second lieutenant's commission later than his, ranked him.

A mutual understanding by superiors found a way around the obstacle of formalism. No major need be detailed under him. There were enough lusty lieutenants for this kind of work. Captain Pershing was given a free hand. He had his first separate field command, which is the ambition of all line officers. In the old days one preferred to be first in command of a post of fifty men to second in command of a post of five hundred.

As usual Pershing analyzed all sides of his task. He was meticulous in his preparations. Discipline was essential to health in villages where disease germs had an eternal open season of tropical heat, essential lest the men get free with native women, essential to prevent outbursts of individual temper under native baiting. The soldier on sentry go, after occupying a village, must bear taunts, abuse and dares and not shoot unless attacked.

Once Pershing started he made the lesson swift and thorough in his marches around Lake Lanao. Sultans learned that if you fought his soldiers you were sure of a licking. They became intimately acquainted with his tough side as an enemy, and then, after submission, with his fair side in keeping the peace. He was the American sultan to them and most cordial with a welcoming smile. "You strong fighting man, Captain Pershing and I strong fighting man, you big datto and I big datto—we good friends." All was well if a Moro chieftain kept faith in practice with his words.

The American sultan bore no grudges. His soldiers did not steal your cattle or raid your villages. You could go on being chief of your people as before if you kept on the right side of the line he drew. But cross to the other and the American's smile had another interpretation. If a Moro ran *amok* then American soldiers ran *amok,* and they shot straight. And Moros must not steal and raid. If they did they would be found out.

Captain Pershing did not sit in camp waiting for all men to come to him and all things to be brought to him. He was on the move. He seemed to have eyes in the back of his head. And his were the simple judgments of Solomon for a primitive people enforced with primitive simplicity and definiteness. One datto might accuse another of stealing and then the other make a counter accusation. Pershing brought the two together and took account of the stock of their possessions.

With the desired minimum loss of life he ended the ancient régime of free-for-all killing and pillage and established order in the interior of Mindanao. This achievement brought him for the first time some attention in the home press, and might have drawn much more if one of his defects, or merits, as you please, was that he was no personal publicist.

But his success won much attention in Washington. Theodore Roosevelt, now President, and Root and Taft were well pleased with their Captain Pershing. For a similar service a British officer, hailed as a Kitchener type, might have been made a major general and knighted. Under our law he might not have the reward of advance of a single number on the army list of captains.

Meanwhile Secretary Root had been quietly busy. Corbin was no longer mighty in Washington. Refusing the way out by retirement or resignation he had been assigned to a field department command to appease his political following.

Both compartments saw the heavens falling when the quartermaster and commissary departments—with consequent reduction of Washington personnel—were merged in one, the quartermaster's, as in other armies. All the compartments turned all their influence in a chorus of outrage against the proposal to establish a general staff system for the actual coördination of preparation for war and its conduct. The clerical monarchists declared a general staff to be foreign, monarchical, undemocratic, unAmerican. They utilized all their channels of appeal to Congress to save the nation from a future military dictatorship.

But the majority of Congress, taking a more intensive

interest in the army in its new responsibilities in the wrestle with the problems of our insular possessions, created a general staff. "Coburging" permanently as "a swivel chair artist" in Washington was over. Expert knowledge in all branches now served a chief of staff instead of a compartmental chief. Drawn from the line, staff officers must return to the line after four years on the staff.

Who, if not Captain Pershing, after he had made peace in Mindanao, should be detailed to service in the pioneering organization of the general staff?

He returned to a different world in Washington from that he had known before. The old Army, which he had known as a second and first lieutenant, had sung its gallant swan song. Elders who held high rank lived in the memory of brave days of another era. Declining years, as they kept slower step, had sapped physical vigor in many instances. President Theodore Roosevelt was acutely aware of the handicap. His dynamic emphasis had free range in private references to "fat old colonels who fall off their horses or cannot stand a five-mile march."

But age gave rank. There was the appeal of the injustice and the blow to pride of a junior being lifted above a faithful officer who had waited his turn through the long, arduous years. Even if he were a colonel or a general only for a few months before retirement, that meant the reward of rank for which he had waited.

Regular officers recognized the theoretical soundness of promotion by selection, but they feared that political influence would enter into the choice. Too much promotion by selection must open the way for abuse. Ambitious officers would become politicians before they were soldiers, undermining the very principle of a constitutional army.

While the President, as commander-in-chief, had not the power to promote an officer under the rank of brigadier a single number he could nominate any officer from a lieutenant to a colonel to be brigadier, subject to confirmation by the Senate. President McKinley had nominated Leonard Wood to be a brigadier.

An army doctor over the heads of hundreds of seniors of the line! This stirred the wrath of the Regulars and a storm of protest throughout the country, which did not prevent confirmation. There was less public protest, and much less from the Regulars when Frederick Funston, for his brilliant leading of the Twentieth Kansas regiment and for his capture of the insurrecto chief Aguinaldo, was raised to a brigadiership from no Regular rank at all.

If there were to be promotion by selection then the Regulars agreed that J. Franklin Bell, a first lieutenant of Regular cavalry at the outbreak of the Spanish War, was entitled to a brigadiership for his dashing and vigorous initiative in the Philippines as Captain Albert L. Mills had been for his in the Cuban campaign. Nor was there any objection when Major Tasker H. Bliss, another West Pointer, had Root's backing for a brigadiership in return for his great work in Cuban reconstruction.

Thus it was the big reward or no reward for scores of officers from lieutenants to colonels who had earned recognition. The President asked Congress to remedy a practice contrary to the principles of efficiency, and made Pershing an example in point for his argument. "Promotion by seniority" was to be content "with the triumph of mediocrity over excellence."

"On the other hand," the President wrote, "a system which encouraged the exercise of social and political favoritism in promotions would be even worse. But it would surely be easy to devise a method of promotion from grade to grade in which the opinion of higher officers of the service upon the candidates should be decisive upon the standing and promotion of the latter.

"Just such a system now obtains at West Point. The quality of each year's work determines the standing of that year's class, the man being dropped or graduated into the next year's class in the relative position which his military superiors decide to be warranted by his merit.

"In other words, ability, energy, fidelity and all other similar qualities determine the rank of a man year after year in West Point, and his standing in the army when he graduates from West Point; but from that time on, all effort to find which man is best or worst, and reward or punish him accordingly, is abandoned; no brilliancy, no amount of hard work, no eagerness in the performance of duty can advance him and no slackness or indifference that falls short of court-martial offense can retard him.

"Until this system is changed we cannot hope that our officers will be of as high a grade as we have the right to expect, considering the material upon which we draw. Moreover, when a man renders such service as Captain Pershing rendered last spring in the Moro campaign, it ought to be possible to reward him without at once jumping him to the grade of brigadier general."

Thus Captain Pershing had been singled out before the country in a message to Congress, which did not enact the President's suggestion into law, while Captain Pershing kept on ploughing in a fertile field for his industry.

As a staff officer he was serving under Major General Adna R. Chaffee, then Chief of Staff. Up from the ranks in the Civil War, ever fit, Chaffee was renowned as the commander of our troops in the March to Peking for the relief of the legations. He was the antithesis of Corbin, an exemplar of the code of the old army at its best. When all the other foreign armies were looting in Peking, he drove his men he caught pilfering back to barracks with his ringing "You're American soldiers, not thieves."

That China campaign was the one army experience in his time that Pershing had missed. He had the inheritance of the old army bred in him in fashioning the new in which West Point became only the primary school for the ambitious. All the graduate schools for the younger officers

53

were being strengthened with stiffer courses, leading up to Leavenworth Staff College for the chosen, who were ready to work sixteen hours a day, and to the new War College in Washington.

Lack of rank did not prevent further spread of educational opportunities for Pershing. He was sent afield to connect up general staff work in the Southwestern Department at Oklahoma City, and then back to be a student officer at the War College. Everything was being done to prepare him for high command should war come.

7

"Invaluable"

BEFORE PERSHING RETURNED to Washington the eyes of the world's army and navy staffs and the statesmen over them were on the plains of Manchuria and the China seas. In the Russo-Japanese War of 1904-05 public sympathy sided with little David Japan against Goliath Russia of the Czar, which had threatened the envelopment of all northern China.

More than thirty years had passed since the Franco-Prussian War and more than twenty since the Russo-Turkish War in a period of rapid progress in the power of weapons. There had been no great recent war in which huge numbers of troops were engaged, only little second or third class wars. The numbers in our war with Spain had been small and our arms not modern on land.

In astounding success the Japanese had driven the Russian army far from the Korean border, won the battle of Liao-Yang and now was hammering on toward the end of the siege of the fortress of Port Arthur. Before Mukden, in the winter of 1904-05, armies larger than those of the Germans and French at Sedan in 1870 or the Russians and Turks at Plevna in 1878 faced each other on the longest battle line so far in history, nearly half of that of the western front from the North Sea to Switzerland in 1914-18.

Staffs of the huge European armies were ravenously eager for exact professional information from Manchuria. The lessons which the German staff learned from it, and the French failed to learn, gave the Germans their advantage in heavy mobile artillery and machine guns in the early period of the World War.

As one staff officer said, while he would not be willing to give his eyes—he would need them for observation—he would be willing to crawl across Manchuria in order to be an attaché with either army. In place of a returning officer whose tour was up Pershing was appointed military attaché to Japan. "The detail came without solicitation and would not have been accepted had it not been for the fact that it gives me a chance to go to the front with the Japanese Army, an ambition which I have entertained ever since the beginning of the war."

Meanwhile the impersonal Captain Pershing who had been fond of the company of women but remained heart-free had fallen in love at the age of forty-four with Miss Frances Warren, daughter of the veteran senator, Francis Warren of Wyoming; and they sailed for Japan immediately after their marriage.

He arrived at Japanese headquarters in Manchuria for the final stages of the Japanese victory in the Battle of Mukden which was unprecedented in the numbers engaged in continuous action for two weeks.

Then Japan was still politely, decorously, humbly asking her way, while she fought for it, to a modest place among the world powers. Ito, Inouye and Yamagata, leaders of the *genro* (elder statesmen), whose midwifery had conducted the birth of a new Japan out of the old, and skillfully nursed the growth of the child, were in the prime of power. They had Emperor Mejii's ear and held the leash on the army in the Bismarckian precedent. Experience had taught them the wisdom of courting world good will. The army, which was far less a law unto itself than later, accepted the *genro* dictum, which became the Emperor's own, that foreign military attachés and correspondents should be received at the front.

The Japanese officers were then mostly—all the high commanders invariably were—of the old aristocratic samurai caste with the disarming and winning samurai etiquette of manners. Truculence had not yet appeared. There was no talk about Japan's destiny as the ruler of Asia. Japanese secretiveness was none the less irritating be-cause it depended upon the subtle finesse of indirection, never answering direct while asking direct questions.

Attachés and correspondents with the army were bound by a silken web of restrictions which we found sheathed steel wire. We were taken to points of observation where we could see the general movements of troops; we had lectures from staff officers outlining the progress of divi-sions to the front which left off with their deployment into battle. Deployment would reveal knowledge of close con-tact, fire discipline and the effects of then modern fire— the most vital point of information attachés sought— which the Japanese staff did not propose to share even with the British in the fellowship of the Anglo-Japanese alliance.

The polite reason given why an attaché or correspondent might not be with the infantry in attack was that a Japanese soldier might mistake his white face for a Russian's. How-ever, when a correspondent, who had not the dignity of an attaché to preserve, did break bounds in his zeal the Japanese soldiers on the firing line received him quite cordially.

It was with the First Japanese Army (Kuroki's) to which we were both attached that I first came to know Pershing. The attachés' camp, which had representatives of all the major powers, was in a Chinese village about a mile from ours in another village. We provided our own food which was largely American and cooked by a Japanese who knew American cooking. The attachés were guests of the army. They got alleged European cooking, which was a gastronomic horror, in a mixture of Japanese and European cooking. So our invitations to dinner to anyone in the attachés' camp were uniformly acceptable.

Also our guests had a chance to blow off steam. Their temper was not only tried by their Japanese hosts, but none including the British allies liked them, contrary to the old precedent of natural sympathy with the army which you accompany in a war. As Pershing remarked, he once had the impulse but not the nerve to tease one of his British colleagues of the Anglo-Japanese alliance with the suggestion that "blood is thicker than water."

In the attachés' group with the First Army were Lieutenant General Ian Hamilton—his laurels won in South Africa still fresh—who was later to be the British commander in the ill-fated Gallipoli expedition; Baron Colonel Corvisart and Major von Etzel who were to command corps opposite each other at Verdun; Captain Hoffmann, later Ludendorff's right hand man and the prime force on the German side of the council table in framing the Treaty of Brest-Litovsk which officially put Russia out of the World War; and Major Caviglia, who distinguished himself in high command in the offensive after the Italians recrossed the Piave. And in the first year of the Russo-Japanese War our own attachés with the First Army had been Colonel Enoch H. Crowder, afterward Judge Advocate General and Provost Marshal General of the Draft in the World War and Captain Peyton C. March, our Chief of Staff in 1918.

The Battle of Mukden had not been decisive. The Japanese army had only driven the Russian army back. Week after week, month after month, attachés and correspondents waited from the bleak Manchurian winter on into the deadly heat of the Manchurian summer for that battle while we were restricted to a five-mile compass of movement. Departure, to which the Japanese objected, might mean missing a greater battle than Mukden.

A common love of exercise brought attaché Pershing and the author together. No two other men in either camp seemed to want so much of it. He was the most pleasingly human and companionable of all to me. He had a sense of humor, which is more than a saving grace on occasion. It is a life saver. Before we had settled in our present camp, while moving, my baggage fell down a railroad embankment. This was enough on top of cumulative irritations to produce a psychosis on my part. To hell with it! Let the Japs, the Czar of Russia or the old Dowager Empress have it. I was through.

I noted that Pershing was grinning. "Don't you grin!" I said. "And by Heavens, don't you laugh. If you do all is off between us forever." He replied; "I was just looking at the scenery and thinking." After I had let some more poison out of my system we both laughed and he lent a helping hand to recover the baggage.

Even the most liquid efforts of the Manchurian rainy season, which seemed properly to belong to the tropic zone, did not prevent our having our walks. One day, after I had been shut up for stifling hour after hour under the drumbeat on the roof of my tent, the flap opened and Pershing, his slicker dripping, said in a merry challenge:

"I have done half my stretch and will do the other half on my way back to camp. But I prefer not to walk back alone. You'll feel a lot better for it,"—as I did after plowing through the mud with the plower and home to my own camp.

He had been habited to clean tent life on campaigns in the West in contrast to his present quarters in a Manchurian village house in the midst of village smells of a most unsanitary people. I had a tent of the lightest strong material, rain proof and mosquito proof, which I had had especially made for Manchuria, as a correspondent's privilege in providing all for myself. If I were to dispose of that tent when I left the army he would like first chance at it in view of his plan for a camping expedition with Mrs. Pershing as a holiday after the present detail was finished; and thus the veteran tent was to have its final service.

Once when I asked Major von Etzel and Captain Hoffmann, the German attachés, to dinner, only Major von Etzel appeared. He explained that Hoffmann was not well. The next day I saw Hoffmann who looked perfectly well, and I congratulated him on his prompt recovery, he said he had not been ill. But he expressed no regret that he had missed the dinner.

When I mentioned this to Pershing he grinned.

"You are not up in the social relations of my German colleagues," he said. "Your invitation went to von Etzel as the senior in rank. So he accepted it for himself. Hoffmann would not have gone, anyway, not with von Etzel or von Etzel with Hoffmann. Can you beat it? The two are living in that little room, sleeping in beds across from each other, and they have not spoken for weeks except when officially necessary. What a life! You'd think they'd have a good 'bawling out' and then make up for convenience's sake if not their Emperor's."

The French attachés hugely enjoyed the feud, and the Austrian, although a Teutonic ally, just as much. To them it was an example of Prussian boorishness stewing in its own juice. "Even if one Frenchman hates another," said a French attaché, "they have enough *savoir faire* to be polite."

All the European prejudices and racial characteristics had their reflection in that group of accomplished chosen officers in the pinpricking frustration of their confinement. To his further amusement the great grandson of Frederick Pfershing noted that some attachés of noble families felt their caste superiority to those who were not. But the attachés all liked him. He got on with all.

It did not trouble him that he was old for his rank as captain or that it placed him at the foot of the table. I never heard any complaint against a law that prevented any promotion for his services in Mindanao or any mention of the tribute paid him in the President's message to Congress. Of the Moros I recall his saying: "They were human —a human problem." It would have been out of all the bounds of possibility that he would have had a star in his baggage, as did a colonel who had been with the Japanese the first year, in his hope the President would nominate him to be a brigadier. Captain Pershing was no grouse; he had the joy of living as the French say. He did not forget his good fortune in being an observer in spite of all the restrictions.

I recall once asking how he thought the American soldier would compare with the Japanese who had amazed the world by their fanatic courage and skill. His answer was decisively indignant. "Better. The American is the best soldier—the best material if well trained." This was no national boast. It was convinced professional opinion. If well trained!

Certainly he had none of the pretense that sometimes goes with learning. But he gave me many surprises in flash of comment which showed the vast extent of his reading beyond a strictly professional range.

How sound and down to earth he was on that subject in which the theorists, the men of words, are so often misled! Grand strategy depended upon the nation's political objective, the mission of the army, the terrain, the gaining of the objective sought, the numbers, the supplies, the arms, the roads and distances to be marched as against the enemy's power, positions and material. Clearly he was there in Manchuria as a faithful industrious reporter, a gatherer of information which would be of basic professional value in knowledge of the contact of troops with modern arms.

He absorbed information from the other attachés who had been longer than he with the army. Niggard as were the Japanese staff lectures they were to be studied for useful points in collaboration with others gained. Given the conditions as they were, make the best of them.

"Invaluable!" as he said of his experience in Manchuria in later years. The plower, who was given to crowbarring a stone out of the way to keep his furrow straight, had an example of its application in the Russian commander Kuropatkin (relieved after Mukden) who had such a fertility of ideas that the Japanese could depend upon him never to see an initial plan through.

The Japanese had a good reason for being friendly to the American. They were three hundred miles from the border of Russian Siberia, five thousand miles from the enemy's capital. They had nothing of the enemy's which would compel him to make peace when they needed foreign loans to carry on and their arms plants were relatively meager in output compared to later days. The Russian army was being heavily reinforced and the Japanese reinforced with old reservists and hastily trained youth on the way to the old resort of "robbing the cradle and the grave."

Already the Japanese army was too near "fought out" for a decisive victory. Should it be able to force the Russians back another hundred miles nearer Russian Siberia, it would be fought out and still facing a Russian army.

Japanese policy must depend upon the prestige of past victories of an invincible army in world opinion and not risk world disillusionment by a military disaster. It was vital to court the good will of America as a mediator. If Captain Pershing could have talked secretly with Washington he would have had some illumining information to impart. The decisive battle was not won in Manchuria by the Japanese but around the council table in the Treaty of Portsmouth preparing the way for the Japanese Man-chukuo and the Japanese sweep into China thirty years afterward. American policy in 1905, which coincided with British, when no hazard of prophecy envisaged a Russian revolution, saw little Japan as the only check on colossal Russia's Asiatic expansion in safeguarding the Open Door in China.

The Pershing one knew in those weary months of wait-ing was a capable, thorough, studious, alert officer and a very likeable man. And I do not forget how he was some-times a little late. There was something which he was doing and he wanted to finish.

"Will Pershing be on time?" we asked in the course of the ceremonial on a hillside looking down on the army drawn up on the plain in honor of the Japanese soldiers who had fallen in the Battle of Mukden.

Each battalion was allotted the space for a full battalion, but this was occupied only by the battalion's survivors among those who were in the battle. Those with the few-est survivors were in front. Some battalions had not enough survivors to fill half their space. According to the Shinto dogma the dead, happy in their immortality for having died for their Emperor, looked down proudly on their vacant places and heard their praises sounded. This was the teaching nursed by the Japanese staff, but personal inquiry revealed that many Japanese soldiers were human enough not to believe it. The worry of the staff was that the survivors had had enough fighting and wanted to go home, preferring the prospect of remaining on this earth a while longer.

The Shinto ritual was about over. With its completion the high officers and the military attachés were each to place a sprig of evergreen on the altar. Pershing had not yet arrived; but he appeared doublequicking with a half minute to spare, looking the pattern plate of military form.

8

Reward and Test

Then "Colonel John J. Pershing U. S. A. Rtd. (Retired)" surely seemed the limit of rank that he would have on his calling card at the close of his army career. Congress was past the mood of further considering President Theodore Roosevelt's request for selective promotion by grades. The Spanish War had become a memory, the Philippines were pacified.

But if the persistent "T.R." could not get a lesser promotion for Pershing he should have the big one from captain's bars to a star. This would jump him over pages of officers above him on the army list. Old colonels of sixty would be saluting as their superior a man of forty-six.

It goes without saying that father-in-law Senator Warren, as chairman of the Senate military affairs committee, did nothing to halt the speedy confirmation by the Senate which was without a hitch. No public objection had appeared. Young regular officers were enthusiastic. Elders might growl a little, but agreed that if any man was to have the elevation Pershing deserved it. Just in behalf

64

of a son-in-law Senator Warren would have met a caustic flow of comment from some of his colleagues.

Nor was Theodore Roosevelt making anybody a brigadier because he was anybody's son-in-law. He was on record in his tribute to Pershing to Congress before Pershing met Miss Warren. As he reiterated to me there were two outstanding men in the army, Wood and Pershing, and "by George," he wanted Pershing's abilities utilized.

As a Congressman would put it, the widespread congratulations Pershing received from both army and civilian friends showed how well "he had looked after his fences." Those whom he had met had reminders they were not forgotten by Lieutenant or Captain Pershing in the big batch of Christmas cards he always sent.

Now a brigadier at forty-six, the youngest except Wood, who was his junior by a few months, he had eighteen years of service as a general officer before him. He would have high command in case of war, and in any event one day doubtless be a major general and chief of staff before his retirement.

With the brigadier's star fresh on his shoulders he was briefly at the Presidio on our Pacific coast, and then detailed as brigade commander to Fort McKinley in the Philippines. With the islands peaceful in a tropical climate the tendency was natural for a large garrison to take it a little easy; but not under Pershing, who had his troops out in target practice against potential enemy targets and in maneuvers in simulation of actual battle practice.

A bridge over a swollen river was a part of the game which the rains were not to interrupt. "It rains during wars as well as in peace," Pershing said. A young engineer, told off to build a bridge, reported he was unable to because he could not get the first rope across to the other bank.

"I never ask the impossible of any officer or soldier of my command. When you get an order you must find a way to execute it. Come with me!"

Mounting his horse cavalryman Pershing led the way in a charge of the two through the jungle. He tied a rope to his saddle and swam across the torrent with it. The bridge was built.

Two years at Fort McKinley, and he was homeward bound by Suez on a special mission to Europe. The staff wanted a report from the former attaché with the Japanese army on the European armies. This took him over much of the ground which later he and soldiers of the AEF were to know even better.

Again attached to the General Staff at home, for the first time he appeared unfit for duty. The aftermath of an attack of sprue in the Philippines, and tropical service which wears the white man down, could no longer be denied. Let him take the time to get well, to which he was entitled, said both President Roosevelt and Taft who was now not only Secretary of War but President-elect. Pershing received an order to go to the army and navy general hospital at Hot Springs and six months' leave.

After six months he had completely recovered, and again it was the Philippines for him, this time back commanding the department of the Moro provinces both as soldier and practically civil ruler. Again he kept on the move in close touch with problems on the spot, again burned the midnight oil over reports, rewriting and rewriting his own to make them brief and clear, as the former champion of brevity on the general staff, in recollection of long-winded documents from the "swivel chair artists" of the old days.

"God! Isn't it awful? Words, words and then this fellow is only passing the buck" as he would say. Military reports were no place for the pseudo-metaphors with which he had had to wrestle at West Point. A cardinal military virtue was definiteness. He doggedly strove to give an example.

Mrs. Pershing shared his travels and life at his stations. He was devoted to his family with the pride in his children of a man who marries late in life. Helen was eight, Anne six, Warren five and Mary two in January of the fateful year of 1914 for the Pershings and the world when they were once more at the Presidio. There they could settle down, it appeared for a long term, and send the elder children to home schools; and there they read the news of the outbreak of the World War.

Chaos had been fast developing in Mexico. Francisco Madero who had overthrown the Diaz régime and made himself President had been assassinated. Huerta, under the shadow of being a party to the murder, sat on the rock of Chapultepec in his place. Three rival northern chieftains, Carranza, Villa and Obregon held defiant sway in northern Mexico.

In the spring of 1914 President Wilson, refusing to recognize Huerta, and determined that he should not hold the succession to the Presidency through assassination, had the navy bombard Vera Cruz and then troops landed in occupation. Huerta's eventful exile did not end the Mexican crisis with Carranza, Villa and other chieftains at each other's throats.

Pershing was ordered to El Paso. There was no telling how long the emergency would hold him there. He would be afield patrolling the border; he might see action in Mexico. It was best for the present that Mrs. Pershing should remain with the children where they were established at the Presidio.

In August, 1915, he had word of a ghastly tragedy. The house that his family occupied was a ramshackle old wooden building. The flames from a fire that broke out in the night fed on tinder. Mrs. Pershing perished with three of the children. Only little Warren survived. Afterward Pershing's lips appeared a little thinner and pressed tighter together. He no longer looked notably younger than his years. Now he had only the solace of the boy and devotion to duty.

On the morning of March 10, 1916 when the slender little figure of Newton D. Baker, former Mayor of Cleveland and so-called "pacifist"—whose choice as Secretary of War had astounded the country—appeared from the White House, after his call on President Wilson, the newspaper men told him "Hell has broken loose in Mexico." What was the pacifist going to do about it?

The previous night Francisco Villa had crossed the border and killed women, children and soldiers in Columbus, New Mexico. After the little Secretary had taken the oath he asked the two veterans of giant stature, Major General Hugh Scott, Chief of Staff, and Major General Tasker H. Bliss, Assistant Chief of Staff, for their recommendations. International law had been gravely violated, they said, and a punitive expedition in pursuit of Villa was the only answer.

"Let us proceed," said Baker. Who was to command? "Pershing," both said, and General Funston of the Southern Department agreed although the command nominally should have gone to a major general. There was Pershing's record, his line record, his whole record. In the last fourteen years, excluding the year and a half in Japan, he had spent ten years in the Philippines. You could trust his sagacity in faithful obedience to directions—again more than a soldier for the most ticklish task that had come to him.

For the first time his name was in front page headline spreads. The expedition had the spell of the chase. It might lead to war with Mexico. Would Pershing get his man? Triumph for him would be to march Villa back as a prisoner at his stirrup leather.

But the one outcome the administration did not want was war, which apparently, as later evidence proved, was being encouraged by German propaganda to divert us from our growing sympathy with the Allied cause. This was not all. Pershing, who had been sent to get the Moro chiefs as a means to peace in Mindanao, was not wanted to get Villa. For this was not the way to peace with Mexico in the view of the Washington administration.

BRIGADIER GENERAL PERSHING, COMMANDER OF THE MEXICAN
PUNITIVE EXPEDITION.

If Villa were taken he would be a white elephant on our hands. The only warrantable course would be trial for redhanded, deliberate murder on our soil and his execution, or we should have proved ourselves weak to Mexican revolutionists in their present mood. If we executed him that would arouse their ire in further hate of the Gringoes.

Read between the written lines, without closing the ear to oral intimations, and it became clear that Pershing was expected only to disperse Villa's band as a warning against future raids across the border. So Pershing was bound to be in the public position of failure in his objective, failure to bring home the bacon. He would be like the general who marched his men up the hill and then down again. But that was all in the day's work, all in the soldier's part to go where he was told to go and do what he was told to do—in this case not to do what he was advertised to do.

It needs no imagination to understand how easy it would have been for him, without seeming to do so, to have allowed personal ambition to break the bonds of discretion by a conflict with the truculent, threatening rebel chieftains, and thus have opened the road of war for a march to Mexico City. Action would not have been unwelcome to his men in the deadly monotony of their isolation on the hot sands. The bonds of discipline must be strong, but not too exasperating, not petty, not pinpricking.

For eleven months he held his force in the broiling heat at the end of a two hundred mile line of thin communications, which he protected. It was ever ready as a pendulum to swing either way to cut off any hostile force of size from moving on our border which all our national guard and all the regulars we could muster were tiresomely patrolling. When we went to war in France we had not also to look after war with Mexico, which the Kaiser and his generals would have hailed as the best news they had ever heard from America.

69

Pershing had had the experience of the command of ten thousand men, the largest integral field force since the Spanish War. Although it would have been capable of over-whelming any Mexican force we had had a lesson in how weak we were in more than numbers against a first-class military power. Ours had been a spectator's interest in the rapid progress of arms in the World War. Aviation would have been most valuable for scouting in Mexico. But we had only two obsolete planes on the Border. They could rise in the air, but not remain aloft long.

Getting what information he could from the official communiqués on both sides, Pershing was in Mexico when the Battle of Jutland was fought and during the first great offensive of the British new army on the Somme, which won little ground after months of struggle, and during the German army's further triumphs on the eastern front.

A week after Germany's declaration of unrestricted sub-marine warfare, which cast the die for our entry into the war, his troops had marched back across the border in veteran fitness and precision. With the death of Major General Frederick Funston came his promotion to the vacancy in the list of major generals and his appointment as Funston's successor at San Antonio in command of the Southern Department.

There he was upon our declaration of war when our people accepted the word of our new Allies that the weight of our commercial and financial aid would assure victory. There he was while we acclaimed the visiting Balfour and Joffre missions in our fresh enthusiasm; there when the word was passed that Marshal Joffre suggested we might send over a handful of men to "show the flag"; there when, May 7, 1917, a month after the declaration of war, he received orders to proceed to Washington to report to the Secretary of War.

When I saw him in Senator Warren's apartment the morning of his arrival in Washington before he reported to Secretary Baker he said, "You have been seeing some big doings since we last met," which had been before the World War. "And you will be seeing some soon," I replied. For the public took it for granted he was to be sent to France at the head of the handful of men, which canny old Joffre, edging along, now announced might be a division for good measure, not that they were really needed to fight.

"I only know that I have been ordered to report to Washington," he said. So far and no further until the next order.

There was not a spare ounce of flesh on his frame. At fifty-six he looked capable of another race with the Indian runner. The tan of the Mexican sun was still on his face. He was in a khaki blouse but I visioned him in shirt and campaign hat on the long grind in Mexico, ever watchful, his eyes missing no detail.

He asked me some questions about the allied military situation as the result of my two years' experience on the western front. The answers pictured it as very serious. From what he knew he remarked that apparently the Allies had a long way yet to go.

9

In Room 223

PRESIDENT LINCOLN had never met Grant until Grant came east to command all the Federal armies, his headquarters to be with the Army of the Potomac. Baker had never met Pershing until that May morning of 1917, and President Wilson was yet to meet him.

After we had been months in the World War Baker made a pertinent remark out of his experience which had taught him the old lesson that an officer's high promise in peace was far from always being fulfilled in war. Baker said he could often tell more about an officer's vigor and fitness for a larger sphere in war's test by watching him walk up and down a room than by reading his record.

Grant's introduction to Lincoln before they met had been Grant's succession of victories in the west freeing the Mississippi to the sea. Grant had won his every battle as a preparation for battles still to be won to end the war. Pershing's introduction to Baker had been his discreet conduct of the Mexican expedition through weary months of worry and alarms.

A heartbeat, Major General Frederick Funston's, had been between Pershing and the future command in France. Referred to as a soldier of fortune, the adventurous young Funston, after an exploring trip in Alaska, did not wait for war to come to him but went to the nearest war, which was in Cuba in the late 'nineties. Because of his experience with the insurgents General Miles had chosen him to go to Cuba on his staff.

When Shafter was sent in command to Cuba in place of Miles, Funston's home renown led to his being named colonel of the Twentieth Kansas regiment of volunteers which was sent to the Philippines. He had not had any regular service or been in the National Guard.

With the outbreak of the rebellion he proved himself a born soldier and tactician under fire. The hotter the fire the better he seemed to like it. "Fighting little Fred Funston" won public imagination. His Kansans appeared to be trying to keep up with him in his charges and the rest of the army to be trying to keep up with the Kansans. He won the Congressional Medal of Honor, promotion to be brigadier general of volunteers. The newspaper men knew that if they kept close to Funston there would be action.

Then Funston disappeared from his headquarters. He was taking a little holiday without leaving any forwarding address. Any insignia on his shoulder straps would have been a spoil sport on a secret hundred mile hike slipping unseen through the jungle.

He had asked Major General Arthur MacArthur, commander in the Philippines, for the privilege of taking a few men to surprise and capture Emilio Aguinaldo, the insurrecto leader, in his remote mountain hide-out. Should Funston be discovered far beyond our lines he would be surrounded, a prisoner, if not killed. It was not in him to surrender. So doubtless he would have been killed. Should he succeed the insurrectos would have lost their leader who they thought led a charmed life.

73

MacArthur bade Funston go ahead, and said in case of success he would tell Washington that he had given his pledged word Funston should have a regular brigadier's star as his reward instead of the temporary one of volunteers. One day Funston ushered Aguinaldo into MacArthur's office in Manila. Funston became the youngest brigadier in the regular service. As a brigadier he was given to none of the so-called "gallery play," which many Regulars had associated with him, but was a modest, learning general officer, winning the respect of his subordinates, never courting publicity. He had done well in the ticklish command of the force of occupation at Vera Cruz in 1914. Outranking Pershing, he had been Pershing's chief until his death in command of the Southern Department in the siege on the Mexican border.

The memory of his Philippine exploits still lingered in the public mind. He had got his man, who was as much wanted as Villa had been unwanted by the government. Funston who had got Aguinaldo to get the Kaiser! It would have been difficult to pass over this senior in favor of his junior. Such was Funston's health that had he lived to be sent to France he would have hardly survived under the strain.

All other major generals, except one, could be dismissed as out of the reckoning. Most of them were near the retiring age, little known to the public. None had had Pershing's line experience.

The exception was Leonard Wood, the ranking major general, ambitious, personable, magnetic, able, who drew men to him in a group of Wood admirers wherever he went as living up to his great achievement as an administrator in Cuban reconstruction. Leaders in civil life who met him saw him as a general they could understand, speaking their language. His public fame literally held that of all other generals in eclipse.

He was the friend of Theodore Roosevelt, the chosen

of all the Roosevelt following and practically of all of the civil world who had stormed at President Wilson as they worked for preparedness while the World War wore on without a decision. Around him in the Plattsburg camp he had drawn a group of the élite and spirited youth of the country for military training.

His conviction and enthusiasm as a crusader led him to open criticism of President Wilson's pacific policy. In private letters and oral outbreaks the pungent phrases of which he was capable had full play at the expense of "the spineless rabbit" in the White House. It is only fair to say that evidently the President did not object to the Plattsburg camp. At least Secretary Baker gave it his support.

Inevitably President Wilson heard repetitions of Wood's personal references to him. They could not have had a happy appeal to the commander-in-chief of all the armed forces of the United States. In contrast was Pershing's subordination in Mexico and throughout his record. There was also the question of Wood's health after the injury to his skull when he hit his head against a metal desk lamp in rising from his desk in the Philippines, which was the eventual cause of his death.

The President, who could also turn a phrase, is credited with remarking that he did not know much about fighting; but "Teddy" of the Rough Riders who did had picked Wood and Pershing as the two ablest officers in the army. He would abide by his predecessor's opinion as an expert, but both Wood and Pershing could not command in France.

The first great heartbreak in the war for an officer was the jumping of the junior major general over the ranking major general who had once been jumped from a captaincy in the medical corps to brigadiership. If Wood had remained a discreet subordinate, and he was not under the suspicion that his campaign for the Presidency would begin with his sailing for France, he might have been the one to go.

As Pershing stood before Baker's desk Baker did not have a second thought about wanting to see him walk up and down the room to make sure the fatigue of the Mexican strain had not given him a lagging step which would be a handicap in the command of the handful of men we were to send to France—now become a division. We had no such field unit as a division in our army, the fighting unit of all armies, but we could gather enough officers and men for one and embark them if we could gather enough ships.

Only the command of a division thus far to serve with the French army! But two or three days later Pershing was to have a different mission. Colonel Fabry of the Joffre mission at first had told the officers of the War College that we better send money not men. The French staff, which saw ours as a bushwhacking army for chasing bandits, was "not particularly interested in having American troops in France." At first Marshal Joffre and General Tom Bridges of the British mission agreed that we "could not raise, train and transport an army of sufficient size to have an effect in the European theater of war."

Beyond the common demand for money the Allied missions were not even allied among themselves. The Secretary of the Treasury kept on signing checks as the missions of the lesser Allies arrived, on the heels of the big, to ask for their share and also frequently for a handful of troops to cheer their people. The new Kerensky government had a particular appeal in having delivered Russia from the Czar's bondage into the fold of free government.

The experts of the Allied missions disagreed about general military policy, tactics, arms, training in relation to our part. Each mission thought of its own needs as expressed by group or personal view. On the inside the War Department was subject to their discussions instead of unified counsel, while on the outside our people had a vision of all in the unity of common sacrifice and sentiment in which they must be maintained. After the ceremonial initiation was over the Department was gradually being inducted into the Allied family secrets.

Papa Joffre became more disturbingly gloomy, lowering his ponderous head with each confidential intimation of the real truth of the situation on the western front. He had been sent to us after his retirement because of his Marne prestige and before that kept in command long after he used to fall asleep over his papers at French headquarters in the middle of the day. He had ceased to have any real influence on the French staff in spite of all the respect in which they held him. He could not say which was the most practicable port in France where we should land our troops.

Arthur Balfour was the prince charming of the British Mission. His art concealed art. He never pressed for little points, but kept big points ever in mind. His was an ambassadorial perfection, if there is any such thing, gained through his distinguished career, with its finished touch of Scotch canniness.

If we could not learn from the missions, which we thought had been sent to tell us, what we had to do to win the war, we must find out for ourselves. Our Allies were still enjoying their inward exultation that we were in with our great numbers and resources. The rest was on the knees of the gods as the fortunes of war so largely always are.

Balfour and Joffre were courtiers of our power, measuring its potentialities across the ocean, cautiously feeling their way in revealing the truth by degrees lest the shock of it in full should lead us to renig, and praying that we should make our effort enough to win.

Pershing was to precede the division we were to send, with a staff of experts to prepare the way for it and to get our own answer as to what would be enough. It was the same sort of a military inquiry that a commission of economic experts might make in a study of economic conditions abroad in relation to foreign trade. Thus far and no further had we advanced in the first month since our entry into the war toward armed land action in Europe.

Room 223, across from the Chief of Staff's office, was assigned to Pershing as a temporary office until he sailed for France. The racing steps outside in the corridors were those of the energy of the nation concentrating on the War Department with all manner of suggestions for quick victory from the speedy mass production of planes to blast the Germans out of the trenches to washing them out with fire hose. The fire hose might not have been unwelcome to the Germans who had no bathing facilities in the trenches.

It was well that Room 223, in which Pershing was to select the band of experts who were to accompany him, was small with little space for lingering callers and no ante room where they might wait their turn. There would have been many more of them if it had been generally known that inside Room 223, at a little desk, was the man who could give the word which meant service "over there" at once. No nation had more or better experts in all branches of civil life than our own and no major nation had so few experts in war.

The most important choice was that of Chief of Staff, the right-hand man of the commander of the American Expeditionary Force which was having its birth in that little Room 223. Between him and Pershing there must be a marriage of minds. He must know how Pershing's mind worked, so he could act for him, save him detail and hold the staff section chiefs together in team play.

In view of West Point class loyalty, which was strong in the days when the classes were smaller, there was some concern lest Pershing should give the big plum to a certain classmate who had notably enjoyed his personal friendship. Professional opinion held this officer to be more of a theorist than organizer.

Major James G. Harbord, who was at the War College,

received word to report to General Pershing. He had never served directly under Pershing, and had met him only in camp after the Spanish War and once crossed to the Philippines with him.

Harbord was not a West Pointer. He had risen from the ranks as a student private. He was hoping that he would not be marooned at a desk in the War College, but in case we were to see much fighting in France he might have a regimental command. Moreover, Harbord was known as a Wood man. He had served long under Wood and been much depended upon by Wood.

After Harbord passed through the swing doors into Room 223 his curiosity as to why he had been summoned was soon satisfied. He was not only surprised but astounded when Pershing announced that he had him in mind as his Chief of Staff. Then Pershing asked him if he spoke French. Few American officers did except such as held over in their recollection from West Point classes. They had never envisioned our army in France, but concentrated on Spanish in heritage of Cuba and the Philippines and in view of our close Latin-American neighbors. Ambitious officers in isolated posts had labored over pronunciation with the aid of the phonograph. Pershing never forgot what a struggle he had with French at the Point.

After Harbord said he did not speak French Pershing's glance was the characteristic one when he "drew in" and postponed decision. "Anyhow, I'm going to take you with me to France," he said. Soon Harbord was sitting opposite Pershing at the little desk, being tried out. The marriage of minds took place; the honeymoon was in a coöperation of immediate adjustment to the job in hand. Harbord who knew how to serve Wood knew how to serve Pershing who was of a different type.

In his modest way Harbord always wondered just why Pershing chose him for Chief of Staff. He thought that the fact they were both cavalrymen had something to do with it. For Harbord's information be it noted that Pershing said: "I picked him because he was the best man. Didn't he prove he was?"

Harbord had an outstanding jaw. Pershing liked men with strong jaws around him; and Harbord had a vast store of information, as a thorough student, in his capacious forehead. He could analyze the essentials out of confusion. He wrote a clear, concise order; and had a power of expression valuable to Pershing whose decisions were not always accompanied by expositions.

Both Pershing and Harbord had a wide knowledge of army personnel. They had the records of officers from the secret files as they consulted in choosing other members of the staff as assistant chiefs and subordinates. Harbord's suggestions were sometimes met with, "I know him better than you. He won't do." or "I want to look him over further," or "They won't let me have him."

A conspicuously able officer was a jewel with whom any chief was loathe to part. From chiefs of the line as well as from the staff came the embattled answer: "We cannot spare him. He is indispensable here." or, "I got him first. Let Pershing find his own."

It must be born in mind the idea was only beginning to percolate among insiders in the Department that we might have to send a large army to France.

Although from the outset we had planned an army of a million men, over which our little force of Regular officers must be spread as drill masters, the impression given was that they were for home defense against a German invasion, when the German army was quite well occupied, cut off by our own and the British navy, and we had not had a hostile shot fired on our soil except by Villa since 1815. Of course the insiders realized that if our army did any fighting it would be in Europe, provided we had to help win the war for our Allies on European soil, but it was not to talk about that yet.

Since billeting was unconstitutional for our army, we should have to build cantonments. Though our soldiers slept on the bamboo floors of native huts in the Philippines the plan before Pershing settled down in Room 223 was to have all our soldiers in France in tents. What a lot of tentage would have been required! Home cantonments must be built before we had the million in training and reserve officers to train them must be trained by regulars.

Older officers of the line would be the commanders of brigades and divisions forming at home. Pershing sought younger officers, men in the forties or late thirties as his experts—men who had the spirit and the teaching of the new army which had succeeded the old army after the Spanish War. Their records in the line, on the staff and in graduate schools were the test. Officers in the late thirties and forties mate experience with physical vigor and minds still capable of learning. Usually they are the ones in power as directing seconds if not in high command at the end of a long war. A wise commander-in-chief strives to utilize the most promising at the start. A sifting process follows.

Only two officers of the General Staff at the time were available for the little group which was to find out what we had to do in France in our part to win the war. Others had had previous staff experience. Reserve officers were included among the experts in all branches from combat to supply in initiating the vast organization we were to have in France before it had fulfilled its mission.

10

On the Way

WITH THE PASSING of every day, while the pioneer staff was forming and then waiting for word of the ship on which they were to sail, Pershing received more gloomy information as the experts of the Allied missions became more candid if not less united. Major Fox Conner, who had been attached to the Joffre Mission, had been early in its confidence. When Joffre before his departure had tentatively mentioned a force of 500,000 men in France Major Conner realized this was not an underestimate.

How was the staff to reach France through the submarine danger zone? Few except British passenger ships were running, and not many of them. There was a delay until one was to sail. Her name was to be kept secret, but all on the inside in Washington were whispering that the ship was the *Baltic*. The *Baltic* must be very carefully guarded lest Pershing's destination be changed from France to Germany as a prisoner on a U-boat with Admiral von Tirpitz as his host.

Across the desk in Room 223 it occurred to Pershing

and Harbord that as yet the busy War Department had overlooked any written instructions for France to the commander of the AEF. So far they had been oral from Secretary Baker. Pershing and Harbord drafted instructions, and took them to General Tasker H. Bliss, acting chief of staff, who signed them. However Baker had some under preparation by Major General Francis Kernan, Assistant Chief of Staff.

"Here are your orders," said Baker when Pershing went to him for the final word before sailing. "The President has just signed them." Those signed by the President were supreme. They were more definite than the other set. They gave Pershing command of American forces not only in France but all Europe. And they mentioned specifically that the identity of our army must be preserved, subject to "such minor exceptions in particular circumstances as your judgment may approve."

As Harbord said in his book, Pershing having been designated as commander-in-chief,—What was he to command if not an army? Not a part of another army. But here was the written commitment of his superiors to the independent America army. Baker had been a little closer than Pershing in Room 223 to the growing pressure to infiltrate our troops into the French and British armies. Already he had given the answer that our troops were to serve under the American flag in France.

In common with Pershing Secretary Baker had a knowledge of our military history. Baker, who had majored in history at Johns Hopkins, had read military history thoroughly after he became Secretary. He would not repeat the mistake of Secretary Stanton in the Civil War of interfering with his generals.

"I shall give you only two orders, one to go and one to return," Baker said. A subtle mind might take this as an intimation that if Pershing failed another general would succeed him.

Pershing was to be no less of an autocrat in France than the commander of a western post under Indian attack in the old army in the west. He was to build his own kingdom in France as absolute monarch. No such power and responsibility had ever been given to a single man in our democracy.

Baker's own destiny was tied to Pershing's. And Baker, who knew his politics and the swift turns of public emotion, remarked whimsically that in case of success all would be well, but in case of failure both might be hung to the nearest lamp post.

Pershing had not yet met the President after he had been two weeks in Washington. Was he to go without seeing his commander-in-chief? Baker went to the White House with him. At first the President talked with Baker about shipping. Then he turned to Pershing and said that he had a very difficult task. Pershing replied that this was what soldiers were trained to expect.

Only four months before the President had spoken of the "peace presently to be made" by negotiation on the eve of Germany's bolt declaration of unrestricted submarine warfare. Further illusions had been broken after our entry into the war. His dream of a league of nations must wait until the war was won by force. Before him was the expert in armed force which had had little part in his philosophy.

Pershing spoke of the honor and responsibility conferred upon him and said the President could count upon the best that was in him. The President replied; "General, you are chosen entirely upon your record and I have every confidence you will suceed. You shall have my full support." And Pershing made his bow after this brief conversation.

The President would not have Lincoln's privilege of a short journey beyond the Potomac to see commanders and army in the field; and it was not in his nature to give the human touch to that farewell that Lincoln would have

given it. And the President's destiny and that of the world
were also to be tied to Pershing's.

On the afternoon of May 28, 1917, more than six weeks
after our entry into the war, those of us who were already
on board looked down on a drizzly afternoon from the rail
of the main deck of the *Baltic* upon Pershing and his staff
leaders coming aboard from a tender for that voyage to
learn what we had to do to win the war. The total of the
pioneer AEF was one hundred eighty-seven. Of these
seventy were enlisted men of the Regular Army—"our combat troops"—ten more than the number of field clerks and
attached civilians.

Among the attached civilians were some whom Pershing
had not seen. He soon spotted them. Who were they? What
were they doing on board? Officers who had given them
authority had to explain their value, why they were just
getting a trip to France.

It was work, work for all—work during the forty-eight
hour wait off Halifax, still work after two American destroyers came out to convoy the *Baltic* zig-zagging through
the danger zone. The interpreters had classes in French.
Boards were meeting for discussions and to assemble the
questions which should be asked Allied experts; a preliminary staff organization formed for team approach to
problems.

I recall a talk with Pershing after the zig-zagging of the
Baltic had begun under the destroyer escort. He had been
reading my book on the Battle of the Somme in which the
British new army had made its first great offensive only to
be stalled after little gains and enormous losses.

"It is horrible," he said, "horrible beyond the power of
words to express to think that the civilized world should
suffer such bloodshed and destruction, horrible that our
country should have to join in."

He was silent for a moment, the lips compressed, taking
the practical soldier measure of the outlook.

"The only way to end it is by force, and we must end it as soon as possible." There was an emphasis on the last word of that old phrase. "It will take us time before we can make our power felt."

The British new army had begun its first great offensive under the compulsion of necessity before it was ready, and that nearly two years after the outbreak of the war.

"As I see it now we shall have to plan for an army of a million in France," he added.

This would include recruits who had yet to go to the cantonments after the cantonments were built. Ships must be provided for them after they had been trained. The ships would have to zig-zag through the submarine zone escorted by destroyers. The U-boats were getting ships faster than they were being built. But Pershing was a rock of confidence that the navy would conquer the submarines. He knew the navy. He knew the American people and the military force they could bring to bear, in time. That emphasis on the *possible* at the end of the old phrase was quite warrantable.

11

Behind the Cheers

CONSIDER FIRST this picture before we look in on Pershing in the little private house which was the first headquarters of the AEF in France.

The red carpet was spread from Liverpool to London and Boulogne to Paris for the man fresh from the Mexican sands. Star Spangled Banner and God Save the King on landing at Liverpool: the guard of honor on the pier commanded by a general who was a descendant of the Major Pitcairn against whose regulars the Minute Men fired the shots which were heard around the world. His troops were the Welch Fusiliers. And it had been the Welch Fusiliers at whom we had not fired at Bunker Hill until, according to legend, we saw the whites of their eyes.

From Liverpool to London in the royal coach; met at the station in London by silk hats and gold braid of high rank; hotel suites with servants waiting; audience with the King who was in a field marshal's uniform for the occasion; dinners and luncheons to meet the Prime Minister and cabinet ministers and those high in power through their own efforts or heredity; and honors paid at Westminster Abbey not overlooked. No officialdom knows so well how to do this kind of thing in gold braid or silk hat as the British, out of ancient tradition in giving the impression that it is as old as the very soil of Britain.

On the arrival in Paris the people made the official attentions an incidental formality. A crowd surrounded the station and the waiting cars to receive the pioneer staff. It was significant of how Marshal Joffre's services were being pigeonholed as memory in that officialdom twice moved his car farther to the rear.

Vive Pershaing! If Pershing had shot a blast of lightning from the *Baltic* which had blasted the German army back across the Rhine the cheering throngs that banked the route of the procession could have shown hardly more ecstasy in their welcome. Flowers were thrown into the open cars; women broke through the police lines to kiss the hands of our officers. The voice of all France spoke in the roar that greeted Pershing's appearance on a balcony overlooking the Place de la Concorde.

Official honors, British style, were followed by official honors French style. He should sign the Golden Book in the French military holy of holies, Napoleon's tomb. Not given to histrionics he was histrionicly most effective to French sentiment when Napoleon's own sword was lifted from its place for him to hold in his hands. He hesitated diffidently and then raised it to his lips. This was as an augury of victory from the temple of France's soldier god.

His own President had spoken a few words of farewell without breaking bread with Pershing. But President Poincaré was far more hospitable in the dinner at the Elysée; and the Premier and cabinet ministers and the great in silk hats and gold braid had their turn to meet him at more dinners. He missed being in the box for a gala performance of the grand opera, but he did find time to appear for that of the *opéra comique* where all the audience

GENERAL PERSHING LANDING AT BOULOGNE, JUNE 13, 1917.

rose and turned toward him in applause which could not have been more heartfelt for the Czar of Russia early in the war when Russia was still an asset as an ally.

No matter how acute the war crisis the opera and the official functions continued. To curtail them would only fan the whispers of doubt which fed defeatism in public opinion. The display diverted the public mind in France and England. It thrilled America. Grandiloquent gestures that promise victory are better than nothing when there are no victories to report.

Old American hands in Europe—not the Europeanized Americans who had practically become expatriated—wondered how all these attentions by the supreme masters of old world ingratiation, at its best when they were fighting for their lives, would affect Pershing? Even peace time routine courtship and hospitality had often led rich Americans, who would round out their careers as ambassadors abroad, to the joy of their socially ambitious wives, to be easily taken into camp. Quite unconsciously they became the ambassadors of the country to which they were accredited. One American ambassador to France seemed most interested that he had been received by the old noblesse.

In all military forms Pershing had the punctiliousness of cadet captain Pershing at West Point. He had the dignity of his rank. Socially and in conference he was polite, the smile in play. At first he had the impulsive moments in which he was so sympathetically receptive that the actual promise of commitment was on his tongue's end, but the word did not come.

All the while he was being measured by those high in civil or military power. It was vital for them to know just what kind of a man he was, as it had never been to know any American except President Wilson. Before he came they had received through their embassies in Washington such accounts as were available about a man of whom Washington had seen little in recent years. Once he was in Europe they would have personal slants on him.

But soon they found it difficult to get through behind the smile. He met premiers in the same way he would a mayor of a home town. Whatever was the real ability behind his smile he had poise, he was self-contained. After the smile he listened without saying aloud a Missourian show-me, simply himself in character.

"They're telling me," he remarked. And he was not telling them, but a pupil who would learn from the masters.

That little private house, which had been picked for him by the little military mission we had in France before our entry into the war, was ready for him on his arrival. In contrast with the frenzied cheers, the glowing functions and ceremonials, it held the distilled essence of military reality. It was far away from the center of business and traffic in Paris on the left bank of the Seine in the old Faubourg quarter. There was a good view of Napoleon's tomb from its front windows. It would have been excellent for housing a party of tourists in peace time.

The few remaining taxi-cabs in Paris did not come that way. A hurrying member of our pioneer staff might have to walk a mile in the summer sun before he got any transport. In all the whole AEF had only ten automobiles, no trucks and not even a modest station wagon. If the French thought the AEF was so very small that it ought to be hidden from public view the location was near perfection.

French and British GHQs (Grand Headquarters) had their huge staff establishments in the towns of Chantilly and Montreuil; and generals occupied châteaux in relative size to their rank, taste or needs. Long lines of motor trucks gorged the road to the front where the roar of the guns had the eternal effect of the roar of Niagara. More than four millions of men were under arms on the Allied side in France. We had the seventy enlisted men among our one hundred eighty-seven, and some engineers who had preceded us to France.

Why all this fuss about so small a reinforcement when fifty times its number would be employed in a trench raid to get some enemy prisoners who might reveal information about the enemy battle orders and plans? Why about a major general with no army when so many local lieutenant generals and generals in command of armies were available? Why about a former second lieutenant of our old army in our west which excited the risibilities of young writer Rudyard Kipling, about its slouchiness in contrast with the pipe clay soldiers in the Victorian heyday—before the South African lesson and our Spanish War lesson under Corbin—when Victoria's brother, the venerable Duke of Connaught, used to review troops under a sun umbrella?

Pershing was receiving the answers in his little office, which was hardly larger than Room 223 in the War Department; receiving them in reports from his staff, his conferences with civil and soldier leaders the while he sought time to work, away from the demands of dinners and functions which must be attended.

"I should like to hear one piece of good news for a change," he said wistfully when bad news had had a field day.

While his coming was being trumpeted as assuring victory the Allied troubles were being dumped in his lap. "Off the record" never told so much which must not be publicly told. The food might be excellent, the host lead off with a pleasant anecdote, but in the end it all lead in effect to "The situation is very serious. We need all the help you can give."

From the King and President Poincaré, from Prime Minister and Premier, from the war offices and from the front came candor as the introduction to appeal. There might be a little good news that the submarine sinkings were not so heavy the last month; but if the truth was told in public reports the prospect was that if the sinkings continued at the present rate with no increase in ship building Britain might yet be starved out. There was encouragement, too, in hearing that we had scraped together enough ships to send over fourteen thousand men in our first contingent of troops as a start in replacing Russian man-power in the war.

For it was clear that the Root mission to Russia was laboring in vain to put backbone into Kerensky. Allied leaders, off the record, made no bones about their conclusion that Russia was out of the war. And France?

Much had happened on the western front since the French staff, just before our entry into the war, had said it did not require American troops in France. In March, 1917, before our entry, there seemed a conclusively substantial basis for thinking that we need only supply financial and economic aid as the decisive weight in the balance.

Day by day, just before our entry, we read of the retirement of the Germans from the Somme line, which they had so stubbornly held through the summer of 1916. Now, at last, the Kaiser saw the hand writing on the wall. Here was confession of weakening man-power and resources which forced the German army on the defensive. Mighty Russia, galvanized for a fresh effort by the Kerensky revolution which had delivered her from the shackles of the Czar, would strike heavy blows on the eastern front.

On the western front the British army would be at its peak in the summer of 1917 for a far more powerful offensive than that of the Somme. France had her new commander-in-chief, Nivelle, hero of the lightning plan of attack. Its success in recovering Fort Douaumont at Verdun had been a Napoleonic stroke which made the old long preliminary bombardments obsolete.

Where it had been "they shall not pass" at Verdun in 1916 now it would be the Allies who would pass. The combined British and French offensives of 1917 would at last break the trench line which had held fast against all previous Allied offensives and against the great German drive against Verdun. Optimism in the Allied world touched the blue sky in the prospect of the long-nourished hope materializing in fulfillment at last.

On the western front the Allies had by far the nearest approach yet to complete unity of command under Nivelle. It had sentimental support from Lloyd George because Nivelle had an English mother and spoke English like an Englishman. Sir Douglas Haig, the British commander-in-chief, was to accept Nivelle's leading in coöperation with Nivelle's plan.

It was a most roseate plan on paper, having the imagined approval of Napoleon come to life out of his tomb. It showed that the school of *Toujours l'attaque*—always the offensive—was in the saddle. There were the confidently plotted advances on the map, seven miles for the first day. The advances of the succeeding days need not be mentioned for reasons that soon became apparent.

German withdrawal to the Hindenburg line had been in preparation for stonewalling at a minimum cost in defense and a maximum for the offensive. The German staff also had learned the Nivelle plan for its guidance. They knew just what they had to meet and where.

On April 4th, two days before our entry into the war, the Nivelle attack began. Against a German army, worn down by fighting, such a plan, especially if the German staff had no foreknowledge of it, might have succeeded, but not then against a German army with its heritage of victory and fresh from winter rest.

That first day the fate of the attack was cruelly sealed against the cross fire of machine guns and torrents of shell fire set for the targets of futile French gallantry in a welter of blood. The gains were counted in yards and not miles. Nivelle kept on at further terrific cost. Mangin, great soldier—now to be called "The Butcher," which he was later to live down—was unable to take the one key position indispensable to any important gain. Nivelle was relieved, unity of command long postponed, the combined Anglo-French offensive over on the western front for 1917.

Such was the news that the Joffre and Balfour missions had to digest in America while they rode through our streets to cheers as loud but not so knowing as those Pershing received in Paris. It accounted for some of the disagreements of the missions among themselves as they gradually inducted the War Department into the truth and Joffre raised the limit to 500,000 men.

But the whole truth was not known to Pershing until he was in Paris. Mutiny is the most alarming word that can be spoken about an army. It bears the sinister suggestion of defeat from within. There had been mutiny in the French army after the Nivelle attack. Committees of junior officers and men went past their superiors demanding to be heard. They would not submit to further needless sacrifice, these veterans, after all they had endured.

More fortunately than has ever been realized for France, for America and the Allied cause, General Henri-Philippe Pétain had been made commander-in-chief of the French army. A career as a line soldier in colonial wars and garrisons as well as in France was back of Colonel Pétain when the war began. Political influence had not oiled the way to the promotions the war had brought him. All had been won in action.

When division commander Pétain became corps commander he still kept close to his men. He was not so great that they did not see him with his wound stripes on his arms in personal tours of the trenches.

Professor Foch, with all his ability, Weygand, his shadow as a staff genius, or even Papa Joffre, with age prematurely upon him, could not have dealt with that mutiny as skillfully as Pétain. Foch's maps would have been no aid to him in this human equation. Pétain knew his soldiers and the right tone in which to say *mes enfants* to them on this occasion.

The penalty of mutiny before the enemy is death. In this case thousands would have to be shot. But it was not a mutiny in another sense. It was the expression of a common soldier protest of a plebiscite without a questionnaire, of the men who hold and break the walls of fire. Officers can not hold them when it is their will to fall back or drive them forward when it is not their will to advance.

And these soldiers were French and therefore their nature French in the French democracy. Little Corporal Napoleon in the great days of his youthful leadership said that his tent flap was up to those who had protests to make, a saying which is not so famous as his encouragement that every private carried a marshal's baton in his knapsack. He did not add that if all the privates became marshals there would be no privates left.

The scarred veterans of the Marne and Verdun had shown the same bravery in the recent immortal effort which had failed as in their victories. They had not mutinied in battle, but after the battle was over. It was "they shall-not-pass" Pétain—the fair and knowing Pétain—who was to give authority to the judgment he passed upon the offenders. A stern but understanding commander-in-chief heard the case.

Some of the ringleaders were shot, others penalized. But there was no offensive fighting spirit left in the mass of the French army. Instead of punishment the veterans should have their turn to rest and recuperate back on the farms and villages. At one time a third of the French combat forces had leave in the fighting season of 1917. But so deftly had the "mutiny" been handled that it was not known for a long time even at British headquarters.

The point of all this about Pétain is background for the future relations of the two commanders-in-chief. At their first meeting Pétain's welcome lacked the effulgence of courtesy and fellowship which had been usual from the eminent leaders. Pétain was most punctilious, but formal.

He too was measuring Pershing and with a distinctly professional eye.

Later they were to warm to each other as steel touched steel. Neither was a talker. Pétain's English was hardly equal to the West Point French Pershing had remembered. Yet they spoke the same language. In common they had known desert sands and jungles. Both mated line with staff experience. Both were inherently and devotedly constitutional soldiers of a democracy, simple, straight soldiers, through all the complications of high command, who carried an air that detached them in their profession in a moral strength that held respect. If a narrow, political minded, short sighted commander had been in Pétain's place the preservation of the independence of our army in France would have been much more difficult against Lloyd George, Clemenceau, General Sir William Robertson, Foch, Lord Reading and all the combinations and intrigues of mistaken, well-intentioned and purely mischievous ignorance, of which more later.

For the present, there in the little isolated private house, it was known that the French army could only hold its lines this summer of 1917. The Italian army, weary already, was stalled in the face of heights it had attacked in vain. The Rumanians, after Mackensen turned their first eager offensive into a rout, and the Servians held fragments of their countries which did have the merit of being larger than the sliver of Belgium where the Belgium soldiers were mired and the enemy was too. Rumania had evidently been ready to yield when we entered the war.

On the vast length of the old Russian front the Germans needed little more than a police guard. Hopes of starving them out by sea blockade had so far failed and now they anticipated replenishing their larders in the grain fields of Ukraine.

It was not only that the Germans were deep everywhere on Allied soil, but so far as any offensive was concerned, the British were fighting the war single handed. They kept on slugging in the Passchendaele battle, drawing in against their masses German divisions from the western, Italian and Rumanian fronts to prevent the Germans reaching the Belgium ports.

Pershing had ample reason to appreciate the irony of all the attentions paid him on his arrival. It was small wonder the man who was given to overlooking the flight of time, preferred to get to work to having the audience rise to applaud him at a gala performance of the opera. Used to grappling with facts he had plenty now. There was a brief interval in which grimness was touched with a gloom that was out of character.

"The map does not tell it all," he said in an outburst. "It's the situation under the lines of the map. The third year of the war! With Russia in, Italy in, Rumania in, and all the Allied armies in with their full man-power, they could not win. Apparently there is no hope of increasing Italian man-power, certainly not the French. Look at what is expected of us and what we have to do and what we have to start with! No army ready, no ships to bring over an army if we had one. How supply and transport an army across France after it is here?"

The survey of the outlook and the task pressed upon him, a bright light in the room upon his face, the close-clipped hair and close-clipped moustache. At times the jaw did not seem pronounced, but in keeping with his regular features, and a little pointed. His closed hand came down on a pile of papers, rested there clenched. The jaw squared, the lips tightened, and the eyes were so steely and set on a point that it would not have been surprising if they had bored a hole in the wall.

"The German army is no superhuman army. It has been beaten before and can be beaten again. We have raised great armies and can raise another which will strike the decisive blow. But it will take far more time than our

97

people realize. We are the last nation to come in, and I do not propose to fritter away our strength in detail."

No one knew better than Pershing that the ecstasy of the crowds upon his arrival in Paris was no personal tribute. Behind the cheers was a prayer. For there was no keeping the truth from the French people about the Nivelle disaster. They had it from the soldiers on leave and in mourning for the sons they had lost.

To them Pershing represented the power of America, the land of magic speed and achievement with vast man-power and resources, now on their side, the land of the skyscrapers and untold wealth. They knew war in terms of a ready army marching to the front anywhere from ten to three hundred miles away. They did not think in terms of sea distances, or how long it takes to make an army out of the raw when every able-bodied French male served as a conscript and remained at call in the reserve of an ever-ready army.

It did not matter that Pershing himself was silent—he was a soldier and soldiers do not talk—while hard-driven French propaganda to revive French morale spread the news from America which pictured us as about to perform miracles. While we signed checks by tens of millions for the Allies, our factories would turn out tanks and rifles in mass production to arm the mass production of soldiers. Pershing's exasperation came to a head in the repeated tales of the mass production of fifty thousand planes with the wonderful new Liberty motor to blow the Germans out of the trenches, to which the French staff, in propagandic urgency, was inclined to give credence when the Liberty motor was only on paper as yet.

"This must be stopped," he said. "It is promising what we can not do. We are under handicaps enough without this one. I know the object of making the most of the reports which do not come from the War Department or any sound source. In the end disillusionment will defeat the object of such propaganda. It will lead to a loss of confidence in us, to a dangerous reaction. Europeans who are given to think we are a nation of boasters will have proof they were right."

Pershing had the support of Pétain in his view. The French press piped down. Not only this, but the French bureau of censorship was not to have its way in being the censor for the American army, too. We should have our own censor. Our people at home were not to be mislead, or the French, if we could help it.

12

Initialed "J. J. P."

"You're Right. I won't do it again," Pershing would sometimes say with a disarming, boyish kind of penitence when it was made clear to him that an impulse had carried him too far.

In the course of his education in France he was learning that he must give up much of his time to people who had a certain influence or certain personal vanities which had best be propitiated lest he be subjected to pinpricking in the rear. He was not only working with Allies now, but he had to listen to suitors and the heads of missions arriving from home and sugar their disappointments when the place they sought or the plan they had in mind was unacceptable. That is, he must be a diplomat in a position which was becoming more and more ambassadorial.

"I didn't know the man with a flowing tie who came in to tell me how to run my army was such an important person," he said, after he had been informed of the status of a caller whose interview had been terminated somewhat abruptly. "It had been a busy day. He did not look to me as though he had much experience in commanding armies himself. So I was brief."

There was no doubt on the part of the pioneer staff or ever to be who was running the AEF. It was the man who wrote the bold J.J.P. under instructions or comment on a pad in letters as clear as though they were block—as they remained twenty years later after he recovered from his illness in Arizona, and one may be sure they would be when he signed the Golden Book in the next world. Rarely was he referred to by those close to him as the Chief, or the General, practically never as the Old Man, but almost invariably as "J.J.P."

So from now on, this narrative refers to him frequently as J.J.P. He was to be no figurehead dominated by any man or group of men. The J.J.P. was final. Lieutenant Pershing who turned on the critic of Shafter before the charge up San Juan Hill, whose will was that of his commander, expected the will of all under him to be his will.

An army can not be successfully commanded by a committee or by cabals. His own commander-in-chief had placed upon him the responsibility for command. He accepted the responsibility from the outset as one not to be dodged.

In leading up to the issue which he faced at once, the issue with which he had to contend to the end, it may be mentioned that the particular gentleman with the flowing tie, who met short and decisive words in telling J.J.P. how to run his army, was a well-known Franco-American, an architect and interior decorator. He had a gift in the choice of furnishings and their arrangement in a room or suite in a fashionable hotel to make the guest feel perfectly at home when the page showed him in. He had no such quiet fervent interest in the world cause we were fighting for as Pershing expressed, but was entirely concerned with victory for France—a French victory—one for the old noblesse and the élite.

His income made life pleasant for him in France, where in common with many rivals of his type he sought importance by giving the impression he had brought America into the war when Americans at home still persisted in thinking the final cause was the submarine outrages.

In common with other Franco-Americans, who lived mostly or altogether in Paris on American incomes, he did not regard France as his "second country," but as first, the land of his heart and his prime loyalties. These expatriates would admit on occasion that there were some Americans east of the Hudson River who were not crude and did know the difference between vintage wines, which incidentally does not require expatriation. Nor does it to be able to speak French well and to admire the French.

When the German army threatened Paris in 1914 the Franco-Americans of leisure, who did not earn their income in France, hastened to renew their acquaintance with their home land, passing the word to their French friends that they had a mission to arouse sympathy there for France. America was a bore and a trial which they endured until Paris was evidently safe again. Then they were back in Paris with glowing accounts of their service in their exile.

Inwardly the French had not much real respect for them, but since all French men and women were ready for any sacrifice for their country except that of the nest egg of money in the stocking if the worst should happen, the returned missionaries had entrée to exclusive and important French circles which had been closed to them. Now they had another duty to France, another opening for ingratiation. This was to show the American Army the way to save France.

Their way was to surrender our leadership to French command, to infiltrate the soldiers of the home land as recruits into the French army. How could Pershing who came from Missouri, where everybody was crude, who had only commanded a little force in Mexico, when he spoke only a little French, and that with an American accent, command a huge army in a land where the language was French?

Such was the attitude of some of these Franco-Americans, that it would seem that Secretary Baker ought to have held a verbal French examination in choosing a commander-in-chief of the AEF. In the judgment of a purist academic board the one who spoke fluently with a Tours accent would have had it over one with a Parisian accent, no matter what his army record was. To carry the idea further a commander of an allied army ought to be a linguist speaking the languages of all its allies. But French would have been enough, all that was necessary, to the Franco-Americans. And we do not ask whether Wellington spoke German or Blücher spoke English at Waterloo. Later General ("Bull") Allenby who captured Jerusalem spoke neither Hebrew nor the tongue of his Arab allies.

No skepticism is in order about the Franco-Americans' good intentions if we reflect that the pavement of war is slippery and spiked under a spray of fire and war is hell. Among them are not included the young Americans who enlisted in the French ambulance and in aviation or those who enlisted as privates in the hard-fighting French Foreign Legion for the cause and adventure.

And there were the Americans in France, including those who earned their living there and wished they could return home to educate their children as Americans, all those with knowledge of France and French, who were a check on American or French provincialism in promoting mutual understanding, and such French officers who knew English well as Captain Charles de Marenches and Colonel Adalbert de Chambrun who were attached to our staff. These did not think Pershing was crude or that he came from a crude country.

More to the point in a broad sense was the question "What did Pershing or our pioneer staff know about big war?" Americans are much given to specialism, to leaving an expert job to experts. There was logic in the presumption that, lacking experts of our own, we should accept the direction of the experts of the French staff. It was a view widely held, and held and exerted by a group at home throughout the war. Echoes of it were heard long after the war. In building a great bridge over a broad river you do not turn to an engineer who had only built one over a narrow stream, but to one who had a record in great bridges.

The sum of it was "The French staff experts know and we do not know." Before the war the French staff had the organization of a large standing army and preparation for the movement of its immense reserves in corps and divisions to the front with a clockwork precision. During the war they had had nearly three years' experience in actual conflict with the rapid change in tactics and the effective use of arms from month to month. War's test should have eliminated the incompetent and brought the competent forward.

But cool evaluation of your allies' strength and qualities in relation to the enemy's is as intrinsically wise as for a lawyer to strive to know his opponent's case. It has nothing to do with lack of loyalty to your cause, your patriotic sentiment, your ideals, but is the basic premise for military success when that is the last resort, to win victory for your cause.

Let us consider tradition, history and results with all respect for that professional French staff, which shared first rank with the German as in a class by themselves. The tradition was that of Napoleon, the supreme genius of victory, a very spell of tradition, as ours is the tradition of Washington, Scott, Grant. Lee, Sherman and Jackson. There is no escape from these traditions although they go back to days in which decisions were made in a few hours on short battle lines. They are in the blood.

On the threshold of the World War French staff councils

were divided between the war of movement and the war of trenches, or to put it a little more definitely, between the offensive-defensive and the defensive-offensive. The first leads off with an attack as the best initial action for defense when no war can be won entirely by the defensive; and the second, which modern arms favored, was to allow the enemy to batter himself against prepared positions before striking him after being weakened by his costly assaults.

The value of the second the Germans learned in the Marne battle. A classic later example of its application was Mackensen's in giving the eager Rumanians play to over extend themselves in their initial offensive and then closing in on them as weary prey burdened with wounds and death.

There had been no warrant of sufficient superiority of numbers for the Germans to think they could surround the French army and force its capitulation in 1914. The German staff in 1914 acted on the heritage of their sweep to the French surrender at Sedan in overweening self-assurance and arrogant contempt for the army which they regarded as that of a decadent nation.

The French staff had been under the handicap of political interference, graft and deadwood both in the staff and field command. It had failed, as has been observed before, to learn the lesson of the barrage, the machine gun and concentrations of heavy mobile artillery in the Russo-Japanese War of 1904-05. Subject to French sentiment it sent its soldiers against the German green into action in red trousers and blue blouses, led in many cases by "fat old colonels" who had reached the easy chair and slippers stage.

The railway sidings the Germans had built at the gateway to Belgium before the outbreak of the World War carried no weight with the French staff. The French conviction that it was a feint to cover the real attack against the Verdun region was confirmed by the Germans openly saying they were preparing to strike through Belgium.

Thus the German staff had taken a hint from Bismarck's remark that the best way to deceive diplomatic opponents was to tell the truth as they were bound to think you were lying, not to mention that the method is helpfully confusing in that your lies may be mistaken for truth.

So Joffre mobilized east of Rheims to meet the main German attack in that direction. He exposed his flank; he exposed his army to the pinchers. The error was the same in principle as though Hancock on the evening of the first day at Gettysburg had decided not to hold Kulp's hill, or on the second day Meade had allowed the Confederates to get Little Round Top, or Lee, in the Wilderness campaign, had given Grant the elbow room quickly to outflank and surround him, which was more warranted by Grant's superiority of numbers than the German in their invasion of France.

But, before the German army was massed for the sweep through Belgium, the Napoleonic tradition had its turn. Joffre had decided for the offensive-defensive stroke. He put his head into a noose. He sent an army into the disastrous and wasteful offensive in Alsace. This was really a proof of his lack of confidence in his own soldiers. He thought that they must have a victory to stir the spirit of the whole to fighting pitch. The army which advanced into Alsace was in an untenable position and forced back in exhaustion, which weakened it for its part in resistance when the main issue was joined after the German right wing had swung through northwestern France.

Now the defensive-offensive was forced on Joffre to break the enemy's stride before he could answer with an offensive. Defeat, not victory had been the result of the Alsatian venture as a filip to French soldier morale.

Then it was for the French soldiers to retrieve the French staff's error. The fate of France was in their hands in the crisis when command really passed to them. Man against man, their unsurpassesd light artillery making up for the lack of heavy artillery, there holding the Gap of Miracourt, on into Champagne and now the Marne, the youth of France, the regular and reserve officers of the line—democracy had its turn against the army of the war lords in immortal professional skill and courage. They checked the German avalanche, held the Gap of Miracourt, the loss of which would have been fatal.

Joffre had the interior line for communication, quick reinforcements, and control of his armies while the German had outrun control by the staff. Now Joffre could strike back in the offensive end of defensive-offensive tactic. The Germans' turn was the defensive-offensive in preparation for any future offensive as they intrenched on favorable positions.

Paris had been saved, France saved, but at needless cost. Joffre who had skillfully directed the final defensive, was the savior, the hero of France, of Britain, of all the people of the world who were for the Allied cause. White-haired and benign, he was "Papa" Joffre to his soldiers to whom he gave rest and confidence in the victory which had come under his command. But the Germans were deep in the soil of France, far deeper than they might have been, and with more cost to them and less to the French.

The point is that no army staff is infallible. When it thinks it is it is in for an awakening. The cocksure almighty German staff, looking down its nose at all rivals, committed most glaring blunders as the test of battle revealed in comparison with maneuvers and studies in the old holy of holies of the inner circle of war lords in the shadow of the Brandenburg gate in Berlin.

But the pioneer staff of the AEF could not look for personal instruction from the German staff. And the last effort of the French staff, applying the lessons of nearly three years of war, had ended in the Nivelle disaster which was excellently worked out in staff detail on paper. A staff must learn from its past mistakes and the fresh ones as it proceeds. The French was a great staff of a great army.

That architect and interior decorator of the flowing tie who volunteered his advice might have better understood Pershing's attitude if J.J.P. had had time to explain what was taken for granted in his own mind as first premise to his task.

The modesty of the officers of our pioneer staff in their approach to their problems was often remarked by their professional colleagues of the Allies. Instead of an attitude of "We've come over here to show you how to win this war," as had been somewhat anticipated, it was "We have all to learn."

Anyone under J.J.P. who departed from this attitude would have broken faith with J.J.P.'s own attitude. Good relations must be cultivated with our allies, since we were to fight at their side. At times he appeared shy and humble as well as grateful before the veteran masters with their great body of experience.

The latest word in tactics and organization from staff offices to trenches was open to our pioneer officers. All the vital details of combat lessons, which had been so secretly guarded before our entry into the war, were ours for the asking from both the French and British. For there were two staffs of two huge armies in France. The British had their own independent army, their own system and practices out of their own experience. It was from British officers that most frequently came this kind of an encouraging remark to the novices, "We get stale from having been so long, close to the struggle. You have the advantage that you come fresh to it with an open mind."

Some of the French staff officers were given to confidential suggestions that the British were tyros yet at great war. Indeed they were still worried if the British would ever learn how to fight a big army. Only the French and German staffs really knew. Professional rivalry in the ancient monopoly was slightly resented. So the French thought it wise that we follow the French system exclusively. And the

British officers might say, "That way may be best with French troops, but not ours. You will be the ones to decide which is best for your army."

Our officers were listening to all the conflicting opinions of line and staff within either army and between the two armies. They went into the trenches of course. Some of them went over the top with troops in the Passchendaele battle, (the only big action then in progress) which brought the joking reminder that one soon was over his eagerness of being shot at for the experience. Participating in an attack was the only way for a real lesson in fire discipline and a close view of the Germans to prepare for meeting them in battle.

All the professional experts of the pioneer staff were bringing in their reports to the little headquarters. They labored far into the night under high pressure analyzing their information for J.J.P.'s service in forming his plan.

The importance of that plan cannot be too much stressed. It was to be the law and the prophets for the AEF. By it we should stand or fall. Its wisdom and prevision would be largely the measure of the cost and length of the war to us. (This was one part of the General's *My Experiences in the World War* in which he did not give sufficient emphasis either in the logical processes of his mind, the concentration on the problems of its execution when it was so obviously the only plan, or in the restraint of modesty about what was so great a tribute to his vision.) For the present, at least, he might discount having heard the worst of the truth of the Allied situation, but the closer the grip of analysis the greater the magnitude of our enterprise appeared.

He and his immediate personal staff and chiefs had been given the use of the Ogden Mills house in the Faubourg near our Paris headquarters. There in a house of great wealth, which had known rich functions and dinners, the staff was living as simply on army fare as though they were in barracks. It was khaki in war and no display: down to

business, as he burned the midnight oil over his problems
after the day at headquarters.

Unforgettable is a talk with him one evening when already the quickly susceptible French people were feeling
the reaction now that the welcoming functions were over.
Behind the curtains of censorship they were thinking,
"The American general is here, but how much fighting
will the Americans do and how soon?" In his own interest
those who believed in him foresaw a reaction at home to
guard against.

No American general, except Washington, who was in
command in a major war at the start had been in command
at the finish. McDowell's career ended with the defeat of
Bull Run as the sequel of the North's cry of "On to Richmond!" to end the rebellion in six months. McClellan had
succeeded him as the organizer. After McClellan's defeats
came more successors in command of the Army of the Potomac on the way to Grant. Lee had succeeded Beauregard
in command of the Army of Northern Virginia.

A far more arduous period of preparation than Mc-
Clellan's faced Pershing. Of course he knew his history,
and he was also perfectly aware that our public, which was
so uninformed about the desperate Allied situation and
the time factor in preparation, might become impatient
over the inevitable delay.

"At least," he said, "I shall lay such a sound foundation
my successor will thank me as soldier to soldier. He will
not have to rebuild from the bottom."

He spoke as detachedly as though he were sitting in
judgment on John J. Pershing as a third person. What did
it matter whether he was relieved or not, whether the
harvest of his plowing, sowing and cultivating was reaped
by another man, so we had the grain in the bin?

13
Plan and Goal

"WE HAVE BEEN TO WAR BEFORE," as J.J.P. remarked, "and in long wars. We have raised great armies that fought many battles."

American examples cover the application of all the unchanging principles—unchanging as the arrogant German staff would agree, since it did studies of the Battle of Cannae before the World War to keep the unchanging principles in mind.

Washington fought an eight-year war. Scott's march over the mountains to Mexico City stirred the wondering admiration of the old Duke of Wellington. In the Civil War, which lasted for four years, the largest armies fought until the Franco-Prussian War of 1870-71.

Either an underestimate or overestimate of your enemy's forces may be fatal. Wisdom is in knowing when to attack, to stall or retreat in husbanding your resources; or a commander may accept the alternative of taking a desperate chance as Lee did in Pickett's charge for victory for the political object of European recognition of the Confederacy.

Lee was the master of delaying action: also of the attack at the Second Manassas, in the repulse of McClellan in the Peninsular campaign and at Chancellorsville. Until the Peninsular campaign McClellan had always overestimated his enemy. Having been an attaché in the Crimean War his model was that of the veteran long service European armies. Convinced of the folly of fighting with half-trained men he would train his troops in their likeness.

But McClellan lacked practical vision inherent in a former Regular officer who was clerking in a country store when McClellan was getting the experience in the Crimea, which was seen as further qualifying this brilliant and personable officer as commander of the Federal Army. Grant had the measure of his enemy whose soldiers were as untrained as his own. While he held his soldiers doing their paces on the drill ground the enemy's soldiers would also be training. In this respect he was already on equal terms with the enemy.

His men were equally well armed. They were in the confident fighting mood of volunteers and he would utilize it while it was hot to get the jump on the enemy. It was better they be killed and wounded in action than die of disease in the trenches and lose spirit in the boredom of camp. He knew his men of the western frontier of that day as McClellan did not know his men; he knew them as Washington knew the frontiersmen in leather breeches, with their Pennsylvania rifles, who had marched from the Alleghenies to join him at Cambridge.

The North hailed the rise of Grant's star of victory in the west at Fort Henry and Donelson and in the iron determination which kept on to win the second day of Shiloh. His men's morale had been steeled by victory itself. If they fought hard enough under Grant the enemy would yield. The killed at Shiloh on either side outnumbered those of the French and Germans for the numbers engaged at Verdun or the French and British on the Somme.

Courage and the will to win without skill were enough at Shiloh, but these would not have been enough against equal numbers of the veterans of Grant's and Lee's armies which faced each other at the outset of the long grind which began with the Wilderness campaign. What short work Lee's or Grant's army would have made of equal or superior numbers of the tyros on either side at Bull Run Shiloh! No "bloody shirt Yank" or "unreconstructed rebel"—if he really saw a lot of fighting—would dispute this if he were to rise from his grave on Decoration Day.

Grant had a trained army which he knew he was to operate against a trained army in the Wilderness campaign. He had so many guns he had not room for them on his front; he had back of him, mobilized and in prodigal production, the industrial north close at hand with the sea open for imports. Lee had back of him the exhausted resources of an agricultural land under blockade. Yet consider all the trouble Lee's skillful, half-starved veterans made Grant, including Cold Harbor, in the next year over the small area of southern Virginia.

Pershing, who was utterly unlike McClellan in character, was cast for a long McClellan period of training against "the greatest military machine in all history." But that was a phrase.

The German army was the best prepared army for the time at the outset of the World War. As a military machine for the time, with the weapons and tactics of the time, be the force small or large, it was no better than Militiades', Alexander's, Caesar's, Pizarro's, Cortez', Frederick the Great's, Wolfe's, George Rogers Clark's frontiersmen across the icy waters to Kaskaskia or Vincennes in the conquest of the Northwest in the Revolution, Washington's at Yorktown, or Grant's and Lee's in the Wilderness or Pershing's regulars in cleaning up the Lake Lanao region in Mindanao.

On Clark's expeditions the goosestepping Germans, with

all their discipline, would have been as house dogs trying to keep pace with sage hunting dogs. Each force was trained for the job in hand. A force's efficiency is primarily in this and sufficient numbers and munitions.

Our General Philip Sheridan, who was an observer with the German army in its sweep to Paris in the Franco-Prussian War of 1870-71—which established the awesome German military prestige—said he did not find much to learn from the Prussian cavalry in comparison with ours in the Civil War. Our cavalry he had in mind was not that of 1861-62 when the infantry used to pass its gibing remarks about no one ever having seen a cavalryman in battle. Sheridan meant the cavalry of 1863-64 after it had learned a great deal more than how to stick on a horse.

The German army, with its long war experience by the summer of 1917, was expert in the mass warfare of millions. We had to train an army to meet the millions and we had neither munitions nor weapons. No Donelson or Shiloh could be expected immediately from J.J.P. who must have an army ready to meet the German army on even terms.

With their home bases only across the narrow English Channel it had taken the British two years before their new army was in force for its first major offensive. How long would it take us with our home base across the Atlantic? Any action on our part in 1917 was out of the question. We could not begin to exert real pressure until 1918.

Could the Allies, with Russia out, hold the trench line of the western front as the iron wall to protect our drill ground and give us time for preparation? The stalemate had been unbroken for three years. All Allied and German offensives had failed. With Italy able to stonewall she ought to account for the Austrians who also had to maintain the Serbian front. The French might not be equal to another large offensive, but all the soldiers Pétain had given leave would speed back to the front for defense at the first threat of danger. The British army, strong enough to keep up its

ENERAL PERSHING AND HIS STAFF IN FRANCE. READING FROM LEFT TO RIGHT, FRONT ROW: RIGADIER GENERAL HAROLD FISKE; MAJOR GENERAL JAMES W. MCANDREW; GENERAL PERSHING; RIGADIER GENERAL FOX CONNOR; BRIGADIER GENERAL GEORGE VAN HORN MOSELEY. SECOND OW: BRIGADIER GENERAL AVERY D. ANDREWS; BRIGADIER GENERAL LEROY ELTING; BRIGADIER GENERAL DENNIS NOLAN; BRIGADIER GENERAL ROBERT DAVIS.

offensive at Passchendaele, had numbers, skill and British stubbornness to maintain their ground.

The one consolation, the one piece of good news in the midst of all the bad J.J.P had heard, the one indispensable factor, seemed to insure that the iron wall, steeped with French and British blood, was invulnerable.

Where was the war to be won? Positively there on the western front, in face of frequently expressed skepticism that there was no room to flank on that solid trench line: a break through was impossible.

This brings us to the view of the "Easterners" as they were called, with the wish the father of their thought springing from the appalling loss of life in the trench stalemate without any decision. They were asking for the Napoleonic stroke. They told us what Napoleon would do if he came to life in the World War just as politicians tell us what Washington or Jefferson would do in present domestic situations at home.

Napoleon was pictured with his eagle eye instantly seeing a wide open invitation to send a great army to roll up the German army on the flank by way of the Mediterranean, through the Balkans or somewhere in that direction. The Easterners did not bother much with details on this point. Doubtless they were willing to leave that to Napoleon's ghost.

In our own history McClellan had tried the same plan in his abortive Peninsular campaign. Sending a great army on the long voyage through the Mediterranean was quite different from occupying Salonika, or Allenby's later campaign in Turkey which was for the protection of the Suez, the Mesopotamian oil fields and other political objectives. If the Germans could have spared the troops to support Turkey there were not railroads nor highways for this movement.

Foch, Haig, Pétain, Pershing, and all the practical soldiers of staff and line were a unit that the war would be won on the western front. Once the break through came then enemy opposition as a whole would collapse (which it did) as surely as a stab in the heart cuts off the circulation in fingers and toes.

The Easterners were mostly the statesmen seeking some short cut to the victory which had so long been postponed as they felt the drain on man-power and resources with no visible result except more blood letting in the trench stalemate. They included the members of the arm chair school of theorists who draw lines on maps which do not indicate roads, and also the gallant Lawrence of Arabia who did not see why the method of the raids of Arab tribesmen in open country should not apply with huge armies.

The Easterners' plan was as fatuous as though Joffre, in the height of the Battle of the Marne, should have detached a large portion of his army by sea to invade Germany in the rear. The Germans had the interior line for the quick transport of troops back and forth. All the German staff had to do was to entrain divisions from one front to another on their railroads. The French had no shipping of account, the British were fully occupied in supplying their army in France even across the English Channel. If they had the shipping for transport through the Mediterranean the Germans would have been able to attack with all their force the weakened Allied armies on the western front, and then have had ample time after winning this decision to meet any army from the southeast.

There were other practical details the Easterners overlooked. Where the British had established port facilities in France they would have to build piers and depots in harbors which had hopelessly inadequate port facilities. They would have had to build highways and railroads for hundreds of miles advance of at least fifty divisions. One European division of 12-15,000 men with all its guns and trains occupied fifteen miles of road, not to mention the lines of trucks to keep up the flow of ammunition and supplies and the personnel to keep the roads in repair under the heavy strain, which was one of the problems on the established hard roads of France.

Granted the material and the labor for the eastern expedition it would have been many months before it could have come in contact with the German army with its back to its bases. In a temperate climate, if not in Lawrence's sunny Arabia, soldiers must have shelter in winter and stormy weather as they rest out of action; and there was no billeting any number of account in pastoral and half primitive lands with scattered villages of miserable houses.

No such adventure could have had the favor of the practical Napoleon who built the *routes nationales,* the long straight national highways of France, as Caesar built the Roman roads, for the rapid movement and concentration of his troops. No one better realized than Napoleon that an army lives on its belly, and the truth of the old maxim that you hit the enemy's main army where you find it, and when you have overwhelmed it the rest is a matter of mopping up. And he had had experience with an overseas expedition in his Egyptian campaign.

So the Easterners' plan was out of consideration if for no other reason than that there was no shipping for it. It is referred to because pressure in favor of tangent adventures—including the later ill-fated Siberian expedition accepted by President Wilson to please Lloyd George for political reasons—was to be exerted along with that against the independence of our army.

The object of all Pershing's preparations should be the German army on the western front. But where in the long trench line should we concentrate? We must have room; there was none on the northwestern part of the line. There the British occupied all the ports and roads. The French were in front of Paris occupying all the roads. They would trust no one else to defend their Paris in the last resort. We must turn to the ports of southern France.

We were to have our sector as the British had. Where? Obviously to Pershing it must be on the French right to the south and southeast toward the Alps. There we would train and form for our offensive. The first proposal favored driving through Alsace. But this was met by prompt French political objection. Alsace, partly German, primarily Alsatian, was the "lost province" which was to be the French prize of victory.

French Alsatians might express their gratification in glowing words to the descendant of an Alsation as commander of an American Army to bring their land back under the beloved tri-color of France; but, in the process, they did not want their villages smashed and their fields torn by shell fire, or Strassbourg cathedral to suffer the damage inflicted on Rheims. Moreover, this would make French repatriation more difficult. Let the battle fields where Alsace was to be delivered back into the French family be not in Alsace, but elsewhere. It was better that French villages than Alsatian should suffer destruction.

Our sector should be in French Lorraine, which was probably the more warranted in tactics. J.J.P.'s eye, surveying the map, was on the exposed salient in which the German drive of 1914 had enclosed St. Mihiel. Beyond was the great German fortress of Metz which he had seen from the outside if not the inside on his Europeon tour.

That was not all. There was another objective vital to the enemy's possession if he were to hold his trench line and not be flanked. J.J.P. would aim for the Briey iron fields which were a source of German supply; and at Mézières-Sedan-Metz railroad system which was the bread and munitions line across France to the German army in northwestern France from the old battlefield of Ypres to Champagne. Win these and the German right wing of the army would have to fall back or be cut off.

Such was the plan, such the line on which J.J.P. would hammer as Grant had hammered. The distance we should have to go to reach these objectives was not far. But it had taken nearly four years for the Army of the Potomac to go the seventy miles from Washington to Richmond. The question, as those who knew German military history posed it, was whether the German army would not crack suddenly when the tide turned against it, instead of holding out with the stubbornness of Lee's veterans when, on the cards, their cause was lost, but they would not admit that it was lost while they had a shot in the locker and a piece of corn bread left.

Sir Douglas Haig, the British commander, held tenaciously to the view that when autocratic German discipline broke it would break badly. The answer to this was to come with time. J.J.P., once he was ready, would undertake no piecemeal offensives; the enemy should have no breathing spells, but the pounding should be without cessation as it was in Grant's campaign from the Wilderness to Appomattox. His goal of St. Mihiel, Metz, the Briey iron fields and the Mézières-Sedan-Metz railroad system was set; and nothing should divert him from it. Should another commander come in his place his successor should find that his starting point was where his predecessor left off.

14

Plan Ready—Goal Set

To THE INSPECTORIAL eye of J.J.P. they were a weedy, untutored looking lot, these men of our first troop contingent whom he saw land June 28, 1917, at St. Nazaire. They were ship worn. They had lost sleep in the submarine danger zone. But here they were safe through it and in France.

Not all the stiff legs were in step, and there was much variation in the slant of the rifles as they marched over the cobbles on their way to the strange old French barracks. A few were evidently old hands. This was to be expected, and this, too, was in keeping with the plan.

We were to profit by the misfortune of the British in sending the flower of their Regular Army, officers and men in their first expedition to France in August, 1914, when they did not realize they had to build a huge army. We should not sacrifice our little nucleus of trained officers, commissioned and non-commissioned, and our veteran capable Regular privates, in one lot, but scatter them as drill masters and organizers of the whole.

"They're sturdy rookies—fine material," said **Pershing**. "We shall make great soldiers of them." He spoke as one who not only meant what he said but knew how.

But how long would they have to train before they met the enemy? This, too, was already outlined in the plan: many weeks of drill beyond the sound of the guns; then into quiet trenches for the primer lesson of trench routine; then into livelier and still livelier trenches, and finally in an attack. They had far from the initial preparation of the members of the freshman class who report for the scrub on the football field. They had yet hardly learned how to kick and pass the ball.

And a standard was already set for them of discipline— West Point discipline—and of morale. And the discipline to J.J.P. implemented the development of the morale. They should be so trained, so disciplined, so hardened, so sure of their skill that far from being in any awe of the German veteran's prestige they should be steel riveted in their confidence that they could out hit and out endure him. The proof of mastery over him in the first actions would give them the edge of morale in future actions.

How long would it be before we had enough men so prepared to strike in swift repetition of blows for the goal set? This was on the knees of the gods partly, on shipping, the War Industries Board at home and the energy and determination of our people. The recruits who were yet to go to the cantonments at home after their period of training there must go through another period back of the lines in France before they would be ready for even quiet trenches.

Well might J.J.P. ask for patience. He might have said, "We must have time if we are to make sure of victory, time as the only way to a speedier victory." But that would have been further trouble for much belabored old Premier Ribot in his eightieth year, the present Premier of France in the course of many changes of cabinets. It might have brought despair to the French people. Pétain's main fear, which he expressed to Pershing, was that under a weak and foundering French government, there might possibly be a revolution, defeating his own policy.

Our own people at home would have been shocked at the long delay to victory J.J.P.'s plan envisioned. He had not only to consider the home sentiment, but that of all the Allied peoples, and silence was his way when he could not bear false witness.

Having heard that some American soldiers had arrived in France, Parisians wanted to see with their own eyes that we had sent over more than a general and staff to France. The French had become Fourth of July conscious. Word was spread that the Fourth was the same to us as July 14, Bastille day, to them. The fame of Lafayette, as a great historic and romantic figure had been revived. Paris, all France, would celebrate our Fourth. This was good French policy, too. It would attach American sentiment and our army closer to France, and detach us from submitting too much to the influence of ally Britain, in memory of a Lafayette gallantly personifying the aid France had given us in fighting on our side to win our freedom against British coercion.

Wouldn't General Pershing please send some of his soldiers from St. Nazaire to Paris for the Fourth? J.J.P.'s natural inclination was against "a victory parade" before his men knew how to march well. His soldierly pride was sensitive to the awkward exhibition they would make before French officers and the Parisians who might think under their cheers "So this is the American army!" in ironic discrimination. It would be different if he could show a troop of the cavalry and a regiment of the infantry of his Mexican expedition as they returned across the border.

But the French appeal was fervent and convincing. Hands across the sea! Washington and Lafayette! The opportunity was not to be missed. George Washington would have approved. All America and France would approve. J.J.P. agreed that a battalion should come.

In the Court of Honor of the Invalides the battalion in campaign hats was lined up, and also a battalion of French veteran World War French infantry in war helmets, in the presence of the old veterans of other wars and the great of France of the time. President Poincaré was there and white-haired Marshal Joffre, whose part in the war was over, in contrast with the tall Pershing for whom the war was just beginning.

A flag for the American battalion from the town of Puy where Lafayette was born; a flag for Pershing from the Order of Cincinnati, started by officers of our Revolution as an inherited honor, of which Lafayette had been a member; then to Lafayette's tomb in the Picpus cemetery where Pershing got the credit for Captain Stanton's "Lafayette, we are here," in the speech Pershing had assigned Stanton, who was "good on his feet," to make! J.J.P. was present, just on time, not having been too stubborn in sticking to some subject in hand which he wanted to finish before any interruption. No speaker failed to mention Lafayette at the luncheons and dinners in honor of the day. The dead Lafayette was serving France now as the living Lafayette had served America.

The march to the cemetery was a *mardi gras fête* for our soldiers. The swarming crowds, breaking sympathetic police lines, allowed little opportunity to see whether the Americáns marched well or not. They were American soldiers—American soldiers in Paris. Men and women linked arms with them without any interest in whether they kept step. Women dropped wreaths of flowers over their shoulders, stuck flowers in their rifle barrels, hugged and kissed them.

The next day they were on their way to Lorraine to start the long ordeal of training before they were introduced to the ordeal of battle. The last of the ceremonials of reception, of capitalizing promise before fulfillment, was over. There was no radio then, but the home newspapers had not lacked "colorful" copy. "Lafayette, we are here," and "Washington, we are over there,"—over with fourteen thousand rookies in the war of millions, a qualification which no one understood so thoroughly as J.J.P. himself.

His plan was made. The requisite men and material to carry it through had been computed. His original estimate as to the size of the American army he had tentatively made in crossing the Atlantic had not been too large.

Before the echoes of the Fourth of July celebration had died away at home and in Paris he was writing one of the two most significant messages that went over the wires from GHQ to Washington during the war and in all our military history. For none, if he had been so replaced, would his successor have been so thankful.

Here, in the two cables, was the fully considered official answer for Secretary Baker from the man whom he had sent to France to learn what we had to do to win the war. Baker read them without blinking. They were not a great surprise to him. But it was not for him to pass them on to Congress, still less to make them public to discourage the Allies and encourage the enemy.

Congress was not yet prepared for all the truth. Confident our weight in the balance and signing checks to the Allies' credit would be enough to bring Germany to terms, Congress had not made more than the $100,000,000 emergency appropriation for our preparation until seven weeks after our declaration of war.

In the cable of July 6th, Pershing said:

"Plans should contemplate sending over at least 1,000,000 men by next May . . . This estimate would give practically half-million men for the trenches. Inasmuch as question affects all Allies whose common interests demand that we exert maximum military power consistent with transport problem, suggest early agreement be reached among

Allies which would provide requisite transportation . . . and limit sea transportation to food and military supplies and the exclusion of every kind of luxury as well as other supplies in excess of immediate needs of countries dependent upon overseas supplies."

A million men in France! This might appear as wild from a soldier eager for big battalions on his side as the statement of Colonel William T. Sherman, at the outset of the Civil War, that we should need 300,000 men to subdue the South—which led to Sherman being called crazy. Sherman thus learned the value of silence for the soldier and did not bother to say "I told you so" after his huge underestimate posted him as an over optimistic prophet. If policy had warranted it and Lincoln had had as candid a commanding general and as young and vigorous a Secretary of War as Baker he might not have waited for the defeat at Bull Run before summoning three hundred thousand more volunteers.

Pershing's first cable might have been construed as preparing the way for the second cable of July 11.

"The further our investigations proceed as to general conditions and the state of the French resources, the greater appear their deficiencies and the smaller their abilities to aid us in material and labor. Therefore deem it of the utmost importance that this be realized at home. Dock facilities available for our use will be very cramped when we send continuous convoys of troops and supplies. Therefore construction of additional dock facilities should be pushed. The railroads we are to use are also deficient in equipment and need repair. Material and rolling stock should be shipped without delay. The French have practically no material available so that both material and labor must come from the United States."

A statement sent with the long General Organization project, July 11, covering the detail of the plan to reach the goal set was still more ominous.

"It is evident that a force of about 1,000,000 is the smallest unit which in modern war will be a complete, well balanced, and independent fighting organization. However, it must be equally clear that the adoption of this size force as basis of a study should not be construed as representing the maximum force which will be needed in France. It is taken as a force which may be expected to reach France by 1918 and as a unit and basis of organization. Plans for the future should be based. especially in reference to the manufacture, etc. of artillery, aviation and other material, on three times this force—i.e., at least 3,000,000 men."

Marshal Joffre's handful of troops to show the colors raised to three millions, which Marshal Foch, the Allied generalissimo, was to conclude were not enough three months before the Armistice! And evidently the three millions were to be in France in time to make sure of winning the war not in 1918, but in 1919. If the Allies had been told we should send three millions of reinforcements it would have cheered them mightily, but not if the weary French, especially, thought they had to wait another two years for victory.

How colossal the vision! What a Herculean effort it called for across the Atlantic! Three millions, and all the means to get them across and all the supplies and munitions they would require, reached astronomical figures. Only a planetary war could surpass our part in the war in which we were involved. And J.J.P was as forthright and composed over his block pad as though he were making requisitions for a route march into Mexico.

He emphasized at the outset the plea for ships which he was never to cease to press. Say it again, there could be no American army in France without ocean transport. Ships enough can transport any number of men. No roads have to be built for them. Their pathway is as broad as the seven seas.

But the men and supplies have to be landed as they

would have had to be in the Easterners' proposed Mediterranean expedition; and they must depend upon railroads and highways to the front. The movement within France for the French army to the front averaged little more than a hundred miles. To reach our Lorraine sector we should have to go from three hundred to five hundred miles. From the western ports of southern France arterial railroads ran across France to our sector. There were excellent highways.

In what condition were the railroads? How much more traffic could they bear? Had they adequate sidings? How much spare rolling stock? Just how far were they equal to supplying two million men?

Pershing had the reports of experts in answer to these questions. He had first-hand views to confirm their answers. For three years France had had three millions of able-bodied men under arms. Their energy had been exclusively directed to making war. All civil labor had been concentrated on the essentials to enable them to carry on at the front. France had not only been bled white in battle but in industrial service.

French railroad beds had deteriorated. It was hard to keep enough rolling stock in repair for war needs. Coal for fuel for locomotives cost $80 to $90 a ton when the enemy had possession of French coal fields. There were not enough motor trucks to move supplies for the French army over the highways; there was a shortage of labor to keep the highways in repair to bear the strain.

We must not only bring over our own trucks and the gasoline to run them and forces to keep them in repair. We must bring over railroad locomotives and cars and coal, build needed sidings, strengthen existing railroad beds.

Nor was that all. The port facilities were insufficient at Bordeaux which must be our main entry port of supply. We must build more piers and railroad yards for rapid unloading and handling of freight. France had no hospital space to spare. We must build hospitals to care for our wounded and bring over ambulances and hospital trains to transport the wounded from the front. And we must build storehouses, refrigeration plants, regulating stations, bakeries, repair shops of all kinds, set up telephone lines—all to rise almost exclusively from material brought from America.

Therefore it must be made clear how much more we had to do in France than to train soldiers to reach J.J.P.'s goal. The point was reduced to figures in the broad estimate in the dispatch saying that only about half of the million men in France would be actual combat troops. One half had to make sure all had food and the other half had the means with which to fight.

If we had had to raise and supply an army on our own soil, aside from no need of shipping, it would have been easier to supply four millions at home than one in France in 1917-18. Then technicians, managers and labor would have been at hand working in familiar ways and on familiar ground. So it was in France and Germany. The principle was the same as between Wolfe's army making a stand on a shore county of England instead of having to cross the Atlantic, self-contained, and go up the St. Lawrence for the attack on Quebec.

One advantage we had was that we were in a civilized and populous land with many habitations. We did not have to bring over tents to house us. There were billets, although we did have to build some barracks. Otherwise there was the likeness of our undertaking to that of building a new town on the site of a gold strike, but not only a town, a supply service three thousand miles away for an army of a size equal in its demands to that for a growing city of three or four times its numbers.

The Panama Canal was also mentioned as a project in kind. But that was a smaller one, far less complicated, an engineering one, with nobody concerned in it being shot at, subject to none of the vicissitudes and surprises of war. Its problem was one of definite prevision in materials for undisturbed step-by-step construction, except by cave-ins, with no lack of experts to draw from the home reservoir in peace time.

In 1917, in a period when the job sought the man, our country's resources were already under a strain; our fields, mines, industrial plants pressed for production to meet Allied demands for war material.

The maw of war was insatiable. The millions of soldiers on the Allied side produced nothing but war, no food or raiment for themselves. Pershing's call for material and labor could have been more readily met in the depression of the 'thirties, when we had some ten millions of unemployed, than when we had no able-bodied men who need be unemployed in 1917 and two, three, four millions of them were to be withdrawn from civil life to the drill ground.

The blue prints which the racing experts over the line of communications brought were as a blue cloud descending on J.J.P.'s desk to be woven into the plan which had St. Mihiel, the Briey ironfields and the Metz-Sedan-Mézières railroad for its goal. He might have all the present truth from the front, with no further bad news affecting the sturdiness of the iron wall of the trench line, but he was learning new truths from the experts in transport and supply.

They were working in a land which spoke another language. Usually they had to rely upon interpreters who were not always available at the start. The Frenchman or American who acted as an interpreter did not always speak English or French as well as he thought he could. Often he missed out on the translation of technical industrial terms. The result was even more confusing sometimes when an American or French railroad man resorted to his school English or French.

But this was only one of the handicaps. French habits, customs, concepts and systems were different from ours. At first the local customs tax was collected from an American regimental train passing through a town on the way to fight for France. This was not meant as discourtesy. It was a regulation, and the mayor did not understand that an exception was to be made for the American troops when he had not yet been officially informed there was an American army in France.

Business we were accustomed to do over the telephone the French did by mail and in long hand. Connection over the overworked and limited French telephone system was maddening. It did not help much if the American tried to explain, especially in English, that his message was official and military. His irritation was not minimized by having missed his morning bath for several days when billeted in a French house which had no bathroom and only a little jug of water was available. At first in the want of a typewriter, he had to write by hand when he had been used to a steno-grapher at his elbow. When we had no automobiles except for the Paris staff and the French had none to spare, he had no car to move about in his studies along the projected line of communications.

His request for the privilege of a building site or to make some improvement for our needs met with the answer that it must be referred to the Prefect. Through channels to higher-ups in the French bureaucracy, as might happen in our own, the Prefect referred it to his chief in Paris, and eventually it was passed on to the French army staff by a cabinet officer who might in turn take it up with Pershing.

"He had a salary of twenty-five thousand a year," J.J.P. remarked about a man who had just left his office a roll of blue prints under his arm. "He is on a major's pay now. Used to his own car and chauffeur, he could not get a taxi-cab and had to walk all the way over here from the Place de la Concorde. He has been through enough to make him lose his temper. But he has a fighting eye and never say die spirit."

With the call to America for ships, soldiers and material went the call for labor and all manner of industrial managers and technicians in the whole industrial gamut from boss stevedores to engineers from civil life for what seemed civil jobs. But all must be in uniform, all take the soldier oath.

They, too, were in the army subject to army discipline. They might have a fresh major's leaf or a colonel's eagle on their shoulders although they had never known the drill of an awkward squad; but they should salute a superior, return the salute of an inferior officer, and obey orders under J.J.P. This he saw as essential in the team work of all the experts with their professional rivalry, team work with our Allies, the team work of the whole down to the laborer on the piers at Bordeaux and the platoon in the trenches.

At first the staff gave the name of the Service of the Rear to that of supply. This brought an outburst from those who would have to write home to mother to tell friends they were all safe far beyond the range of fire. J.J.P. sympathized with the objection. He realized the feelings of officer or man who was stuck on guard duty along the line of communications in any expedition: the feelings all the men who were giving all their civil experience and strength in sacrifice of civil pay; of any officer or man of combat troops who was diverted from the front because he had technical training which filled a crying need in supplying the army. They also served. Theirs was hard luck to come to France without ever seeing a trench. The Service of the Rear became The Services of Supply.

Those blue prints of our plan to support two millions of men, even three in France, might well have been convincing to the French government and high command that we were in earnest with all our power to make sure of victory. But to them blue prints were not military action. We were seeing "big" American fashion. We were a strange people. Why did our soldiers need refrigerated beef and even chewing gum?

In that little room in the private house on the left bank of the Seine J.J.P. was on the way to the command, the absolute command, of the greatest of American armies and the greatest of American industrial organizations. Anyone who was in the first GHQ, and looks back to the founding days, is tempted again to say that the rest was a matter of execution in fulfillment of the plan, in faith in his country's power once it was all bent toward the western front.

Then the question was the vast task of the execution subject to the gamble of war. How far would Pershing be able to rise to his task when it was a common saying that the statesmen and generals of high promise who had been broken by the war showed we were dealing with forces beyond the compass and control of a single mind? What was J.J.P.'s capacity for growth? The man who listens and learns, who keeps his feet on the earth, is the one who grows with his responsibilities.

There was J.J.P.'s so-called weakness of procrastination. He would not hurry in making the plan. Haste might make waste. There had been too much haste. One heard remarks that he was paying too much attention to detail. He would work over papers and make decisions which should have been delegated to a subordinate. His answer to this was:

"Yes, I am while I may," he said. "Then later those under me will know how my mind works."

15

At Chaumont

It Was Late September. What a transformation from the little house on the left bank of the Seine! An old French barrack now housed our GHQ at Chaumont, a small city in Lorraine. The atmosphere was as American as that of a great American business concern, only the Americans hurrying up the stairs and along the corridors. in place of French officers and privates were in khaki. Some partitions had been ripped out and some put in to adapt the soldier quarters to our needs.

J.J.P. had his office on the second floor in the middle of the main barrack which was flanked by the two other barracks on either side. His office was not large, hardly more than eighteen by twelve feet. The light from the windows, looking out on the barrack parade, was over his shoulders and in the face of his callers across a flat top desk where he sat in a chair with an arm rest—an arm rest which was superfluous as the seat of power of the AEF.

There was only one chair in the room with a sloping back which might permit lounging. This was pushed against the wall as though it were excess furniture. The few other chairs were not so placed as to invite a committee of experts to be prolix in their reports.

Frequently he stood up to receive a caller and sometimes remained standing. No visitor, after his inquiring glance which succeeded his smile, had the inclination to tell J.J.P. a story to entertain him, although occasionally, J.J.P. forgot time for the moment in renewing an old association and then caught himself as though a man with the work he had to do had no moments to spare.

On the left wall, facing J.J.P. under the light from the windows, was a huge map of France. It did not show the location of troops or plans, only the black line of the trench wall from the Swiss border to the North Sea. Beyond it was the fortress of Metz and the Mézières railroad line to remind him of his goal.

Across the hall from the General's office was that of Colonel James G. Harbord, the Chief of Staff, and also then Major Frank R. McCoy, Secretary of the Staff, another Wood man, later to command a fighting regiment and brigade and have a distinguished post-war career. The two had been used to working together.

Major, Colonel, Brigadier General, Major General, Harbord won enough esteem for his service just to be called Harbord as sufficient identification. So it is Harbord from now on in this chronicle. He may accept that as promotion just as we refer to Jackson or Sheridan without civil concern as to whether they were two-three-or four star Major Generals. Harbord's handwriting was as firm as J.J.P.'s, his J.G.H. in just as bold lettering.

Scattered through the barracks, surrounded by their subordinates and clerical forces were the chiefs of the staff sections. Now we had a general staff for the command of a great army, adapted to our needs from what we had learned in our observation of actual operations from the British and French staffs. The sections were known as the Gs, which represented departments of organization in the same way that production, sales, etc., do in a great industry, and war covers all industry and all forms of combat.

G-1, for example, was in charge of ocean tonnage, priority of overseas shipments, billets and billeting, provost marshal service, welfare organizations, among other details. G-2 had to do with all information about the enemy from battle order to espionage, and the dissemination of information and censorship. G-3 had to do with all strategic plans and study and all of the preparation for combat operations and their conduct. G-4 had the enormous task of the direction of all supply, construction and transportation in France from port to front. It was for G-5 to direct the training of all officers and men all the way from the drill ground to the training schools in all branches and staff direction, which J.J.P. insisted upon being established at once. He never once overlooked the supreme necessity that no officer or no man could be too well prepared for action.

Every morning the chiefs of the staff sections met with Harbord. After a discussion based on their information he took the distilled result to his chief across the hall. J.J.P. could have a picture of the situation in the efficiency chart of Harbord's lucid mind to consider the pressing needs of the moment and questions of policy.

In turn J.J.P. would call on any chief of a staff section to go into further details. Two conspicuous ones who were with him on the *Baltic* and remained with him until the end of the war may be introduced at this time. By the look of him Brigadier General Dennis E. Nolan was a fighting man if his Irish name did not suggest it. It seemed natural for the General to say, "Here, you know how. Whip that bunch of recruits into shape and get them into action." (Nolan had been a major of Regulars when assigned to the pioneer staff; but owing to the rapidity of promotions the author has made it a rule to give the rank which officers eventually received in the AEF.)

He had previously served under Pershing who recognized his other qualities. He had a sense of humor which is always an aid to balance. Known as "Denny Nolan" he was popular among his fellow officers. He had the sagacity, the personal agreeability, the thoroughness and patience which adapted him for G-2, the section of intelligence.

At West Point, under Pershing as instructor in tactics, was a fourth class man who rose like a strong tower for recitations which got the sense of a problem down to the earth. There was no overlooking Cadet Fox Conner and his pleasant imperturbability. The tower had a firm foundation.

"What does Fox Conner think about it?" And you had an answer in a small weighty package of words in a few syllables of the kind used back in Laclede, Missouri, in Pershing's youth. He had been a year with a French artillery regiment. The fact that he spoke French was incidental in his case.

At the time J.J.P. was selecting his pioneer staff in Room 223 Conner was an inspector of field artillery fire in the Inspector General's office. As chief of G-3, which had to do with the actual movement of troops into battle, with strategy and tactics and all battle action, his was the problem of how to hit the enemy harder than he hit you with more cost to him than to you. He never appeared ruffled or in any way hurried. In all the evaluations which officers make privately of one another no question was ever raised as to his ability. Yet of all the chiefs of sections he was least known and the one whom Pershing retained longest after the war.

It was Conner, who with then Lieut. Colonel John McAuley Palmer, Major A. B. Barber and Major Hugh A. Drum worked out our strategy plan in the early days in the Rue Constantine. Palmer, then Conner's chief, was soon invalided home where he recovered, later to have a regimental command in the Meuse-Argonne battle. As for

Drum, soon after Pershing took command of the Southern Department in succession to Funston, Pershing sent for Captain Drum of the infantry.

"Captain Drum, I am told you turned in an organization plan some time ago. I have been unable to locate it."

Drum said that it had seemed to him that the department was too loosely integrated in a series of separate commands on the Mexican border for prompt action in case of an emergency. But he had heard nothing further from the Chief of Staff to whom he submitted the memorandum.

"Have you a carbon?" Pershing asked. Drum said that he had. "Let me have it at once," Pershing said.

A few days later Pershing received the summons to Washington; and then Drum received a telegram to report to him in Room 223. Later Drum became the chief of G-3 of the First Army in the Meuse-Argonne battle.

At first Colonel James A. Logan was chief of G-1, later succeeded by Brigadier General Avery D. Andrews, a classmate of Pershing's who had resigned from the army when young to become a lawyer and later to become the head of a great corporation.

Brigadier General William D. Conner was the first chief of G-4, to be succeeded when he was given field service by Brigadier General George Van Horn Moseley. Brigadier General Paul B. Malone, who was the pioneer in G-5 (training), until he also had his wish to go to the front fulfilled, was succeeded by Brigadier General Harold B. Fiske. All the chiefs of staff sections became brigadier generals in the rapid promotion which kept step with the increase in the numbers of the AEF in the spring and summer of 1918.

Harbord was not a no-man nor was any one of the chiefs of staff sections. J.J.P. did not want to be surrounded by no-men but men of counsel. In one instance at least a staff chief was transferred because J.J.P. found him to be too much of a yes-man courtier.

There were sometimes hot arguments between J.J.P. and Harbord, and J.J.P. would yield when convinced. By this time all the subordinate chiefs did know the workings of his mind. The plan which he had inaugurated in the Rue Constantine became the established guide in widening circles of command. Though J.J.P. was receptive to advice, to recommendations which filled in gaps and tightened organization, each suggestion, each proposed change, was always considered in relation to the main lines of his policy.

He would not be diverted from the main road to his goal. Anyone who proposed taking a detour must show that his purpose was to get around an obstacle the sooner on the way back to the main road. In the colossal undertaking of building so vast an organization for a task that was without precedent in our history, three thousand miles from home, any variation from the main principles would have piled confusion on confusion.

Every paper crossing his desk, every report made to him, was submitted to the test of adaptability to the pattern of the plan. When he appeared to be won away from it temporarily he always insistently returned to it. If a paper submitted to him were long, he might push it aside after running through the pages, with "Does he think that I am to do his thinking for him?" or "Turn it over to—and see if he can find any wheat in this bundle of verbiage."

He himself continued to give an example of brevity. Its symbol was in the block pad always at hand on his desk. He wrote orders and directions in that clear, bold penciling. Words were not crossed out. He knew just what he wanted to say, and in one or two hundred words he might crystallize a dozen pages of the memorandum before him.

Sometimes he would try out subordinates to make sure of their own convictions. He appeared in a receptive mood to a proposal by Herbert Hoover, whose fame as the chief of Belgian relief had led to the American public "Hooverizing" under him as Food Administrator. Hoover would have sentinels put over our soldiers to make sure there was no waste even when they received their food from the rolling kitchens at the front.

J.J.P. even wrote out an order embodying the suggestion. When it was shown to one of his staff officers the comment was outspoken in frank conviction to the effect that it simply would not do. Such an order was against all military experience.

"You say that you're a soldier," J.J.P. said very emphatically. Then the staff officer went into more detail. The trouble was to make sure that sturdy soldiers at the front had enough; that "seconds" (another "helping") were available. Any stinting of food, any captious oversight would lead to a universal growl which would be utterly bad for morale, all in keeping with the old adage that an army lives on its belly. With a grin J.J.P. pushed the order to one side of his desk without further comment, which was a familiar signal that it was dismissed.

16

Counted Minutes

J.J.P. HELD as many as twenty important conferences in one of his long days where ten are a good measure
for a high executive in civil public office. A military
commander is master of his time. He does not have to
lead the subordinate before him up to the point. He may
ask a penetrating question which brings it out at once or
determines whether a conversationalist has any point to
offer.

J.J.P.'s eye must be on every port, on every new installa-
tion in the Services of Supply, on aviation and on relations
with the Allies. He must be in touch with the chiefs of
administration in addition to the staff sections and with
the commanders of the combat divisions.

One subject which had held his attention from the first
was the health of the AEF. This, too, was related to the
Pershing discipline. A sick soldier, trained by his country
for action, is of no use on the battle line. He becomes a
military liability instead of an asset. He may be invalided
for life, an unhappy derelict and a public care.

Pershing did not share the view of some of the line officers of the old army of the west who were inclined to leave
the ambulances behind on a campaign. They saw those
doctors, with their military rank, as doing no fighting and
given to "babying" soldiers into thinking they were sick.
J.J.P. had not forgotten the agony of the uncared-for
wounded and the sick in the Cuban campaign. There
should be ambulances and hospitals enough.

His choice of a Chief Surgeon for France was as vital
as that of any of the chiefs of staff sections or a corps commander, if not all the chiefs of the staff of the whole AEF.
At first the chief was Brigadier General Alfred E. Bradley.
Later Brigadier General Merritte W. Ireland became
chief. The tall Ireland had no circumscribed professional
bed-side manner. He was a blade of indomitable cheer and
energy.

Officer and physician, he could speak the soldiers' language to the soldiers and the physicians' to all the reserve
medical officers, who included distinguished surgeons and
physicians from civil life who had given up rich practices
to serve on a major's pay. But that was not enough. Ireland
must be a disciplinarian and organizer of a force which was
a part of the military whole.

The Red Cross was not directly under him, for the men
of the Red Cross bore no stretchers and the women did no
army nursing. Both the army stretcher bearers and the
nurses were no less soldiers in uniform who had taken the
oath than the men in the trenches. All the service from
bringing the wounded back from under fire to caring for
them in hospitals represented a huge technical and human
organization.

Among the civilian experts, whom J.J.P. had brought
to France with the pioneer staff, was Colonel Hugh Young,
genito-urinary specialist at Johns Hopkins. For J.J.P. realized that the soldier is a male animal peculiarly subject
to temptation on leave. He comes from every class of the

community. Through all time gonorrhea has been the curse of armies. A soldier who returns from the wars with syphilis spreads it in the civil world even to succeeding generations. In the early days in the Philippines where the curse was so widespread among the population we had regiments with appalling percentages of infection. One volunteer regiment of fine western youth had so many that it was considered incapacitated for the firing line.

Prophylaxis was already established in 1914 as a preventive after indulgence; but the French had disdained it, although their army had suffered much, and the British had not applied it in the first two years of the war, but had confined soldier victims in barbed wire compounds under treatment.

Enforcement was a delicate matter. Powerful groups of moralists and idealists in our country disliked to think that their noble soldier boys should stray from the path of chastity and saw that immunity from infection might make them more readily succumb to temptation, which would not be eliminated altogether in France.

J.J.P. had Secretary Baker's support for enforcement which he determinedly carried out against many French protests that we were interfering with natural laws. Not to go to the nearest station for prophylaxis—a confession in itself—was to be penalized as a military offense. No soldier with an infectious disease was allowed to leave France, or if it developed in passage, to leave the home camp until he was cured. And that is enough of this unpleasant subject, which is a reminder of one of the practical aspects of despatching a great army abroad for whatever cause.

Related to health were deportment and conduct and keeping all the units up to soldierly standards. Major General André W. Brewster, the Inspector General, who had won the Congressional Medal of Honor in the Battle of Tientsin, had come on the *Baltic* with J.J.P. and remained with him to the end of the war.

If soldiers could not fight unless they were healthy, they must first have the arms to fight with if they were to win the war. Brigadier General Clarence Williams was Chief of Ordnance. He was the expert in the arms and the making of arms, responsible for their supply, from rifles and guns to tanks. At the time Pershing sailed for France we had not enough modern guns for one hundred thousand men and not enough rifles for half a million.

And there was Brigadier General Harry Taylor, Chief of Engineers. And there was Brigadier General Edward Russell, electric and suave, Chief of the Signal Corps, to be in charge of all the wires and means by which the parts of the army communicated from headquarters to the front where the wires were forever being cut by shell fire. At first aviation was under Russell when we had no planes and later under Brigadier General Mason M. Patrick. But crossing on the *Baltic* had been the future ace of our aces who could begin flying as soon as a plane was available, then Sergeant, later Captain Edward V. Rickenbacker.

Regulars these, but along with the calls for more Regular officers was the call for civil experts of all kinds, from home in building and directing the service of supply. Notable among them was Colonel William J. Wilgus, a distinguished railroad engineer, who was already in France before the pioneer staff arrived. It was he who worked out the original plan for increased port and railroad facilities across France. An early cable by J.J.P., before he was in touch with Wilgus, asking for a first-class railroad man in France was answered weeks afterward when W. W. Atterbury, Vice-President of the Pennsylvania Railroad, who had been made a Brigadier General, sent his card in to J.J.P.'s office. Colonel Wilgus very graciously yielded to rank and served as Atterbury's subordinate.

In addition to all this varied personnel in making an American world in France and all the supplies required was that of the welfare organizations and their needs:

Y.M.C.A., Red Cross, Knights of Columbus and Salvation Army. Secretary Baker had been very insistent about welfare and that it be done by the established private organizations. There should be canteens and gathering places where the soldiers off duty could have relaxation and entertainment and buy chocolate and cigarettes in addition to their rations.

When E. C. Carter, the chief of the Y.M.C.A. in France, proposed that the "Y" should supply cigarettes free to the soldiers J.J.P. replied:

"Our soldiers have money to buy their cigarettes. I am opposed to handouts or making my soldiers appear as paupers."

Carter foresaw difficulties. The soldiers might not always have change in their pockets; their pay might be delayed, which unfortunately did happen in the early days. But J.J.P. persisted with the frank question, "Are you here to serve?" Carter said he was; and so the soldiers were to pay for their cigarettes until later on other organizations gave them away, which did not add to the popularity of the "Y."

"Are you here to serve?" was the test for the chaplains of all of the different faiths under Bishop Charles H. Brent, for every man or woman 'at least who had taken the oath and was in uniform if not always for some of the very social-minded Red Cross women volunteers.

In the adjoining little room at the left of J.J.P.'s office were his aides. There was Colonel Martin C. Shallenberger; and there was Colonel James L. Collins who had been with the General in Mexico. Collins was probably closer to him than any other man in his career. Slight and willowy of figure, softly spoken with a manner that asked his way without wishing to intrude, he was easily J.J.P.'s most daring no-man.

Usually aides do not speak much unless they are spoken

to. Collins was a most circumspect, modest, attentive aide except when he thought the occasion called for argument. When J.J.P.'s glance signified that the subject was closed, Collins would keep right on arguing. New members of the personal staff would be amazed until they concluded that "Jimmy can get away with it, but I should not like to try it on myself."

Not only would he walk into Pershing's tent in Mexico but he would follow him into his bedroom in France with his "General, you can't do that." Looking straight into Pershing's eye, holding as fast to his conviction as a bull dog to a bone, he would keep on telling Pershing that he was wrong. Collins' utter honesty, loyalty and courage had unchanging appeal to J.J.P., who, in common with other leaders, found that the higher they rose the more they were isolated in the silk of flattery for selfish aims.

If J.J.P. should dismiss Collins then Jimmy would have done his duty as he saw it to his chief and be back with troops. When J.J.P. persisted in his own view Collins would have fought to the death to see it carried out and fought with anyone who questioned any decision of his beloved chief. J.J.P. summed up Collins when he said, "There is a lot of wisdom packed in his head. He has the gift of being right."

Another man who had been with J.J.P. in Mexico was Captain George E. Adamson, his confidential secretary. No one could have a more honest face as a secretarial sphinx. J.J.P. was used to dictating letters to him, and he knew his General's ways and how to get his General's papers in order, which was no little task.

Although Collins spoke Spanish he was not good at French. While Collins remained the sage, Colonel Carl Boyd became the active aide. Boyd had been one of our student officers with the French army before our entry into the war. He spoke French well, easy, colloquial French. He was a handy aide who could sew on a button with a tailor's swiftness and precision or interpret a conference in technical terms with a French general or in political terms with a French statesman. He was adept in the noise-less speed with which he slipped in and out of J.J.P.'s office or glanced in at the door to do his part in helping end an interview with the finesse of a private secretary.

But a private secretary serves only in office hours. His chief never had to ask, "Where is Boyd?" Boyd was on call at all hours his chief was awake. He lived in the house at Chaumont where J.J.P. also had in his mess Harbord, his Chief of Staff, his Adjutant General, and Boyd and Collins and Colonel Robert H. Bacon.

For exercise, in the early days at Chaumont, cavalryman Pershing rode every morning, as a rule with Harbord. Sometimes they talked when J.J.P. had some point he wanted to discuss and again there was silence. There might be silence from the time they mounted their horses.

Both were at the barrack offices at eight or soon after eight. But the day's work was far from done when J.J.P. left his office. Officers with whom he wanted to talk might come to dinner or for evening appointments. After dinner he frequently worked until midnight or even later. Boyd was quite used to the appeal, "Won't you slip this memo-randum on the General's night desk?" Report had it that J.J.P. would not go to bed until he had read the last paper on his night desk, that is, if the paper were brief.

There was one item in J.J.P.'s office which Boyd had placed directly opposite him on the wall. It would seem that he could not look up from his desk without seeing the large clock face. If J.J.P. never had to wait on Boyd, Boyd very often had to wait on him, and so did others.

"General, the car is ready." But that was no argument at all when J.J.P. wanted to finish what he was writing on his block pad. He would hold fast to that task in hand. Boyd would hover about his desk gathering papers he had signed and others he might need on the trip.

"General, it will take an hour to get there and now we have only a half hour." Silence—the General oblivious of the interruption. "Shall I telephone explaining?"

"No," or, sometimes with a somewhat testy added: "They have more time to wait than I have, and this cannot wait."

"Maybe I'll be late for this appointment," J.J.P. replied on one occasion at least, "but we'll not be late for the battle when the army is ready."

The pencil signed the J.J.P. to the order,—with Boyd making sure no other paper to waylay him was within reach, —and down the stairs he went, looking the embodiment of soldierly form and punctuality with pilot-bird Boyd just a step behind him. He might be off to another one of the many councils with the French to iron out wrinkles of disagreement, or down the line of the SOS (Services of Supply), or on an inspection of a division in training.

17

Mould of Discipline

SECRETARY OF WAR Newton D. Baker once said that he did not understand how any man who had such great vision as Pershing and so signally fulfilled it should have thought so much about buttons. Baker himself was quite careless about clothes and while he took no interest in what other men wore, in common with Pershing he had an observant eye which missed no detail. It is not certain but that after he had been Secretary of War for a time he would have noticed if a general reported to him with a button on his blouse missing, or not in the buttonhole, as not quite in keeping with the military profession.

Possibly if J.J.P. had neglected the buttons the AEF not only would have been unbuttoned, not to say naked, in the face of fire, but lost its legs and even have been disemboweled. That all buttons should be in their buttonholes was a part of the Pershing pattern of discipline to which every officer and every private must conform. The elaborate detail of written instructions in conduct, training and organization ever had in mind that he had to make a homogeneous army in haste out of civilians unused to military life and its primary essentials against the veterans of many battles.

Soldiers who have been much under fire are a law unto themselves. Their discipline has become so instinctive that they are pardoned for paying less attention to the forms. Franco-Americans, who at first had been alarmed lest we should send over an undisciplined mob of an army, were soon critical of the Pershing discipline as comparatively far more rigid than the French.

The discipline of every army is that best suited to the psychology of its soldiers. The kind which succeeds with the French would not succeed with the Germans and the kind which succeeds with the Germans would not with the French. Anyone who knows French drill ground and barrack life knows that French discipline for the conscript is as firm as it was in its essentials in Napoleon's Grand Army.

It was said that Pershing's soldiers would never call him "Papa" as the French soldiers called Joffre. To them the Pershing smile was a legend. He was a steel machine of a man. Shorter and uglier terms of characterization were to rise from plodding columns and dugouts in sardonic and profane comment.

What soldier had ever seen him smile on inspection or in a glimpse of his profile as stiff as the vizor of his cap, speeding past in his automobile on his rounds? If anyone ever had the luck to see him smile, surely no one ever heard him smile. Surely he could no more laugh than a stone image.

But he was a very live stone image of flashing eyes, sometimes given to rough words on an inspection. Throughout the army the word that the Commander-in-Chief himself was coming to inspect a unit had a threat almost as serious as an enemy offensive. If there was a button unbuttoned, a rifle that was not clean, he would spot it.

No top-sergeant could say in more stern reprimand, "Do

149

you call yourself a soldier?" Not only privates but officers, including colonels and generals, heard this. He was harder on Regulars than reserve officers. The Regulars had no excuse. It was their business to "know better."

The soldiers might be waiting miles away for inspection while Boyd with his eye on the clock was urging J.J.P. that time was passing and he would be late. He was not invariably as late for the time set as many supposed. Often a commanding officer, in his eagerness to make sure his troops were ready before the General arrived, and even anticipating that some generals had a habit of being too early rather than late, had his men waiting for hours in line before the time set from GHQ. For years after the war these memories of standing in the rain, after the grinding drill day after day, were to linger in the minds of soldiers.

On occasion an inspection was not announced until his arrival. An example of this in the early days was that of the aviation group in Paris which had become the subject of scandalous rumors. Although we had no planes yet, this group was thinking of itself as a *corps d'élite* in a precious world of its own. It had established itself in luxurious quarters in Paris with a super-abundance of women clerks and lavish spending.

As Pershing entered the building a young officer came gayly trotting down the stairs and started to pass him by without saluting. J.J.P. caught him by the arm and turned him around until their eyes met.

"Salute your superior officer!" said J.J.P. The offender gasped as he recognized the Commander-in-Chief, and tremulously saluted. And J.J.P. read him a very brief and very trenchant lesson on what the salute meant in the army. It was a symbol of instant readiness to obey orders. After the wrath of the military god had swept through that building the subsequent orders issued from GHQ brought a swift reformation which endured.

The reserve officer who had been the able, experienced

chief of a civil hospital never quite forgave J.J.P. for his
response when he entered a ward and the surgeons and
nurses came forward to greet him as they would the mayor
or governor.

It had been a hard day for J.J.P. He had seen some very
bad marching. Some troops had appeared very slouchy.
Some field exercises were most discouraging. It was a day
when he thought, "Will I ever get them ready?"

He flabbergasted the hospital chief, the doctors and the
nurses, all of whom were used to hospital discipline, with
his, "You are expected to stand at attention in your places
on inspection."

In after years when I mentioned this to J.J.P. he did not
recall it among the many incidents of his inspections. He
said, "Send that officer to me and he'll find I'm not so in-
human. He had to make an efficient hospital which I am
sure he did. I had to make an efficient army. All officers
had to join in the example to keep the slack up to the
mark."

France had known the invasion of many armies. It had
repelled many invasions and sent its victorious soldiers
under Napoleon to Russia and down the Italian boot leg,
but never had there been so strange a picture on the soil of
Europe as that of our pioneer First Division, which was
the first to go through the paces of training to become efficient in every detail of warfare as it had been developed
through three years as Allied and German steel and industry had ground on each other in unceasing struggle.

We were there to learn all we could from our Allies, but
J.J.P. did not forget that his troops were American making
an American Army. The object of all the Pershing discipline
and the severe training was to capitalize our military and
national inheritance of the spirit of initiative which began
with our first settlers. It was in Washington's crossing of
the Delaware, in the vain Federal charges at Fredericks-

burg and Pickett's charge at Gettysburg, in Grant's and Stonewall Jackson's aggressive tactics, and the charge up San Juan Hill in which Pershing had a part.

The American soldier will always charge, but to charge is not enough. It was not enough for the Federals at Fredericksburg or for Pickett at Gettysburg. Sheer bravery of initiative of itself would have meant massacre against the skilled German veterans and at least the temporary loss of morale in vain sacrifice. J.J.P. would continue to drill into the American soldier's very bones not only his sense that he could be master of the enemy at the start but that he could continue to hold the mastery, retaining all his own quality at its best while not only benefitting from the merits of the French but also from their mistakes.

Most significant was a conversation he had with a French general one day when they were watching the pioneer division at its exercises. J.J.P. was in one of his determinedly inquiring moods. He understood French fairly well if he did not speak it well; and in conference when you have a mediocre knowledge of the language of the man with whom you are talking, interpretation allows time to think and also to check the interpreter's rendering. The interpreter had translated J.J.P.'s *"on dit"* with *"il dit,"* whereupon Pershing interrupted with, "No, not 'I say' but 'they say.' "

And what "they" said was that French soldiers, so long used to the trench offensive and to hand grenade action in trench fighting where the length of the rifle makes it clumsy to handle around a traverse, had failed to shoot at Germans with their rifles when the Germans were within a hundred yards because they were out of grenade range.

Thus the rifle had become an almost obsolete weapon to the French. In peace time training, the French conscript, on account of the comparatively immense size of the French army, had nothing like the allowance of practice ammunition for the target range of our Regulars and National Guard, owing to the great cost. Therefore the French were relatively poor shots compared to the British regulars, who also had a large allowance of practice ammunition, and proved their marksmenship in the way they punished the German advance in their stubborn covering of their retreat before Von Kluck's overwhelming numbers in 1914.

The rifle had always been our soldier's weapon in the tradition of the rifle of our frontiersmen against the "Brown Bess" of the British regulars. Accuracy of rifle fire gives the soldier confidence. If he has a better rifle and can shoot better he takes more toll from the enemy than the enemy takes from him.

Pershing's "they say" became an "I say" in the training of the American Army.

The rifle was still the soldier's own weapon, which was always with him. It had always inflicted far more casualties than any other weapon upon the enemy and was to in all of our actions in the World War. The machine gun fires rifle bullets, and its accuracy, shot for shot, is accordingly important. J.J.P. had discovered for the French their own neglect of rifle fire. They were to realize its value afresh in their resistance to the great offensive drives of 1918 and later when the Allies turned the tide in their favor.

One popular conception, and one often expressed in France, was that Pershing's real contribution was in stressing the value of accurate rifle fire. Invaluable as this was, it should not be singled out alone for emphasis when it was a sound and characteristic application of immemorial principles and only one factor in the development of the great plan and his generalship.

18

In Face of Disaster

OCTOBER CAME and still the pioneer division was drilling. The French were becoming impatient with us. It was ages ago in war's short memory since the acclaim of "Général Pershaing" upon his arrival and the march of a battalion of our first contingent through the streets of Paris. Instead of "Lafayette, we are here!" the French were asking, "Where are the Americans?" They judged we were hidden in the folds of the Lorraine landscape when the press noted that they had been reviewed by President Poincaré.

M. Georges Clemenceau, still an intransigeant and out of office, included us also in his diligent personal tours in informing himself about how badly the French government was conducting the war. He thought our men should be put in the trenches immediately. But J.J.P. would not be hurried. He would send them in soon in quiet trenches under proper conditions.

Meanwhile, we were far behind the arranged schedule both in the arrival of combat troops and of labor and material for the installations for the SOS. America was the last major nation available to aid the Allies. If our soldiers in their first contact with the enemy should make a poor showing the effect would be serious for Allied morale.

In dribbling lots the first detachments of other divisions, the 2d, the 42d and the 26th, were beginning to arrive not in the sunny France of their imagination but in the chill, overcast, spongy moist Lorraine climate. They had their first experience in being billeted in French peasant houses and barns over the manure piles and their first experience of drill in mud—Lorraine mud—and practice trench mud.

Supplies for them did not keep up even with their small number. They lacked winter clothing and food luxuries. It frequently took six weeks or more for letters to reach them from home. Colonels and even generals had to walk when they were entitled to cars. The French telephone service was hopelessly inadequate for communication with GHQ.

Not only the soldiers but some high officers were suffering from war disillusionment, discouraged by multiple frustrations. The War Department, after sending them abroad, had evidently forgotten them. At the time voices were even being heard in Washington against any attempt to reinforce the nucleus we had already in France in view of a lack of shipping, while with the shipping available it was bringing many items which had not been asked for in place of those which were vital. One of J.J.P.'s cables was a reminder to old time bureaucrats in Washington that our needs in France were for a combat army and not a peace time army post: "For All Departments: Recommend no further shipments be made of following articles . . . bath bricks, book cases, bath tubs, cabinets for blankets, chairs except folding chairs, cuspidors, office desks, floor wax, hose except fire hose, step-ladders, lawn mowers, refrigerators, safes except iron field safes. settees, sickles, stools, window shades. Further stop orders will follow soon."

But it was not J.J.P.'s way to make any complaint except to the War Department. Influential visiting Americans who were shocked at the conditions they saw and suggested that they should tell the truth at home soon found that this would be decidedly without his assent.

As he said, "Mr. Baker has his own troubles. I will not add to them. He has reposed confidence in me and I mean to justify it."

Division commanders as well as other officers of high rank had voiced pessimism to our senators and men of influence who had come to see the AEF. To J.J.P. this was defeatism. He rounded on the known offenders personally in no uncertain terms and determined to reach all in a letter of warning. He said that he realized that optimism cannot be created by order but, "it is not an overstatement to say no officer worthy of command would give expression to thought or thoughts of depression, much less communicate to untutored civilians false ideas of the morale of our troops . . .

"A conservative firmness and faith in our cause is not inconsistent with a serious estimate of an enemy's forces or even of a grave strategic or tactical situation, but I hardly need add that a temperament which gives way to weak complainings, which views with apprehension the contact with the enemy, which carps at the individuality of our Allies, and querulously protests at hardships such as all soldiers must expect to endure, marks an unfitness for command of such an officer, and indicates his practical defeat before he goes to battle.

"The officer who cannot read hope in the conditions that confront us . . . who shrinks from hardships, who does not exert his own personal influence to encourage his men . . . should yield his position to others with more of our national courage. The conscience of such an attitude should in honor dictate an application for relief. Whenever the visible effects of it on the command of such an officer reach me in future, it will constitute grounds for his removal without application."

So another principle was established. Officers ceased to pity themselves or pity their men, for one sure way in military command to make men pity themselves is for an officer to pity himself. A certain general officer's talk may have been responsible for a report that was made public to Americans at home to the effect that J.J.P. thought that the German trench line which it held for three years could never be broken.

This led J.J.P. to break his silence with, "The German lines can be broken, they must be broken and they will be broken." To break them was the goal of the plan for which he was sent to France and he had never faltered in his faith that they would be broken.

Meanwhile, as the October days passed, the Allies were confident, though Russia was out of the war, that their own trench wall for the protection of the drill ground would hold fast. The British army, slugging on at Passchaendale, had drawn immense numbers of German divisions to its front for the relief of the French after the mutiny and break in their morale following the Nivelle disaster.

But now in late October the French soldiers under General Pétain had so far recovered heart that they undertook a limited defensive in the Chemin des Dames sector where Nivelle had failed, with success as an augury of confidence for the winter quiet. By spring, if more soldiers and material should arrive, the American Army should have trained divisions for offensive action in further strengthening the wall against the day when we should be able to turn the tide. The French at last had the good news that on October 21st our pioneer division had entered the front line for their first trench experience in the very quiet Luneville sector.

But that was reckoning without knowing what was in the mind of Marshal Ludendorff. Unknown to the Allied intelligence services, he had been training crack divisions for a special task. In the third week of October seven of these divisions were being mobilized with all their guns and ammunition along the mountain road under the heights of Caporetto.

The High Command of the Italian army, which was supposed to be securely set for the winter in their trenches, did have an inkling that there was some movement on the enemy's part, but did not take it very seriously until on the morning of October 21st the German and Austrian armies sprung the most skillful military surprise so far of the war, which led to what seems a still incredibly titanic disaster for the Allies.

Instead of the preparation of a long artillery bombardment the attack was introduced by a brief terrific one, immediately followed by the German infantry charge scaling the Caporetto heights which were supposed to be impregnable. The Allied military commanders and statesmen then knew such days of suspense as they had not known since the German drive to the Marne. On the second day in the enveloping movement of the German and Austrian wings the offensive was through the Italian trench line out on the plain. All the ground which the Italians had gained in two years of gallant piece by piece advances had been lost. The Austro-German forces had taken 300,000 prisoners and 3000 pieces of artillery.

Fear pervaded Allied councils lest Italy as well as Russia should be out of the war. In her distress it might be her only alternative unless French and British divisions arrived.

But now as winter closed in, the German army, having put Russia out of the war and occupied three-fourths of Rumanian soil, could leave ally Austria to hold the Italians, and for the first time turn its full strength against the wall protecting our drill ground in the hope of a decisive victory before America was ready to exert her strength on the western front.

19

A Valley Forge in France

CAPORETTO HAD magnified the prestige of the German army under a new demonstration of the genius of Hindenburg and Ludendorff on the background of Tannenburg and their subsequent triumphs over Russia. On each occasion they had developed tactics suitable to gain their objectives. Hitherto all offensives on the western front by either side had failed to break through, but now over all Allied councils was the growing fear that this one might succeed. Only the inner circles realized the danger to the full. The Allied publics and our own were shielded from so stark a presentiment.

Such was the shadow under which J.J.P. was to labor through the winter of 1917-18. There is another American likeness, that of Lee's Army of Virginia under the shadow of Grant's huge preparations for the campaign of 1864-65. Our soldiers in Lorraine, that winter, knew hardships enough, if not so severe, as Washington's soldiers who certainly had not to submit to more rigorous drill than Pershing's.

Where would Ludendorff strike his blow? First reports suggested that it might be against the sector which the Americans had chosen for their own. But it was not long before we knew he was mobilizing in western France where he would throw the weight of his concentration suddenly somewhere between Champagne and Flanders.

In the event the German offensive should break through to the English channel ports, or separate the British from the French army or threaten Paris, our own little army in distant Lorraine would be isolated. If Germany had completed many new submarines during the winter increased submarine activity might cut us off both from further reinforcements and supplies from home.

For the submarine was far from conquered though the number of sinkings had been reduced. If they had not been reduced from the immense toll at the time we entered the war then Ludendorff would be able to strike against a Britain which was already practically starved out. March and April would mean favorable weather for the U-boats as well as for the German land offensive. Therefore, through December, January and February the Allies would wait in suspense while they prepared against the inevitable blow.

Chiefs in our front zone could not fail to be impressed by the depressing rumors. Chiefs of the SOS were "worn to a frazzle" by their manifold difficulties and lack of material. But it was not well for them to appear discouraged in J.J.P.'s presence. He himself never let down in industry or determination which he imparted to others. The worse the news the warmer the brief smile to the visitor and the sharper the succeeding steel glint in his eyes. He would have his outbreaks of temper in brimstone language which of themselves carried a certain confidence of an invincible spirit. For a period before Caporetto the inclination in Allied military councils had been to disregard our little army. It appeared to be hardly worth the attention that it required. Drillmasters were supplied for its instruction, but the general attitude was that this stubborn American general was playing at making an army which would never be of effective service. If America could find ships to bring over more soldiers and material, why well and good, but the British were not inclined to spare further shipping for us.

The Allies made the most of their propaganda in America that if they were beaten it would be our turn to suffer German conquest while secretly they realized, in their own logic, that we could not really be fighting for our self interest because of the protection of our isolation across the Atlantic. Moreover, they saw us in a chaos of disorganization at home taking months to build cantonments to house our soldiers before we could begin drilling them. We were a fractious, sentimental, emotionally unpredictable people.

One source of secret concern of the Allies was that, inasmuch as we saw no reason why we should suffer heavy casualties in the European shambles, we did not mean that our soldiers in France should be too much exposed; and we were relying, eventually, upon the cumulative power of our preparations as a diplomatic asset for the ending of the war on our own terms.

If we meant to fight in earnest it appeared to the military councils after Caporetto that all the preparations we were making in our SOS no less than at home seemed to be based either on a grand gesture or a view that the war might last forever, or at least for another two or three years. This the Allies could not endure. When their resources had been under such heavy strain and the French army's man power was so far on the decrease and it was amalgamating weakened divisions rather than expanding their number, and the British army had reached the peak of its man power, they faced the honest fact that the Germans could muster a superior force to their own on the western front.

In periods of optimism the Allies had pulled apart, each thinking of its own share of spoils in victory. When the outlook was bad they pulled together. They had never had such reason for unity as after Caporetto. At home we had come gradually to understand their own lack of coördination which was such a handicap in our own home policy as well as in team work with them. It was as though each Ally, including ourselves, was fighting a war on its own. In the hope of better coördination the mission of experts under Colonel E. M. House, with General Tasker H. Bliss as the military representative, was on its way to London while the Italians were being driven back to the Piave. The mission arrived to find the statesmen and war ministers of Britain and France hastening to Italy. There they met at Rapello.

At last, after more than three years of war, the proposal of Lord Kitchener, which naturally Lloyd George claimed as his own original idea, took form in the Supreme War Council. At least, through it as a clearing house of information and of counsel, one Ally would know what the other was doing and whether its call for aid was genuine or just in keeping with habitual policy.

Caporetto had led to the fall of the French government then in power. Old "Tiger" Clemenceau had become premier. The Supreme War Council itself consisted of the Prime Minister of Britain and the Premiers of France and Italy. President Woodrow Wilson would have made the fourth if he had been accessible. Colonel House could not remain permanently in Europe to act for him. The premiers of the smaller Allied countries were not included.

The Council itself was to meet monthly at Versailles where there was a permanent organization of military representatives and experts. General Bliss with his broad experience, his scholarship, his wisdom, was to be our military representative; and, owing to the absence of any direct representative of the President, to have a statesman's part though he did not actually rank with the chiefs of state and sit in their secret sessions. The commanders-in-chief of the British and French armies were naturally disturbed lest the Council, through its military representative, should attempt to exercise field command. General Ferdinand Foch, as the French military representative, was supposed to command an Allied reserve force ready to move in any direction to meet a crisis at any point after the German offensive developed. But no one of the Allies was willing to part with any troops to form the reserve.

General Bliss, upon his arrival in London, had been alarmed by the candor of the statesmen about the critical situation and astounded at the waiting attitude of the Allies and a kind of fatalism, without any directly planned action to meet the approaching emergency.

Now the Allies did look toward America where they found that not only were the cantonments built, but we already had many divisions sufficiently well trained to be sent to Europe for their prefatory training before entering the line. Indeed, we had a million men ready for transport.

Here was the man power to replenish that of the British and French. The British had the ships for transport. Not only this but the British and French had the guns which we lacked. Their munition plants, which they had started building early in the war, were now in full production while their man power had a sufficient complement of guns and rifles.

No American planes, no Liberty motors, had yet been forthcoming from the United States for the AEF. We were training artillerists and pilots but they would be dependent for their guns and planes upon the Allies. This put the Allies in a position to demand that we send over our masses of infantry and machine gun units at their disposal. Only by the infiltration of our men as recruits, as they saw it, could we be of service in time to prevent the German offensive from overwhelming the Allied armies.

On its face this appeared logical. It was natural reasoning in the Allies' own interest. Our policy had been clear, as stated by President Wilson to the author and by Secretary Baker, and fast in J.J.P.'s own mind, that in case of a great emergency all our troops would be at the Allies' command.

It must not be forgotten that from the day of the arrival of the Allied missions in America, after our entry into the war, on through to Caporetto, the campaign, if never direct, had not ceased for the infiltration of our troops into the Allied armies. Bringing influence to bear on the spot on that "stubborn man," J.J.P., with his "thin lipped smile," as Clemenceau described him, and pressure on House and Bliss after their arrival in Europe was accompanied by all the methods of diplomatic play which nations with their very lives at stake could employ through the Allied embassies and missions in Washington. ·

Not only was there an effort to undermine Pershing, but tentative advances were made to have him recalled. Meanwhile, Secretary Baker himself had already learned that war may induce prevarication even among allies. We were about to have a real test of solidarity from the White House through the Secretary's office to GHQ in France.

Mr. Baker had read the history of the Civil War with its record of Secretary Stanton's interference with his generals, the Halleck intrigue against Grant and the difficulties which President Davis had made for General Lee. Fortunately President Wilson had faith in Baker, who in turn had faith in Pershing, in marked contrast with the changes in the French government and commanders and Lloyd George's persistent dislike of Sir Douglas Haig, the British Commander-in-Chief, which almost amounted to a personal hate, though he never had the courage to utilize his power to dismiss Haig. Indeed Lloyd George had a personal distaste for soldiers as soldiers, and appeared to think he himself was a born general.

Premier Clemenceau, who throughout the war had kept in close touch with the front and had come to know all the British and French generals in person, did have some knowledge of military affairs which might be subject to the qualification that half knowledge may be sometimes dangerous.

Baker modestly announced that he had all to learn when he became Secretary of War, but he had a marvelously quick perception in judging men and a genius for mastering the essentials of any situation. It soon became clear that Pershing would never be recalled on the suggestion of the Allies and his policies had the administration's support, but the covert siege in Washington did not cease.

Since Secretary Baker had such great confidence in General Bliss, who had been at his elbow as Chief of Staff and wise counsellor, naturally the Allies had a purpose in striving to set his opinion against Pershing's. They made it appear that he agreed with the Haig if not the Robertson plan, which will be mentioned later. When Pershing and Bliss met at the first meeting of the Supreme War Council J.J.P. relates how General Bliss suggested that if they had a difference they might submit it to Secretary Baker. J.J.P. replied that this would only show that they were incompetent to make a decision themselves and both should be relieved, to which Bliss nodded his assent. Thereafter there was no question of Bliss' support of Pershing and his policy to the utmost.

Bliss soon learned, as Pershing had already learned, the interplay of intrigue in the conflict of allied interests which has its most valuable historic revelation in his own letters to Baker written while he was a member of the Supreme War Council.

Bliss too had vision. He was strangely a prophet of what we later saw happen in post-war Europe. He saw Pershing as the Commander-in-Chief in the field and his own part was simply to aid in his support by promoting Allied unity and in bringing all the power of America to bear to win the victory now we were in the war.

"Build a Bridge to France" was the latest slogan in the succession of drives at home. We had to build the shipyards before we could build the ships. In the extremely cold and stormy winter of 1917-18 at home we were far past the stage of our first war enthusiasm and at grip with its realities as the people of the belligerent nations of Europe had been for three years.

Our piers were piled high with ammunition and supplies for the Allies for want of shipping. It was amazing that when we had a million men eager to go overseas to fight for the security of the French soil and English channel ports, we should have had to wait so long to get the ships in this crisis, while the Allies continued to waste time in political maneuvers for short-sighted advantage.

20

"Out" or "In"

THE GREAT DECISION of his command of the AEF
rested with J.J.P. If he resisted infiltration and disaster
came, then he might be charged with responsibility for the
disaster. Meanwhile no one was more eager than he to
hasten our troops to France.

Inevitably there was competition between the British
and French for American recruits. The French, who were
not happy at having so many foreign soldiers on their soil,
wanted their share lest the British become preponderantly
strong to the prejudice of French interests. The French
would introduce our regiments into French divisions for
a very brief intensive period of training before they were
sent into combat. Eventually they were supposed to be
released to join American divisions, but there would have
been an outcry from the French command, when the time
came to carry out the agreement, that French divisions
would thereby be so reduced that they would be too weakened for action.

About this subject of infiltration the experts of our pioneer staff had to make no study in France. One need not have been a cadet captain at West Point or a student at Leavenworth, or at the War College, to realize one basic principle that must apply. To change it would have been equivalent to changing the law of gravity or recasting human nature by fiat. It seemed as unnecessary to demonstrate it as expecting a professor of mathematics to prove that fifty and fifty make one hundred, by counting out two groups of fifty wooden blocks each and then putting them together in one group and recounting them all to show the total was one hundred.

The principle was clear to any army sergeant who had ever been in war, and indeed should be to anyone who did not think that his neighbor was just like himself or to any primary school teacher who did not think all children were alike in character. All the history of allies in war, of soldiers in battle, of human beings under heavy strain, left no shadow of a doubt that the infiltration of our soldiers into the army of another nation would be sheer military imbecility.

Civil War history was rife with regimental and sectional jealousies in both armies; with regimental charges and counter-charges that the troops on "our" right or left failed to support us; with bitter discussions as to which regiment took or yielded a certain position; with the Texans and Virginians and the Maine and Wisconsin men confident they were the better fighters of the two.

It was all as humanly inevitable as that the pitcher should have an edge because the short-stop juggled a grounder missing a double play that lost the game; as that the general manager should have an edge that "we would have got that big order" if the sales manager, who of course was a good fellow, had not nodded on the job.

J.J.P. from Laclede, who had served in all parts of his country, had the advantage of knowing its peoples. In what was later called "The Big Parade," the workman who rode in the subway, the share cropper from the south, and all our other types with differences of inheritance, religion, racial origins and occupational and educational influences were to be in the AEF. Our melting pot was to have war's hot fire under it, and care in the statesmanship of war had to be taken lest it did not boil over and even get upset. This was Secretary Baker's home task which enabled him the better to realize what was J.J.P.'s task in France.

As for infiltration with the French: Imagine, in battle, a western rancher on one side and a suit-maker from New York on the other side of a Frenchman whose language neither knew when the French command had its difficulties in preserving unity free from sectional bias among the Britons, the Savoyards, the Lorrainers and the Marsellaise. Imagine our young officers from our training camps receiving their orders in French in battle or an American and French sergeant trying to understand each other under shell fire. Imagine all the complicated directions for objectives in attack written in both English and French. The confusion which surprise fire brings and the quick readjustments required in the gamble of battle make this difficult enough among the soldiers who have a common language

And food: Were there to be two commissariats behind a single division on the battle line, two sets of rolling kitchens, two kinds of rations borne up to the trenches under fire in an *à la carte* instead of a *table d'hôte* service? Were our soldiers to have the French rations with the bitter French pinard wine instead of coffee? When we tried French rations with one division the wine soured on the stomachs of our boys from prohibition Kansas and others who had always been teetotalers, with consequent loss of efficiency.

The record of the relations of British and French staffs had only reflected the difficulties in *liaison* of British and French divisions side by side in offensives which led to charges and counter-charges of how the other had failed to do its part. Although this may have been a misunderstanding, due to contrasting military methods and racial temperaments, it was none the less serious.

In coöperation with the British we did have the advantage of a common language. But the Australians, Canadians, New Zealanders, and all the contingents from the self-governing Dominions of the British Empire, had their own integral divisions from the start, and the Canadians and Australians had their own corps. Each Dominion's force had its own character and discipline. Their climatic environment and inheritances had fashioned them into what were really distinctive national entities. When the Australians took over a line of trenches from the Canadians or tne Canadians from the Australians, there were hot and uncomplimentary exchanges. The British staff found it wise to keep them apart in the operations.

What with the Dominion forces and with the English, Scotch and Welch divisions and British regiments of long traditions, the British high command had a sufficient problem in homogeneity without the incorporation of Americans. It was surely not less human and national, when war accentuates nationalism, that the Americans should want to fight as Americans than that the Canadians and Australians should want to fight as Canadians and Australians.

We did not share the common bond of being His Majesty's subjects as a part of the British Empire. Even the Cockney, the Yorkshireman and the Devonman are far removed in habits, custom, outlook and even food from the New Yorker, the Oregonian and the Texan, though all do speak their different kinds of English. The Irish also spoke the English language, but we had an example of their feelings when buttons with the British coat of arms were still on uniforms from Britain issued to some of our troops who were Irish born or of Irish descent.

Not only this, but in our army were foreign born soldiers

who spoke more than thirty different languages, including those of German birth and German descent with distinctly German names who fought most gallantly in the AEF along with those of the races of the component parts of the Austrian Empire, from Hungary and Bohemia down to the Black and Aegean Seas.

Their common bond was that they were Americans under the American flag; and if the war had any patriotic moral value to us it was in the common blood test of every soldier's Americanism, whatever the race or races of his origin. And there were Americans of pure English descent through generations who would no more welcome wearing King's buttons than the Irish.

It must always be borne in mind in any narrative of J.J.P. or the AEF, that, after an American soldier had been a few weeks in France, he was not fighting for a European cause but for America and the sooner to have the job over and get home. It was this which accounted for the practically universal opposition in 1939 on the part of all of our veterans who had served in France against our ever entering another European war.

General Pershing's own book gives the faithful, indispensable record of his struggle to maintain the independence of our army. And the background which I have given for his attitude was so obvious to him, when he had so much to tell in his brief, soldierly and honest manner that he did not go into it in such detail.

It must be repeated that he did not object to training his men with the British or French up to the point where this served best in forming our own army and in making our weight fully and promptly felt by the enemy. In a technical military sense the issue may be simplified in the words of in or out.

"In" meant that American troops would inevitably be lost in the ranks of an Allied army. It was this plan which

171

was favored by General Sir William Robertson, the Chief of Staff of the British Army, and Lloyd George, the Prime Minister, who wrote a memorandum to Lord Reading on December 2, 1917, saying: "The C.I.G.S. (Chief of the Imperial General Staff) is very anxious you should place the enclosed (memorandum) before Colonel House. I entirely concur and urge its acceptance. We shall be hard pressed to hold our own and keep Italy standing during 1918. Our man power is pretty well exhausted. We can only call up men of 45-50, and boys of 17. France is done. The American soldiers will not be ready to fight as an army until late in 1918. Our experience proves that meanwhile we must keep the fight going. Even half-trained American companies or battalions would fight well if mixed with two or three years' veterans." But the French thought the British could have easily marshaled 300,000 more men if they had rounded up their slackers. The Allied alarm about the overwhelming power of the coming German offensive, which led Lloyd George to write in February that the war was lost unless America was in time, was either exaggerated for effect upon us or else their intelligence services were greatly at fault. For the truth was that when the German offensive began, the Germans had hardly more than four-to-three against the Anglo-French numbers, far from the requisite superiority by all calculations and by all experience on the western front, for a decision.

"In," considering battalions rather than companies, meant that these battalions would become as much a part of the British organization as though they were British battalions, that is, that a battalion of American soldiers from Minnesota or Ohio would be permanently fighting in the line next to British, Scotch and Welch soldiers under British command. General Robertson's bid was really for all the one million soldiers training in our home camps as recruits to fill in gaps in the British ranks.

"I did not swear this time," said J.J.P. after returning

from a conference with General Robertson as though he deserved a credit mark for keeping his temper. "It is incredible to me how a man who has risen from a private in the ranks himself should make such a ruinous proposal in our common interest in winning this war." Haig, who was the Commander-in-Chief in France, was so well fortified in his experience that he was for the "out" plan. He was ready to train our battalions within British divisions the while we formed our brigade and division staffs in training with the British. Thus our division organization should be ready to receive the battalions back into our divisions, which would in turn be formed into the larger unit of a corps.

But it was easily understandable how Haig, when his army had reached its peak of man power, especially since his demands for an increase had not been met at home, should not want to see those divisions sent to Lorraine instead of serving in coöperation with the British army.

He would have our army sector transferred to western France in line next to the British army. This would mean that all our expenditure of energy and material in building up our line of communications from ports to our future front in Lorraine would practically be waste. It raised a question which had already been answered in J.J.P.'s investigations with his pioneer staff. Ports, roads and railroads in the British region were too crowded to leave room for the maintenance of anything like the size of the army of one million or two million, or even three millions, which now more than ever seemed essential for Allied victory.

From western France we should strike the enemy in front as the British had in the battle of the Somme and subsequent operations in Picardy, as it had in the terrific fighting of the Ypres salient, with the climax in the tremendous losses for little gain in the Passchendaele campaign of the previous summer.

Only from the ports of southern France, which might

yet have to include Marseilles in the Mediterranean, and across France was there room for our Services of Supply, and only in Lorraine room for operations on a large scale which would be in flank of the German army to cut its communications in front of the British and French armies in western France.

To consent to moving our zone would mean that Pershing's eye would be off his goal so clearly marked for him on the wall map of his office. He was against any patch-work expediency upon which the Allies had so often relied, against anything that endangered his vision, and this included the prospect of the reaction of our soldiers in France and that of our people as the news came filtering home about how we had no American Army in France and we had only been supplying troops to the Allied armies at the cost of immense casualty lists and disaster.

In face of all the councils of despair by the Allied statesmen and commanders to impress us, it did seem impossible that the enemy possibly could muster sufficient force, however skillful, for the break through which every offensive had failed to gain during three years. The wall would hold to protect his preparations. But, if at any time it seemed that it were cracking, then his trained divisions, or even his half-trained divisions, would be rushed into the breach in a far more effective contribution than mixing our soldiers with complete loss of national identity into the Allied armies.

At last, at the end of January after three months of dragging negotiations, it was tentatively agreed that six divisions should be brought over by British shipping for training as battalions under the plan which would incorporate them into American divisions. But they could hardly arrive in time for sufficient preparation to meet the German offensive which was bound to be launched as soon as the winter broke in more favorable fighting weather.

21

Baker in France

In the Grizzly dawn of March 11, 1918, the two four-star generals in France, Generals Bliss and Pershing, were awaiting the arrival of their chief. They greeted a slender little man in a derby hat as "Mr. Secretary."

J.J.P. had more than once expressed his desire that the Secretary of War should make an inspection of the AEF. An inspection of the British army by a British cabinet minister meant only crossing the English Channel. But Baker had to take practically two weeks at sea in going and coming; and in view of this he wanted to be sure that he could also spare the time for thorough observation. Before sailing he would be sure that home preparations were far enough advanced to permit so long an absence.

Late in 1917 a storm was gathering about the head of the Secretary who had been denounced as a pacifist when he was appointed, and later derided under the soubriquet of "Newty-Cooty" floundering in chaos. When Congress convened word was whispered in the galleries that "if Baker doesn't break, we'll break him."

He was summoned before a Congressional committee of investigation. His answer to the fire of questions was a disarming candor. For the first time he made some revelation of our difficulties which we had had to conceal for the sake of the morale of our Allies and lest our own public should be too much disillusioned as to the real situation. He was eloquent in his statement:

". . . We were coming into a war which had been going on for two and one-half years, in which the greatest military experts, all the inventive genius, all of the industrial capacity of those greatest countries in the world had been for two and one-half years solving the problem of what kind of war it was to be and where it was to be waged.

"It was not for us to decide where our theatre of war should be. That theatre was France. It was not for us to decide our line of communications. That line was across three thousand miles of ocean, one end of it infested with submarines. It was not for us to decide whether we should have the maneuvering of large bodies of troops in the open. There lay the antagonists in the trenches on opposite sides of No-Man's Land at a death-grapple with one another. Our antagonist was on the other side of that line, and our problem was and is to get over there and get him. . . . They said to us: This is a moving picture; it is something that nobody can paint and give you an idea of. It is not a static thing. . . . France was a white sheet of paper, so far as we were concerned, and on that we had not only to write an army . . . we had to go back to the planting of corn in France in order that we might make a harvest."

Now the country better understood, from his own words, the enormous demand that was made upon us. It had for the first time an appreciation of his character. There was an end to the calls for his resignation. The decks were cleared for his journey to France.

He had requested that there should be no extensive official reception and only the simplest official formalities.

Where there had been such acclaim for the arrival of Pershing, the Secretary slipped into France very quietly, as quietly as Pershing would have preferred for himself eight months ago. He was to see what had been done in writing an American Army on the white sheet of paper and the nature of the planting for the harvest; how in building an American world in France we had divided Gaul into three parts or zones.

Theoretically we were always to have a reserve of three months' supplies in France for the AEF: forty-five days in the base section, thirty days in the intermediate, and fifteen in the advance section. The colossus of America had one foot set on the home shore while the other strove for a foothold on the shore of France. One hand stretched its powerful fingers farther and farther into France to deposit there the material passed across France by the other hand.

Since our soldiers mostly disembarked at Brest and took a more northerly route to Lorraine, the residents along the line of the SOS saw no troop trains coming from the southern ports. They wondered much about the American way of making war. Evidently we made it as builders and not soldiers. In our invasion with our motor trucks and huge machines we seemed to be wasting our impatient energy as prodigally as we wasted our material. The French army managed to get on without ice to store its meat. Six months ago some Americans had arrived with blue-prints and there, seventy per cent complete, was a vast cold storage plant set in a spray of spur tracks on a space where not a handful of earth had been dug.

Why all this acreage of buildings and all these activities which the French army did not require? Why all this huge apparatus just to unload ships? Why chewing gum as well as cigarettes for the soldiers? Could not the Americans fight without keeping their jaws working all the time?

The French along the line of the SOS were amused and puzzled and would have been most disturbed if the Americans were not spending money so freely. And the French were very interested in being told that the little man in the derby hat was a chief without uniform, a civilian cabinet officer above all the generals and soldiers, just as one is in France.

At home he had seen the blue-prints of the plans of cantonments and industrial plants taking form, with blue-prints of more and more waiting their turn when others were finished. So it was in the SOS, from the base sections at the water's edge, where he began his inspection, to the front.

"There's Pershing and there's Baker too."

Baker was standing beside Pershing on a flat car being run over spur tracks from our new piers while the specialist in the project under his eye was pointing out what had been done, its purpose, and then showing him a blue-print of construction that had not yet been started.

Long explanations were unnecessary for his quick understanding. The warrant for the manifold requisitions which poured into the War Department became clear. He saw areas of American corrugated iron roofs in sight of the tower of an ancient village church. There were quiet French villages where the guests in khaki outnumbered the inhabitants. One area had so many Americans that it started its own little newspaper in addition to the famous *Stars and Stripes.*

The question arose whether or not the life of so excellent a Secretary of War should be endangered in the zone of fire. J.J.P.'s view was negative. At the end of a long and crowded day the subject was under discussion. When it looked as though Baker was the only one voting "aye," he said whimsically: "Gentlemen, I don't want to risk your lives as well as my own, but I should like to go." That was not an order, of course, but it was an intimation.

I was chosen to accompany him. We rose at 4:30 the next

morning. I am quoting from a previous book in tribute to an impromptu speech which, under the conditions it was spoken, gave me more of a thrill than any speech I ever heard:

"After we left the house where we had spent the night, we had gone only a few miles when a company of American infantry took vague form on the road ahead of us out of the mist of dawn. Our car stopped. The captain asked Baker if he would say a few words to the men. Their faces were like moist granite in the mist and grey like the moist grey road under their feet. The clinging particles of mist gave their khaki and even their steel helmets a grey film. All things seemed to be reduced to a severe outline, all thought to be chilled in the winter air of a moondead world to which spring would never come.

"The captain was very proud of his men. They were young and fresh. After all their training they were near the promised land of the trenches where the enemy's welcome of gas, shells and bullets awaited them. I had seen the young and fresh Frenchmen going to the front in August, 1914, and the young and fresh men of the British new army, and seen them suddenly grow old in that war which was now so very old. So these young countrymen of mine would in turn grow old in war. I had already become familiar with the sight of them on French roads. They were a part of the routine of feeding flesh into the hopper, a routine which must go on until the war was won; a routine in which even the sight of an American secretary of war alighting from an American army car on a road in Lorraine to speak to an American company of soldiers had become a part.

"I had heard scores of speeches to troops by visiting officials and statesmen and speeches of final instruction and girding by commanding officers to their men before they filed up the communication trenches to take their places for the zero hour in going over the top. . . . The longest speech had been made by a famous orator. This had lasted half an hour, and such was the discipline and fortitude of the soldier listeners that no jaw had dropped in a yawn. Indeed I had heard so many speeches that I thought I could foretell the nature of Baker's remarks, as a matter of course, just as one could foresee that the dressing stations would soon be busy after an attack began. There were certain things a statesman must say to strengthen the morale of troops in wartime, and many more things he must not say, owing to that instinctive self censorship which was the potent auxiliary of the formal censorship."

I took it for granted that Baker's speech would be of the usual stereotyped kind with which I had reason to be familiar in having served as press censor for my first six months as an officer of the AEF. I had never heard Baker speak on an important occasion; and this was not an important occasion to me, this of an impromptu talk to a company of infantry on a road when companies of infantry had so long been so common on French roads. From reading Baker's letters and dispatches I was sure the speech would be in excellent English and sutured in a compact whole; only if Baker were as sleepy as I was he would be a marvel if he could utter a dozen coherent sentences.

"Then suddenly I realized that he was not saying what I expected him to say. The little man, with his hat off had become a foot taller. I was wide awake now, broken out of the routine, myself young to the war, my imagination soaring high and wide. My sophistication was conscious of being shamed.

"Shafts of all kinds of sunlight from coast to coast of the homeland had shot across the Atlantic, illuminating the mist and glinting on steel. I was seeing the mighty pile of the Alps looking down on all the races in their rivalries, hates and quarrels, and seeing the Appalachians and the Rockies as very near the Alps in the map of one human scheme. I felt not only the wonder of that company of American soldiers being in France, but why they were there and the cause that brought them there and made them so rigid and disciplined."

It was a pity that no stenographer was present to take down this talk, which touched the heights of inspiration. Any attempt to repeat it out of memory in his own words would be clumsy presumption.

Later in the morning the Secretary, in tin hat and with his gas mask, passed up the labyrinth of communication trenches into the front line where he chatted with the men, some of whom were from his own State of Ohio. The Germans loosed no artillery "strafe:" no machine gun rat-tat broke the silence. He concluded that the Germans, if they knew of his presence, had shared the view of his unimportance of some of his political enemies. But after we were in our car and driving fast through a road zone forbidden to any but staff cars by day, a 105 shell burst near enough to be exciting.

"That was a shell, wasn't it?" he asked.

"Yes, about a four inch."

"Then I may say I've been under fire, mayn't I?"

And the Secretary who had his troubles at home which he had borne without complaining realized that Pershing had his troubles in France which had also been borne without complaining. And he realized that a greater crisis than the Allies had yet met might be coming in that period of suspense when at any hour the great German offensive might begin.

On his way to London he was motoring to call on General Pétain at his headquarters at Chantilly. Afterward I was to show him over the battlefield of the Somme with which I was familiar. But as the car in which he was riding with General Pershing approached Chantilly a distant roar of guns which seemed to cover the breadth of the horizon announced that the lightnings had burst from the long gathering clouds. There was no showing him over the battlefield of the Somme, which the Germans had evacuated in their retreat to the Hindenberg line in the early spring of 1917, because the speed of the German rush was fast recovering it. The road we took on the way to Amiens with walking wounded and ambulances told its story of Gough's army, which was already in distress.

The next day he was in London, a London shrouded in more than the gloom of a winter fog as the Germans continued to make their startling gains.

22

"All We Have"

It Was Said of J.J.P. that he made no phrases which rang the bell of popular acclaim. Even "Lafayette, we are here," with which he was at first credited, was spoken by another. Naturally not a phrase-maker himself, he would not allow any public relations expert to invent one for him.

"That is not mine," he would reply. "It is not in character."

Phrases as such were alien to the plower's mental processes. They were not in the lexicon of his military training and tradition. It is for the statesmen, the moulders of public opinion, all the guild of wordsmiths, to fashion phrases; and for political platform builders to make grandiose promises.

General Hooker made a resounding phrase, which delighted the North in the Civil War, when, as the new commander of the Army of the Potomac, he voiced the slogan about "bayonets to the front and spades to the rear;" but it became a joke after the silent, swift moving Stonewall Jackson humbled him at Chancellorsville.

Wellington's, "Guards, up and at 'em!" and Nelson's, "England expects every man to do his duty," would hardly be known to every child in Britain if Waterloo and Trafalger had been lost.

What phrases do we associate with Washington, Grant and Lee? Any radio script writer would have an easy day's work in making more scintillant phrases, at least more wisecracks, than ever came publicly from the lips of all three. Washington's prestige weighted his advice to prepare for war in time of peace and to avoid foreign entanglements, which might have received no attention if uttered on the floor of Congress by an obscure member.

And the deed was back of Grant's proposal to "hammer it out on this line if it takes all summer" and his "Let us have peace" after Lee's surrender. "War is hell" expressed a sentiment doubtless old to soldiers in the stone age, but it became famous and associated with his name when uttered by General Sherman after his ruthless march to the sea.

J.J.P.'s "all we have" to Foch will live since it was spoken in the name of all the power of America in the greatest crisis of the World War in face of the appalling, continuing success of the German offensive in the last days of March, 1918.

Marshal Ludendorff, with characteristic German thoroughness, had schooled his hosts in tactics to break the defenses of the western front. From daylight to dawn the ever industrious and obedient German soldiers had been drilled to make each soldier, squad, platoon, battalion and division letter perfect in robot precision.

Three days of fog had favored the camouflage of his final swift concentrations for the full effect of surprise on the chosen front of attack. Instead of the previously prolonged initial bombardments, before offensives, this was brief but of crushing, unsurpassed volume at dawn, March 21, 1918. Infantry groups, with their machine guns and mortars, were driven wedges of steel forcing gaps in the trench line for successive waves of infantry to pass through, with the field guns close on their heels in support.

The "Big Bertha" gun spoke its accompanying propagandic piece. One hundred and twenty feet long, it carried a shell a distance of sixty miles in the bombardment of Paris. Its destructive power was out of ratio to the moral effect the Germans anticipated it would have upon the Parisians the while they read the French army communiqués, which confessed to the deep stretches of French soil which were passing under the iron heel of the enemy.

"Hold your ground! Stand firm! was Pétain's rallying appeal to his soldiers. "Our (American) comrades are arriving. Altogether you will throw yourselves upon the invader."

But the German attack did not direct its avalanche against the French army. It was preponderantly against the British, with the aim of breaking the juncture of the two Allied armies. Pétain, as Commander-in-Chief of the French army, hesitated to dispatch reserves to the aid of the British army in his concern lest the Germans should yet turn against his own front.

Now the protecting wall of our drill ground was threatened. Now, in face of the emergency and in keeping with our policy, J.J.P. hastened to Pétain's headquarters to place all the troops we had in France at his disposition to aid in the defense at any point he chose.

J.J.P. describes Pétain as far from his usually nonchalant and confident self. Haig was appealing to him for aid, but still he waited. It was France first for him as it was bound to be Britain first for a British commander. The one mind in command of the German offensive had relied not only on the military power of his attack but on the factor of the divided minds of the Allied command.

They faced the Ludendorff of Tannenburg, of the Russian and Italian campaigns, the army of Von Mackensen's

185

masterful campaign in Rumania, its record of victories on all other fronts, now in the full tide of confidence that it could achieve a miracle on the western front.

Usually offensives on the western front had made their deepest advances on the first day. On the second they had begun to slow up and on the third we read in the communiqués, "We are consolidating our gains;" and then the armies were back to the old stalemate. This time the advance was deeper on the second day than the first, and continuing on the third day it was well past all the trench systems on the front of attack. Gough's Fifth army had been shattered. Resistance was now on fresh soil.

From London and Paris in their speeding cars, which were slowed up by the back-wash of the retreat, the Allied chiefs of state and generals hastened to Doullens as they had hastened to Rapello in the Italian crisis. Long they had flirted with the idea of unified command. But Lloyd George had opposed it, since inevitably it would be under a French general, and Haig and even Pétain had opposed it. In theory it was right but in practice it was found impossible. Now it was compelled in a desperate situation.

A gap had been broken between the British and French armies. Haig said that unless he received aid he must swing his army back for the defense of the English channel ports. This meant the French would in turn swing for the defense of Paris. The two main Allied armies would thus be separated with the American Army in Lorraine in line with the French. General Foch was chosen to coördinate the actions of the Allied armies just as Pétain, at last convinced they would not turn against his front, was dispatching his reserves to hold the German onrush.

Secretary Baker was back in Paris from London and J.J. P. was in Paris. Quite unforgettable is the picture of J.J.P. seated at his desk in the Mills house which he occupied when he was in Paris. He was flushed with combative indignation as he looked at the map over his desk. "They are that far this morning." If they could keep up their advance for another day they would have Amiens, the important city and railroad center of Picardy. Then they would be on high ground and it would be largely down-grade for them to the sea.

That day the permanent military representatives of the Supreme War Council also met in Paris. They sat around the table to make their recommendations while the battle raged, and the call was not for middle-aged generals but for more men and gun fire.

America had the men. The military representatives drafted Joint Note, Number 18, which they signed. It declared that all previous agreements or conventions be modified to assure that only American machine gun and infantry units should be sent to France as recruits for the British and French armies. This meant our divisions should have no artillery. It prepared the way for infiltration. J.J.P., who was present, registered his objection and then in a flash of decisive temper, he rose and withdrew as an expression of his dissent. This put the issue really up to Secretary Baker as between J.J.P.'s own view and the recommendation of the Joint Note. Secretary Baker approved the note with this provision:

"Such units when transported will be under the direction of the Commander-in-Chief of the American Expeditionary Forces and will be assigned for training and use by him in his discretion. He will use these and all other military forces of the United States under his command in such manner as to render the greatest military assistance, keeping in mind always the determination of this Government to have its various military forces collected, as speedily as their training and the military situation will permit, into an independent American Army acting in concert with the armies of Great Britain and France, and all arrangements made by him for their temporary training and service will be made with that end in view."

187

Even before the meeting at Doullens Pershing had insisted that the crisis had opened the way at last for the unified command which he had favored; and "I am for Foch," he said. Unified command also had the support of Secretary Baker and President Wilson, a most important influence. The afternoon of March 27 J.J.P. was off to see Foch, reported to be at Clermont-sur-Oise, near Paris. Progress was slow along the roads blocked with motor trucks and supplies in support of the French troops. Foch was hard to find. The headquarters of the French Third Army did not know just where he was in the midst of the confusion of traffic and refugees. But eventually he was located in a French farmhouse, hidden among the trees, where spring flowers and a cherry tree were in bloom in the yard. Inside Clemenceau, Foch and Pétain were studying a map. Pershing asked to see Foch alone and when they were alone, he burst into French in the full tide of impulse, without waiting on Boyd to interpret for him. It was sufficient to convey his "all we have" message.

"I have come to tell you that the American people would consider it a great honor for our troops to be engaged in the present battle. I ask you for this in their name and my own.

"At this moment there are no other questions but of fighting.

"Infantry, artillery, aviation, all that we have are yours; use them as you wish. More will come, in numbers equal to requirements.

"I have come especially to tell you that the American people will be proud to take part in the greatest battle of history."

But Foch's function as yet was only accepted as that of an adviser by the Allied commanders. They did not necessarily have to conform to his directions. On April 4 Pershing met Clemenceau and Lloyd George, Haig, Foch, Pétain, Sir Henry Wilson, British Chief of Staff, and General Bliss, in another conference at Beauvais. J.J.P. strongly supported more power for Foch.

"I do not believe," he said, "that it is possible to have unity of action without a supreme commander. We have already had experience enough in trying to coördinate the operations of the Allied armies without success. There has never been real unity of action. Such coördination between two or three armies is impossible, no matter who the commanders-in-chief may be. Each commander-in-chief is interested in his own army, and cannot get the other commander's point of view or grasp the problem as a whole. I am in favor of a supreme commander and believe that the success of the Allied cause depends upon it. I think the necessary action should be taken by this Council at once. I am in favor of conferring the supreme command upon General Foch."

Both Haig and Pétain were a little doubtful but consented to a resolution confirming Foch's appointment which, however, J.J.P. at once noted did not include the American Army, mentioning only the British and French. He said: "The American Army will soon be ready to function as such and should be included as an entity like the British and French armies."

Pétain replied: "There is no American Army as such as its units are either in training or amalgamated with the British and French."

J.J.P., who had a way of pressing his point so that it went home, insisted: "There may not be an American Army in force functioning now but there soon will be and I want this resolution to apply to it when it becomes a fact."

So the American Army was included as what possibly was a gesture on the part of Lloyd George and Clemenceau, and also Foch.

It had been "Lafayette, we are here!" in July, 1917. But, Lafayette, just what did we have at the end of March,

1918, in the list of Pershing's "all we have?" We had two divisions which were in the shock class; two more which had had active trench experience and could be counted upon against a heavy attack. Since our divisions were double or more than double the size of British or French divisions, the four were equal to eight Allied divisions.

Artillery? Our gunners had been trained in French schools and the four divisions now had their complements of French artillery.

Aviation? The press at home had carried accounts of how our fliers would soon command the air over the enemy. The French had read reports from America of the vast numbers of Liberty engines and of planes which would be shipped from home. Not a single Liberty engine had yet been delivered nor had a single American plane yet been sent to France. J.J.P. sent a cablegram, which was almost mandatory in its pleading, that this false promise for propaganda's sake should be stopped. But we were training fliers and they were getting and flying French planes. By the summer of 1918, discounting over-optimism, we should be certain of mass production of Liberty motors. The combat proportion of the four hundred thousand men in France was relatively small because of the immense personnel required in the service of the SOS. But we did have one hundred thousand fighting men as the main asset in the "All that we have are yours; use them as you wish."

General Foch ordered our First Division, which was just out of the trenches, to proceed to the Montdidier sector where he anticipated the Germans might strike their next blow. But the second offensive was to be against the British along the Lys in the old battle ground from just north of Ypres to Gavenchy It began on the morning of April 9 in a direct drive for the English channel ports, while our First Division was on its way to the Montdidier sector. They were getting settled in billets, awaiting the call for the front, when Haig sounded his "backs to the wall" in the crisis of the Lys battle—a phrase which will be forever associated with his name because of his victory.

The British had lost vital ground but were slowing down the German defense in desperate fighting as J.J.P., just before the First Division entered the trenches, made the longest speech that he ever made during the war in France. His audience, on the grounds of a small château, were Major General Robert L. Bullard, its commander, and all the officers of the division. There was vigour in every word.

"You have now been on French soil ten months, and you have carried out a progressive system of instruction under varied circumstances . . . I believe that you are well prepared to take your place along with the seasoned troops of our Allies . . .

"Whatever your previous instruction may have been, you must learn, in the actual experience of war, the practical application of the tactical principles that you have been taught during your preliminary training. Those principles are as absolute as they are immutable. Whatever may be the changing conditions of this war, those principles remain practically the same, and you should constantly bear them in mind.

"Now that you are going to take a place in the line of battle, you will be called upon to meet conditions that have never been presented to you before. When confronted with a new situation, do not try to recall examples given in any particular book on the subject; do not try to remember what your instructor has said in discussing some special problem; do not try to carry in your minds patterns of particular exercises or battles, thinking they will fit new cases, because no two sets of circumstances are alike; but bear in mind constantly, revolve in your thoughts frequently, and review at every opportunity, those well-established general principles, so that you may apply them when the time comes. . . .

"You should always have the interests of the individual

soldier at heart, for he is the principal part of the machine upon which you are to rely to carry you to success. His morale must be kept up to the highest pitch. That morale is effected by his confidence in his officers, by a realizing sense that they are his example. They should really be an example in everything that personifies the true soldier, in dress, in military bearing, in general conduct, and especially an example on the battlefield.

"To get the best out of your men they must feel that you are their real leader and must know that they can depend upon you. They must have confidence in you. Do not hold yourself aloof from your men, but keep in close touch with them. Let them feel that you are doing the very best you can for them under all circumstances, not only in providing their personal wants, in looking forward to a regular supply of food, and clothing, but that, as their leader, you are directing them wisely in the trying conditions of battle.

"You have behind you your own national traditions that should make you the finest soldiers in Europe today. We come from a young and aggressive nation. We come from a nation that for one hundred and fifty years has stood before the world as the champion of the sacred principles of human liberty. We now return to Europe, the home of our ancestors, to help defend those same principles upon European soil. Could there be a more stimulating sentiment as you go from here to your commands, and from there to the battlefield?"

In closing the Commander-in-Chief said:

"Our people today are hanging expectant upon your deeds. Our future part in this conflict depends upon your action. You are going forward and your conduct will be an example for succeeding units of our army. I hope the standard you set will be high. I know it will be high. You are taking with you the sincerest good wishes and the highest hopes of the President and all of our people at home.

I assure you in their behalf and in my own of our strong belief in your success and of our confidence in your courage and in your loyalty, with a feeling of certainty in our hearts that you are going to make a record of which your country will be proud."

This confidence was expressed that same afternoon, when he went to see Foch, in terms which were a sufficient answer to those who had criticized him for his cautious insistence upon such long training for his men before they were put in serious action. He told Foch that it would hasten the formation of an American Army if more American divisions were put in line with the First. In addition to the four divisions already offered, two others might be withdrawn from quiet sectors which would make six, or a total of 150,000 men, who could take the place of exhausted French divisions in the battle front. He might wish that these two had more training but there could be no hesitation in this emergency. He wrote that his "understanding after this discussion was very definite that the plan would soon be carried out," leaving the matter of time and place to Foch's own decision.

23

An Ordeal in Council

HAVING OFFERED all that we had to Foch and having had Foch's assurance that our divisions which were ready would be put in line as an army corps unit, was J.J.P. to be free from his part as an ambassador so that he could look after his manifold duties as a general and organizer of GHQ? Hardly.

He was off to London for a conference with Lord Milner, the new Secretary of State for War, and General Sir Henry Wilson, the new British Chief of Staff, about the number of American divisions and the conditions under which they should be attached for training with the British army. Secretary Baker was in Italy at the time; for if Britain and France were to see the Secretary, the Italians must also have the attention of his presence to strengthen Italian morale and also to give them an opportunity to make a plea for not only material and financial aid but for a share of the troops we were sending abroad.

While Secretary Baker was absent from Washington, Lord Reading, the British Ambassador, was very much there; and Reading was most adroit, the most plausible Briton of his time with much of Arthur Balfour's charm and less concern about the means to an end. Reading could be convincing where Lloyd George's weather-vane consistencies soon made him suspect. In the course of the conference the British had word from Reading that President Wilson had assured him that America would send over 120,000 infantry and machine gun units a month to the British army, which would have left no British shipping to transport our troops for our army.

The question which had evidently been settled by Baker's qualification in the approval of Joint Note 18 of the Supreme War Council, was wide open again. (Be it repeated that infantry and machine gun units without any divisional artillery—which meant the absolutely indispensable gun support if they were to operate as divisions—made infiltration inevitable.) The President, as supreme Commander-in-Chief of all our armed forces, had perhaps unwittingly, from his lack of knowledge of military affairs, sacrificed the independence of our American Army, which was certainly not his intention, since he was capable enough a politician to realize the effect on American public opinion when it awakened one day to find that we had been sending all the youth from our training camps as replacements in the ranks of an Allied army. Reading's cable was a bomb for J.J.P. but he was getting used to bombs, out of the blue, and to mines planted along his path.

The eyes of Lord Milner and J.J.P. met in a straight glance across the cabinet table. Milner was a thoroughbred and doubtless he understood Lloyd George and also Lord Reading. For in all the altercations and intrigues of the inter-allied conferences one point stood out clear, and that was how much easier coöperation was between honest men who kept their word than those who seemed to have no sense that a commitment made today for tomorrow holds tomorrow. The result of the London conference was the famous Pershing-Milner agreement which was faithfully kept by Milner, to whom a pledge given was a pledge to be kept.

The British were to transport six of our divisions for training as battalions and regiments in the British army and then they were to pass under the command of our divisional staffs and in turn into our army. Pershing agreed, in keeping with his policy, that in case of need they were not only to enter quiet trenches but they were to fight as units to meet the demand of any emergency under their own regimental and battalion commanders. Any further shipping that the British could spare should transport troops for our own army in addition to our own shipping.

But the French were quick in their protest that the Pershing-Milner agreement had been made without their consent, and they also insisted that it had been made covertly, without their knowledge, which was untrue. However, since the French had no shipping, they were in no position to transport the share of troops to recruit their own army which they demanded.

General Bliss had been prompt in expressing his opinion that no such "utilization of American troops" as Reading proposed should be permitted. Later Baker queried the President by cable and received this response:

"I agreed upon no details whatever with Lord Reading. I told him that I had agreed to the proposition of the Supreme War Council in the formulas proposed to me by the Secretary of War by cable and that I could assure him that we would send troops over as fast as we could make them ready and find transportation for them. That was all. The details are left to be worked out and we shall wish the advice of the Secretary of War as the result of his consultations on the other side."

Yet J.J.P. was still under the handicap of the supposed Presidential agreement with the Reading plan when on the way back from London he conferred, April 28, with Generals Foch, Bliss and Weygand. Foch was not in as agreeable a mood as when Pershing last saw him.

So far the British army had borne the main brunt of both the German offensives. Its losses had been 300,000 men. Very reluctantly, Foch had at last sent French divisions to the aid of the British ten days after Haig's "backs to the wall" appeal, and after they had been stubbornly yielding ground foot by foot against the pressure of wave after wave of German reserves. But the first French divisions in support, having gone in to hold strategic Memel Hill, had lost it.

Foch wanted Pershing to consent to send only infantry and machine gun units for the next three months. Pershing would consent to ship them for only one month until he had an order from the President, as Commander-in-Chief, to do otherwise. Foch sought to encourage Pershing to change his mind in view of a prospect that would give him at least 300,000 more infantry by July 1. But since the French had the necessary field guns, Pershing asked why our artillery personnel should not also be brought over if we were to create our own divisions.

Foch then turned to Bliss expectantly for his support, but by this time Pershing-Bliss unity was established no matter how much the other Allied leaders disagreed among themselves. Bliss simply referred to Baker's amendment to Joint Note 18 and emphasized the fact that this placed all the troops sent to France under Pershing's direction.

Pershing added significantly, if not wearily:

"I have been discussing this question of training our units for the last eight months, first, with General Pétain and then with Marshal Haig. The method agreed upon leads naturally to the formation of constituted American divisions."

Foch insisted he did not want to be misunderstood. He was all for American divisions and a large American Army but he thought the Pershing method meant serious delay.

Foch had a command of language. He could be dramatic and appealing in word, voice and gesture.

"But do not forget we are in the midst of a hard battle," he said. "If we do not take steps to prevent the disaster which is threatened at present the American Army may arrive in France to find the British pushed into the sea and the French driven back behind the Loire, while it tries in vain to organize on lost battlefields over the graves of Allied soldiers."

At this time the German offensive against the British was already obviously weakening and near its limit, and three days later it came to a complete rest. In addition to our own divisions ready for battle, the French still had reserves and the British were still holding troops in England for home defense, which as a last resort could have been rushed to France. The protecting wall was far from the danger of being broken as it was after the gap that was made between the British and French armies in the first offensive. Pershing again assured Foch that all we had was at his service and that British shipping authorities, as he had learned in London, considered they could transport 750,000 Americans to France in the next three months.

Foch was surprised to learn this and admitted that if it were true there was no reason why whole divisions should not soon be transported. But soon he was back again reinforcing his demand for only infantry and machine gun units. For deep down in every Frenchman's mind, including that of the Generalissimo, was the fear that in addition to Britain's army in France there would also be a great American Army with a preponderant political influence which might prejudice the future of France, after all her sacrifices, in the final peace terms.

Four days later came the very hotly controversial meeting of the War Council at Abbeville. This was after the second German offensive had given up its gigantic effort to reach the invaluable goal of the Channel ports, which would threaten the life-line of the British army to France, establish submarine bases and bring British coast cities within reach of long range guns, of the "Big Bertha" type.

"I have not been to all these conferences without learning something about how they are conducted," J.J.P. said with an unmistakably triumphant smile after the Abbeville conference. "This time I did not wait on the other fellows to make a plan. Go into the conference with one of your own and hold to it. Or, if you are prepared to make certain concessions, do not do so at the start, as these old hands will only press for more."

He was determined, since the second German offensive was over, that this gathering of the chiefs of state, the Generalissimo and the army chiefs should commit themselves definitely on a paper signed by them all that once the emergency was over all our divisions or battalions and regiments, wherever they were, should be merged under our flag and his command as an army subject to the command of Foch. Earlier, when he had only a few troops in training in Lorraine, he had been perforce feeling his way and speaking in a small voice in Allied councils when essentially the cards that counted on the table were the cards of force. Now he had more than 400,000 men in France and he was asking for 1,500,000 before the summer was over, which we were preparing to send.

The hope of the Allies was now indisputably and admittedly in America. Her voice, as spoken by the Commander-in-Chief of the AEF, need not be that of sibilant, ingratiating assent in new world awe of the old world patron. In all politeness and goodwill, since we had come over to win the war, our prospective contribution warranted our having some say about our part in winning it.

Clemenceau, who presided over the meeting, took the floor on France's behalf at once. He was miffed over the Pershing-Milner agreement in which the French had not been consulted. Let the British have the 120,000 Americans who were to come in May, but France must have her 120,000 in June. Although there were 400,000 Americans in France, he remarked quite unauthentically that only 125,000 of them could be considered as trained combatants. He evidently saw that this was the result of the Americans having their own army instead of our troops being in charge of the French, his implication being that if they had been we should have more of them at the front.

It would have been useless to have reminded Clemenceau that the main reason we had not more combat troops was the necessity for the immense personnel of the Services of Supply in a war exhausted land with its rickety railroad beds and depleted rolling stock.

Lord Milner, not concealing his anger, rose in repudiation of Clemenceau's intimation that there was anything mysterious about the London agreement. It was no reversal of the Supreme War Council's Joint Note 18 which the governments had never ratified. No impression was ever given that half the troops would go to France. Then J.J.P. reminded Clemenceau that he had told him he was going to London to arrange for the shipment and Clemenceau had approved of it.

Clemenceau passed these references over. He insisted that where four were in alliance two of them could not act independently. "The appointment of General Foch," he said, "as Commander-in-Chief is not a mere declaration . . . He must meet the present situation. He must provide for the future. . . . I want to know what is intended for June."

Lloyd George now had his turn. He was all for considering what was best for the common cause but the British army had suffered heavy losses. Ten British divisions had been so severely handled they could not be re-constituted. The British were sending all the reserves they had, but these were not enough to fill the vacant places. He would let the decision wait to see where the American troops who arrived in June should be required to face the next German offensive.

Foch, on his part, merely insisted that there should be the same shipment of infantry and machine gun units in June as in May. If there were any more tonnage available it might go to filling up the American divisions. He was sure "that General Pershing, with his generosity and his breadth of view, will grant the fairness of this and will extend for June the agreement decided upon for May." J.J.P. absolutely refused to commit the American Army so long in advance. He would recommend the extension only in case the emergency required it. Always he held to the view that only the emergency warranted any form of infiltration.

Lloyd George, Clemenceau and Foch continued to say that they were all for an American Army, but Foch insisted that Lord Milner, General Pershing and himself get together to sign an agreement that evening definitely extending the May agreement into June. Clemenceau said: "What is important for the morale of our soldiers is not to tell them that the American soldiers are arriving, but to show them that they have arrived;" and the way to do this was to put smaller American units into French divisions. The French must have recruits and America must realize the gravity of the situation. So the day's general discussion ended with an evident intention to compel a continuance of infiltration.

Foch, Milner and J.J.P. retired to an adjacent room. Pershing insisted that placing infantry units to fight under British and French commands would neither relieve the situation nor end the war. He repeated all the sound and obvious arguments out of military history and recalled the length of time that the French were training their own recruits before they sent them into the front line, and how it took nearly two years' training before the soldiers of the British new army became effective.

But Foch became dramatic again. He asked:

"Are you willing to risk our being driven back to Loire?"

"Yes, I am willing to take the risk," replied the embattled J.J.P. "Moreover, the time may come when the American Army will have to stand the brunt of this war, and it is not wise to fritter away our resources in this manner. The morale of the British, French and Italian armies is low, while, as you know, that of the American Army is very high. It will be a grave mistake to give up the idea of building an American Army in all its details as rapidly as possible."

Lloyd George, Clemenceau and Orlando walked into the room as reinforcements, and Milner told Lloyd George in a stage whisper behind his hand,

"You can't budge him an inch."

Now all turned their guns on J.J.P.

"Can't you see that the war will be lost unless we get this support?" Lloyd George demanded.

Clemenceau and Orlando, the Italian premier, pressed the attack. The statesmen of the old world Allies, who had larger numbers of troops and all the world's resources back of them, were now, late in the fourth year of the war, in fear of utter defeat, and joined in working a third degree on this neophyte from the new world. Still they made no progress. Pershing had listened, now and then tight lips parting in a smile over firm jaw, until finally, with a quiet dignity, he rose and said:

"Gentlemen, I have thought this program over very deliberately and will not be coerced." And then he withdrew.

What were the five great men to do? They knew that Pershing had President Wilson's and Secretary Baker's confidence; that President Wilson was bound to support Pershing in any direct test; and further they knew that nothing could be more fatal than any disclosure to American opinion, at the time, of their own squabbles and of their actual demand that the youth of America should become cannon fodder in European armies.

It was Pershing they had to win over, the stubborn American commander to whom Secretary Baker had said: "I shall give you only two orders, one to go and one to return." It was evident no direct pressure emphasized by a cry of alarm or concerted diplomatic approach in Washington could compel Pershing's recall.

That night, as a lone fighter, the others considered the next move in dealing with him. The next day Lloyd George took the lead with an open challenge.

"If the United States does not come to our aid then perhaps the enemy's calculations will be correct," he said. "If France and Great Britain should have to yield, their defeat would be honorable, for they would have fought to their last man, while the United States would have to stop without ever having put into line more men than little Belgium."

Thus Lloyd George might enable Pershing to visualize what would be his own position, in case of such an outcome, before his own people and the world as the result of his tenacious perversity. But Pershing, who had offered "all we have" and still offered all, was unimpressed by this dark foreboding in his unchanged conviction that infiltration was the way to lose the war; and Lloyd George took care to be propitiatory by saying that he did count on the existence of an American Army to deal the enemy the final blow.

The American commander patiently repeated what he had often said before. He agreed with General Foch as to the gravity of the situation. America, which had declared war independently of the Allies, was prepared to face it with a powerful army and to share the burden to the fullest extent. But the morale of our soldiers depended upon their fighting under our own flag. America was anxious to know where her army was. He called their attention to the fact that the Germans were circulating propaganda in the United States to the effect that the Allies had so little confidence in the American troops they parceled them out among Allied divisions. The American soldier had his pride no less than the French or British.

Just when it appeared that Pershing appeared unreasonably adamant he was ready for the concession he felt warranted in return for gaining the object he had had in mind. He would agree on another 120,000 infantry and machine gun units for June, but further commitments must wait on the situation.

The resultant good feeling, with olive branches extended and hatchets buried, opened the way for Clemenceau to present the resolution which J.J.P. had prepared. Its vital point was:

"It is the opinion of the Supreme War Council that in order to carry the war to a successful conclusion, an American Army should be formed as early as possible under its own commander and under its own flag."

And while the troops sent over in May were to go definitely to the British, those sent over in June should be "allocated for training and service as the American Commander-in-Chief may determine."

In the name of Lafayette and of King Louis XV of France, this was a fair request in paying our debt to France in the American Revolution. The following were the instructions of the King to Count Rochambeau before he sailed to America with his army:

"It is His Majesty's desire and He hereby commands that, so far as circumstances will permit, the Count de Rochambeau shall maintain the integrity of the French troops which His Majesty has placed under his command, and that at the proper time he shall express to General Washington, Commander-in-Chief of the forces of the Congress, under whose orders the French troops are to serve, that it is the intention of the King that these shall not be dispersed in any manner, and that they shall serve at all times as a unit and under the French generals, except in the case of a temporary detachment which shall rejoin the main body without delay."

Another item of more recent history which was issued by French GHQ to French officers while the Abbeville conference was in session, is worth quoting: "Americans dream of operating in open country after having broken through the front. This results in too much attention being devoted to this form of operations."

The Germans in their first drive particularly, that of March 21, which broke the gap between the British and French armies, had broken through into open fighting, and also in a smaller measure their attack on the north flank of the British in the drive of April 9. Since the trench lines had been established the ambition of both the Allies and the Germans had been to break through for open fighting, which was the only possible way that decisive victory could be won. J.J.P., with his eye ever on the goal of flanking the German army, realized that the American Army must be trained for open fighting.

The fact that training for it had fallen into neglect, especially by the French army, caught the Allies at a disadvantage after the Germans had broken through in their two first offensives.

So far the Italians had refused to accept unified command. They were still fighting on their own with the aid of the British and French divisions which had been sent to their rescue. Their appeals had been persistent that they in turn should have American reinforcements which would convince their army and people of our military as well as financial and economic support.

Pershing, with his divisions already widely scattered, had been loath to agree to further dispersion, but he now suggested that he would send a single regiment to Italy in recognition of its value in showing the flag for the sake of Allied morale. This offer was gladly accepted. Moreover it put Orlando in a mood at last to grant Foch's authority over the Italian army, making him Generalissimo of all the Allied land forces from the North Sea to the Adriatic.

However vigorously and stubbornly J.J.P. might stand to his guns, his good humor quickly returned after the points of dispute were settled. He had more than that thin-lipped smile for doughty old Clemenceau and histrionic Lloyd George. To judge by the hand-shakes and the *au revoirs* upon their parting those who had used anything but formal diplomatic language to one another might have just concluded a love feast. Among the old hands in war councils and European politics it was agreed that the honors of this conference were with the man from Laclede.

But one issue which Pershing pressed was left hung up in the air for further discussion in the familiar agreement, "on principle." This was the pooling of Allied supplies, which the crisis and the enormous amount of shipping which the supplies required for our expanding program, had made as acute as the hastened rush of our man power to France. It seemed a natural sequel of unified command no less than tactical and strategic direction on the battle front.

The French needed material which the British might supply and the British needed material the French might supply. There was overlapping in one category and gaps in another. Priority had been disregarded in the British and French requisitions on America, when cargo space was so precious we did not want to ship material to our Allies which was already available in Europe and particularly Spain which was not at war. If Spain had mules, why should they be sent from America? If France had surpluses in some lines, why should we not buy them in the nearest market? To this end J.J.P. had made his old friend, Brigadier General Charles M. Dawes, chief of the General Purchasing Board.

However, Professor Foch, brilliant military scholar and master of tactics that he was, had a blind spot about supplies. Napoleon would certainly have never made him a quartermaster general. He seemed to take it for granted that where there was man power soldiers would be trained and they would be fed, ready and armed for his command in battle.

When the economic side of war was brought to his attention he was given to passing it by with something of the indifference with which a master chess player may regard checkers. But the pooling of shipping and supplies as well as other effort was bound to be achieved later out of the sheer necessity of the situation when it took four trains of 25 to 30 cars to move one of our big divisions and no less than 25 French carloads to move all the material which was found unserviceable when a division came out of the trenches.

At the time of the Abbeville conference we actually had 300,000 combat troops in France. We had eight complete divisions; the 1st, 2d, 3d, 26th, 32d, 41st, 42d and 77th. We had five incomplete; the 5th, 28th, 35th, 82d and 93d. Four, the 1st, 2d, 3d and 5th, were Regular; the 26th, 32d, 41st, 42d, 28th and 35th were National Guard. The 77th was National Army and so were the 82d and 93d (colored). The Regular divisions had been formed out of reserve officers and recruits around a nucleus of Regulars, the National Guard divisions expanded by recruits, while the 77th was the first complete division of the new National Army formed from the draft to arrive in France.

24

No Gallery Play

WE HAD BEEN a year in the war. But J.J.P. surveyed a trench line on his wall map which cut deeper into Allied soil in northwestern France than in the winter of 1914-15. Our Navy had done invaluable service against the submarine menace. Our loans had replenished the war chests of the big Allies, saved some of the little ones from capitulation, and the weight of our influence had drawn in new allies.

So far on the western front we had had divisions in quiet trenches and made the defense of the active Toul sector our own under the commanding height of Montsec. The first two German drives had been too remote for us to have a part. Our "all we have" had not had the test of resistance to violent attack. Where would the next blow be struck? It was taken for granted by General Foch that another was coming.

Those of our troops who had been through the winter now discovered that in spring the sun really can shine in sunny France, even in Lorraine. Our arriving troops were seeing France in Maytime, where the peasant women and children labored, in place of the men who were at the front, in the fields which were showing green with growing crops.

Practice in front line trenches was less muddy. Soldiers were receiving their letters more promptly. We had more "Y" huts. Salvation Army lassies were beginning to appear back of the trenches to greet the men coming out from front line service with hot coffee and doughnuts. There were regular American filling stations along the main roads in the American zone. Busy colonels no longer had to walk as in the early days but had cars.

In place of the nerve-wracking efforts to get telephone communications over the French lines, we had strung and were still stringing wires on the poles we had set up. In answer to calls, we had the cheery, quick response of American telephone girls who were brought over to France as being incomparably superior as operators to any male of the species.

Structures half finished at the time of Secretary Baker's inspection were now finished and others being built. Across France from Bordeaux ran our line of supply, and northward from Brest debarking soldiers rode in the 40 and 8 cars (40 men and 8 horses) past the red-roofed villages of old France to be billeted in other villages which were to be their temporary homes.

The larger J.J.P.'s family, the greater his responsibilities. The hastening of troop movements, the new requirements of the crises of the German offensives, presented new problems and readjustments in organization. Cavalryman Pershing no longer rode in the morning. This soldier who had always had exercise had no time to spare for it in his crowded hours. The AEF was now so far embodied in his own person, its mind was so largely his mind, that, naturally, there was concern about his own health and endurance.

He was the subject of entreaties and plots to insure that he should have more relaxation. One day I sent to him in army form an order: Subject, exercise, to the Commander-in-Chief nominally signed by the Commander-in-Chief, requiring him to walk home when he left his office at the end of the day. An accompanying note reminded him that he had an impeccable record as a subordinate soldier. A day later he greeted me in the hall with a grin saying, "I did it. I walked home last night." However, so far as one could check up on him, he did not the next night or again lest he should be still later for dinner after he had finished the task in hand.

There had been changes in the official family which lived with him in his house. We had a new Chief of Staff, Major General James W. McAndrew, who had been the founding chief of the Staff College at Langres, in succession to Harbord who had had a soldier's wish granted for front line service in being given command of the Marine Brigade of the 2d Division. Brigadier General Benjamin Alvord had been invalided home and Brigadier General Robert C. Davis had succeeded him as Adjutant General.

The faithful Collins and Colonel Martin T. Shallenberger, as well as Harbord, having gone "to serve with troops," there were two new aides, Colonels Edward Bowditch and John G. Quekemeyer, both of whom spoke French well. "Peter" Bowditch, as he was best known from his home town of Albany to Manila and Zamboanga, had gone as a youngster with Governor General Cameron Forbes to the Philippines where he had first known Pershing. He was surprised that Pershing had sent for him. J.J.P. had a way of indexing a man's capacities and never forgetting him. After greeting Bowditch, he said:

"In time of peace it is customary to ask an officer if he would like to serve with you as an aide but in time of war he had no choice. Consider this an order."

Captain John G. Hughes was soon drafted as a third member of the family, who made himself ubiquitously useful.

Colonel Jacques Adelbert de Chambrun, the French aide in liaison, was the chief conspirator in moving the family from the small house in Chaumont to the Château of Val des Ecoliers, with spacious grounds, only two miles away from Chaumont. Its owner, M. de Rouvre, who had made a fortune and married into the French aristocracy, remained a good business man. At first, in answer to the proposal to rent his house, he asked a price utterly out of keeping with the family's budget in which rent and mess costs were prorated according to the members' pay.

When Colonel de Chambrun alluded to the service his own ancestor, the Marquis de Lafayette, had done for America, M. Rouvre wanted to know what America was doing for the Rouvres. Colonel de Chambrun replied in an explanation of what America was at present doing for France, and therefore all the French, including the Rouvres. So M. Rouvre consented for a nominal, small rent. While the château was quite warm enough in summer, the cost of making it comfortable in winter with the sanitary accessories to which Americans are habituated, represented a worth while improvement.

But the invitation of the open country was not sufficient appeal for J.J.P. to continue his rides. His exercise mainly was walking up and down outside the house sometimes in company and again alone in reflection. He made it a rule that "shop" should be dismissed at meal times. Talk ran on other subjects with J.J.P. often in a light mood. However, the rule was often broken when consultation was pressing with some subordinate chief. And frequently there were distinguished civilian guests for luncheon or for dinner. To lunch or dine with J.J.P. was to receive the "red carpet" of attention, as it was called, spread only for the chosen, Allied or American.

To facilitate his work and to speed his movements he had his own private train fitted up with an office. Whenever he traveled by automobile a second car followed him in case his own should break down.

Professional public relations counsellors saw J.J.P. as being very badly served in his personal publicity "build-up." When they met him, this supposed human machine, this man of iron, and they basked in the smile of his greeting, they were more than ever convinced of their view.

Here he was, "the boss" of all the mothers' sons we were sending overseas, who might be promoted as the hero of a gigantic and heroic undertaking, but his soldiers saw him only as the grim source of all authority. It was even said that he ruled by fear. So he did in one respect. All would be time-servers or profiteers knew the wrath of God would descend mercilessly upon them for any deviation of any kind from absolute incorruptibility.

The well-intentioned publicity experts therefore thought they had the more reason to apply all the familiar methods by which the personality of a presidential candidate is given mass appeal. From the first J.J.P. did not lack such advice and suggestions from the highly skilled men in G-2 and others who wanted him known to his army as he was known to them. He was a most difficult subject. An example of what was called a missed opportunity was the first tour of our pioneer division in the trenches.

Of course J.J.P. was going into the trenches, but he saw nothing remarkable about that. It was not only in the line of duty but of inherent interest to see the men for himself at the front. Of course it was best that he should go in unannounced lest the Germans might put over an artillery "hate" which might mean the loss of the American Commander-in-Chief. But why should not more be made of all the details for the press showing how the leader was sharing the dangers of his soldiers?

There was still another element in addition to the fact that such personal publicity was not in character. Under the Allied censorship regulations, with which we must comply, only the name of the Commander-in-Chief of an army might be mentioned in the press. Subordinate commanders must remain anonymous on the premise that this would be information of value to the enemy in relation to the battle order, which sought not only the locations of divisions but to judge their competence by the character of their commanders. Consequently, J.J.P. was the more sensitive in his impersonal detachment to have the Commander-in-Chief regarded as an institution rather than a man.

He continued to grow with the size of his task. Here was a bigger J.J.P. than last month who promised a still bigger one the next month. More and more he became consecrated to his responsibility and his devotion to the independence of his army.

Inevitably such was his power that certain influences around him, basking in its glamor, tended toward levitation. Just as it seemed that they might lift him off the earth the man from Laclede was revealed as having his feet still solidly planted on his mother soil.

For history's sake a historian once proposed that every evening, for history's sake, he should explain the reasons for all the day's decisions. This had much the same reception as though he had been asked to limit his working hours to three and spend the rest of his time riding and playing golf and bridge.

"Not in the evening," he said. "I should have to begin at ten in the morning to tell why I had made those up to that hour. What about the others I must make during the rest of the day?"

Action would be sacrificed to the exposition of the workings of his mind and in analyzing experience which often counted for prompt approval or dissent. Men close to him disagreed as to whether he had more power of expression verbally or on paper. In both ways he showed a real command of lucid explicit language when occasion demanded or commanding impulse imposed the right mood. He was certainly at his best in the use of words when he spoke or wrote spontaneously.

The promoters of personal publicity thought that at least photographers should be with him and the press should have stories about him in his random, intimate talks with soldiers. In propagandic prevision they would even have proper occasions arranged for such exhibitions, but they found this was a hopeless campaign against his astounding perversity to anything that had the appearance of playing to the gallery.

He might be hard on his soldiers but if they could have heard some of his outbursts when he let off steam they would have better understood him. Ever the stern father was the protector of his men.

"The task assigned me is to make them soldiers. I am taking the long view. They will appreciate one day that we have chosen the right way. . . . I am not going to have our men sacrificed needlessly because some Allied leaders by paving hell with good intentions would lose this war."

Again, as he took up two papers from his desk:

"I have always had an idea this (French) politician was a handy liar. Now I know he is. Here is what he says to me and what he has been saying in Washington. I don't blame him as a Frenchman for preferring to have American to French soldiers killed. But his plan would waste the lives of both."

With his widely separated divisions, with the personnel of his organization so immense, the situation was quite different than in the Civil War, for example, when all the soldiers of their relatively small, compact armies saw their commanders at times. They saw them riding on a horse, not in an automobile, going at forty or fifty miles an hour.

Out of the windows of the car flying the four star flag, the experienced eyes of the Commander-in-Chief noted much although the columns he passed had hardly a glimpse of him. No division was forming but that he was not at the headquarters of that division, that he did not have a view of the troops in training, that he was not taking measure of the division and its strength and weaknesses as well as of the division commander.

More than once I heard J.J.P., who was sometimes criticized as not being human, say of a subordinate, "He is not human." For he ultimately reduced everything to the human equation and this took him back to the soldier in combat.

The chiefs of the combat forces were the division commanders. The division in all armies is the tactical combat unit. Know the commander of a division and in a sense you know the division, especially in an army where there is a mean level of the same kind of officers and men.

In the World War as in all wars division commanders at the outset in the Allied armies were men on the downhill side of middle age. They could not stand long physical strain. They were post-dated in the modernization of weapons and tactics. The French suffered a heavy handicap in the battle of the Marne not only from old division, but old brigade and regimental commanders. The survival of the fittest brings forward younger men with more active bodies and more active and receptive minds.

J.J.P. noted that most of the division commanders now in the veteran British and French armies were usually in the forties. In one of his early letters to Secretary Baker he had stressed the importance of younger men as division commanders. But the policy was far more easily proposed than carried out.

Baker recognized its merit from his own experience with

the elders. But the elders by right of seniority (many of them in the late fifties), had what was to them the right of the reward of service, of the long wait through slow step-by-step promotion, not to be replaced by their juniors.

There was no sure way of picking the right juniors, who themselves had not known the real test of war itself. Promising juniors might fail to come up to expectation as many did while some elders were bound to surpass them, as some did. It was again the human equation, the question of the man, and how he would expand with the expansion of his responsibilities.

The commanders of divisions in training at home were sent to France for a period of "indoctrination" in the winter of 1917-1918 and then to return to their divisions before the divisions were sent abroad. Pershing met and observed them all. Then Secretary Baker asked him to send a list of those division commanders whom he wanted in France. This was a choice which might exclude old army associates and classmates, but it must be made.

One division commander not on the list was Major General Leonard Wood who, accordingly, did not accompany his division, but the humiliating manner in which he was relieved just as his division was about to embark was in no wise J.J.P.'s affair but of administrative function in Washington and delay in the White House's decision. No one questioned the spell that General Wood had over officers and men under him with his magnetic personality, his ability as an organizer, or that he had made a very fine division. That a man with such a distinguished career should be omitted seemed a cruel injustice when he had an immense public following which had considered that he and not Pershing should have been the Commander-in-Chief in France.

According to General Bliss, when Wood was in London in the course of his own "indoctrination" tour, he expressed himself in high British quarters most pessimistically about the prospect that we should ever have an army in France which should be of any real aid to the Allies. Lloyd George was greatly impressed by him, and reportedly even considered using his influence in Washington to have him replace Pershing. Wood criticized Pershing and continued his gloomy talk after he reached France. This was in the Valley Forge period when J.J.P.'s jaw was hard set against any whisper of defeatism by any subordinate.

No commanding general would want a man with Wood's great name and influence as a subordinate who was disloyal to his chief's policy. Pershing said: "There is not room for both Wood and me in France." He left Wood off the list of division commanders he wanted in France and even threatened to send him back if he arrived.

If a Grant or Lee exerted his personality over 75,000 men, then a division commander in France ought to exert his over 27,000, as would most certainly a Pershing or a Wood. Age was no bar to many of the elders in impressing their leadership as the "old man" upon the division.

But there were elders whose faces seemed almost unfamiliar, and whose names were hardly known, to their men. They simply lacked the quality which gave life to their rank. They were rarely seen in the trenches. This left the impression with the men that they were parade soldiers.

They seemed to have the idea that the duty of the division commander was to be back at his headquarters in touch with his wires in case of an emergency. But he had a chief of staff to look after that and emergencies were rare in stationary warfare in our training sector in the winter of 1917-18. It was most inconvenient for some division commanders when they had to tramp along the muddy duckboards in the rain in complying with Pershing's order that in stationary warfare they should inspect their trenches once a week.

The division commander or administrative chief whom J.J.P. had sent for, often entered J.J.P.'s office in grave concern as to why he had been summoned. Usually it was only to answer questions and canvass a situation. Again the meeting was not so pleasant for the caller. After he had passed out, J.J.P. might exclaim:

"What am I going to do with him? He is not growing up to his job, but where is a better   n? Do you know one?"

Or the comment might be:

"He is doing magnificently, growing all the time," or, "I hope he now understands he is not back with the company command at an army post in peace, but with a huge army in war."

Sometimes he would ask about a high ranking officer:

"What is the matter with so and so?"

A straight answer without regard to personal relations was in order. In one instance it was:

"He not only does not see the forest for the trees, but he is digging himself a hole under the roots of one tree."

"Why, I have considered him one of my broad-minded ones," said J.J.P. "Haven't you met any of my narrow-minded ones?"

On another occasion he said about a commander who had just left his office:

"I told him he ought to read Tolstoy's *War and Peace*. It might develop his imagination. He needs some."

Again:

"I have known him a long time. I am very fond of him, but he has not yet gone as far as Caesar's *Commentaries* in studying the history of war since he forgot the history he learned at West Point."

At times J.J.P. swore he had had enough, he was going to relieve a certain officer immediately. Then the word was passed after it was learned the officer had been transferred to a less onerous, less difficult post:

"There goes J.J.P. again in his care not to hurt the feelings of the 'lame duck' "—that is, of one who is doing his limping best.

There was no tenderness for one who just lagged. But there was tenderness for those who had tapped their last reserves of energy in ambition and zeal under the nerve-and-body-wracking strain, beset by a complexity of frustrations.

"He has given all he had to give but has done noble service. But now he must have time to recover. He is very proud. Manage it if you can, so that he will not be hurt too much."

A problem from low rank to high rank in an organization which included every branch of human activity and every kind of expert was fitting the round pegs of personality in the round holes. This was handicapped by the desire of every expert in any peace craft to hide the fact lest he should not have a chance to remain at the front or to go to the front. A giant, eager soldier who had been spotted as a master welder in the repair of locomotives might find himself back in the SOS (Services of Supply) just as his division was about to go into the trenches.

An elderly general who had hoped for combat command, might be riding about in a car with a flag of a brigadier's star on a mission up and down the lines of communication, which was better than if he had been sent home to unbosom his troubles. To be "sent to Blois" (the classification station for officer personnel) was not always a disgrace. It sometimes meant promotion and service in keeping with an officer's capacity.

Once when J.J.P. became oblivious of the flight of time, he was pouring over a bundle of requisitions which represented an amount of detail that seemed to be the duty of a subordinate. This was his explanation:

"I know him (the brigadier general who was responsible for the requisitions). He is a very able man, just the man for this job, but he has a way of slipping things over which are often a little too much in his personal interest. I have already caught one item. There may be another. He will have a lesson that somebody is on the watch as I shall remind him. I don't think he will make the mistake again."

On another occasion, after a general had left his office, he said:

"I've just asked him how many colonels I've got to make in order to get that job done."

Promotions, especially for the Regulars, kept pace with the rapid expansion of the army. A captain upon our entry into the war had become a colonel. A brigadier general's star had replaced a major's leaf. It was, "Good morning, Captain," to the man who had been a lieutenant when you last saw him.

John J. Pershing's new rank, the highest we ever had bestowed upon an Army officer and bearing the simple designation, "General," was never before awarded except as a tribute of victory. And during all our history only four others had been so honored—Washington, Grant, Sheridan and Sherman.

Promotions were almost epidemic. They were the reward of merit, the goal of ambition. Reserve officers from civil life who had been in our officers' training camps and then attached to the forming divisions in the cantonments would generally have to wait for their promotion until casualties had made vacancies or they had earned commendation in action.

A better incentive and better reward than promotions were soon provided. Hitherto we had had only one important war medal. This was the Medal of Honor from Congress, the equivalent to the British Victoria Cross and the French *Medaille Militaire,* given to an officer or private for gallantry in action. How sedulously it had been guarded as a reward was exemplified in the fact that only one hundred were given to our army in the World War. Yet its symbol of white stars on a blue background in a strip on the breast of a uniform was little known to the American public which in the war and after the war regarded the French *Croix de Guerre* as the supreme reward of courage.

The *Croix de Guerre* was given by hundreds of thousands. French generals carried them about in their pockets to bestow them on soldiers. They were scattered with all the prodigality of Iron Crosses in the German army. Our new medals were the Distinguished Service Medal, which was given for distinguished service whether at the rear or in command at the front, and the Distinguished Service Cross which could be won only by officers or men who showed exceptional initiative and daring under fire. J.J.P. was determined, with Secretary Baker's support, that these should be awarded only on the recommendations of superior officers after a thorough canvass of the evidence by a board of officers. It was this that made our crosses very precious to Allied officers and soldiers, although they remained still unrecognized by our own public.

When Brand Whitlock, the American Ambassador to Belgium, suggested to his old friend, Baker, that he should like a Distinguished Service Medal for a high ranking Belgium officer, and Baker replied that this was a matter for the board to consider and not for him, Brand exclaimed:

"Why, Newt, I thought you had a number in your desk that you could pass out at any time."

No branch had been a source of more controversy and confusion than that of aviation in its rapid development in war time. Not only did experts disagree with one another, but one expert's view one week disagreed with that of the next. Boards met only later to repudiate their own findings. All this prejudiced anything like a dependable organization of this youngest, most experimental branch. It appeared to justify the sapient remark of one very able general officer that "as soon as anybody had anything to do with aviation he becomes as temperamental as an opera star and always up in the air."

J.J.P. had appointed a board to form a definite conclusion on our aviation program. When they reported to him they immediately began a discussion, expecting him to act as an arbiter on technical matters in which they were supposed to be proficient. The discussion was sharply interrupted:

"This is enough debate. I appointed you to work out an aviation program so that I will know what you want. Then I shall adjust it, as Commander-in-Chief, to the requirements of the whole and our resources. You will remain here at GHQ and continue working until you bring me a definite program."

It was forthcoming the next day.

While the Allies were waiting through May for the next blow, J.J.P. continued to make some progress in the pooling of supplies. Clemenceau accepted it on principle for the French. He went so far as to promise us domestic horses which we needed for transport, but the peasants objected to parting with them on the ground that if we brought over our own horses and mules they would be for sale cheap after the war. The British had not yet agreed to Clemenceau's terms for pooling and the proposed organization for its conduct.

25

The Château-Thierry Crisis

So RAPIDLY HAD TROOPS come that by the end of May we had nearly 600,000 men in France counting all the personnel of the Services of Supply. Not only more favorable weather, but the pattern established for them to follow, allowed more rapid training of the divisions which were arriving.

The word passed from village to village and lip to lip through France of the movement of the many trains crowded with the khaki clad soldiers of America. But this was not enough. Although they were here there was no news of their fighting while the weary Allied armies and the people were under the threat of another German offensive which was accepted as inevitable.

Pershing had offered his divisions, but Foch's failure to use them in sectors which might become violent might be easily construed as an intimation of a lack of confidence in them for any severe test.

However, Foch was convinced that the next German offensive would be in the Montdidier sector, and our First

Division (Major General Robert L. Bullard) was still in the trenches in front of Montdidier. It had a disadvantage of ground and had been under heavy fire from the commanding positions of German trench and artillery fire.

The Allies had made no actual offensive, except counterattacks, since the fall of 1917. A distinctly American offensive if successful, would be more valuable for Allied morale, especially that of the Allied troops, than any amount of talk about the hosts of Americans who were arriving. It would show not only that we would fight but that we knew how to fight, which veterans always doubt about unexperienced troops.

Not again was J.J.P. able to spare the time for such attention to division detail as in his council over the plan for the offensive with General Bullard and with Colonel George C. Marshall, Jr., the division operations officer.

The French brought up additional artillery in support. Every precaution was taken for success when failure must have such a depressing result. Our attack gained its objectives, capturing the village of Cantigny in so masterful a manner that it would have had resounding promotion as Allied propaganda, if it had not been overshadowed by the news of the terrific and disastrous impact of the third German offensive.

Master Foch and the French staff had been completely fooled by Master Ludendorff and the German staff. The French staff had been quite unreceptive to the "amateurish" suggestion which came through the battle order division of G-2 of our staff under Colonel A. L. Conger. Major Samuel T. Hubbard, Jr., a reserve officer who had been a thorough student of military affairs, had worked out, through all the complicated sources of information in fitting together the picture puzzle, the conclusion that the offensive would be between Noyon and Rheims.

It was to this line, comprising the blood-soaked Chemin des Dames, that Foch had sent to rest in a "quiet sector" exhausted British and French divisions. French aviation and intelligence nodded. No observation planes were sent out for days. Only the fortuitous capture of a prisoner the night before the attack gave the first inkling that it was coming.

Undetected, the Germans with their infinite pains and industry, had mobilized 300,000 men and all their guns and ammunition. It was a surprise more remarkable even than that of Caporetto; a surprise comparable in our own military history with Israel Putnam's capture of Ticonderoga, Washington's crossing of the Delaware, George Roger Clark's capture of Kankaskia, and Stonewall Jackson's concealed flanking march to Chancellorsville.

On the morning of May 27, after a preparatory lightning barrage, the avalanche swept through the trench lines, then on down the slopes of the Chemin des Dames to the taking of Soissons with a speed that surpassed that of any other advance on the western front during the war.

Thirty French divisions which were hastened to the defense were more or less caught in detail. On the fourth day the Germans were far beyond their planned objectives. They were on the banks of the Marne and beyond Château-Thierry, pushing ahead along the Paris road, nearer Paris than they had been since the early days of September, 1914.

They had taken 60,000 prisoners, 650 guns and 2000 machine guns, not to mention immense quantities of material and supplies. They had cut a railroad important to French transport. Should they break across the Marne beyond Château-Thierry and past Montmirail, they would threaten Paris in another direction and also the American Army with the necessity of retreating from its Lorraine sector.

The people were evacuating Paris as they had in 1914. More than a million were to go before the crisis was over. Official archives in Paris were being packed for transport, trucks were ready to remove documents of the Supreme

War Council from Versailles, and we were beginning to bundle up our own papers at our GHQ at Chaumont. Now it was not a case of confidence by Foch in American divisions but of hastening any available one to stem the tide.

But before turning to their part, we revert to J.J.P. who, after seeing the First Division ready for the offensive, had gone to inspect our divisions which had arrived at the British front. Then, after the German offensive was under way, he hastened to Sarcus where he found Foch and his staff at dinner through which they sat in gloom, hardly speaking a word. It would have been cruel and impolite for J.J.P. to have reminded Foch of his mistake in judgment as to the location of the offensive. He simply repeated his "all we have." Not only our two divisions already sent to face the German advance, but every one within reach and not elsewhere in the trenches was at the Generalissimo's disposal.

J.J.P. might not satisfy his wish to go to the front to see the two divisions in action against the offensive, for he had received a call to be present at an emergency meeting of the Supreme War Council. In Paris, on the way, M. Andre Tardieu, the chief of the French mission in Washington, who was then in France, sought a word with him.

M. Tardieu evidently thought it was time that the American commander be told some plain truths. In his criticism of the American staff and its organization, he was not in the slightest restricted by the recent mistake of the French staff. If there could be any two antipathetic characters it was Pershing, the soldier, and Tardieu, who was a singularly proficient example of one type of French politician. J.J.P. did not mince words. He simply told M. Tardieu that he was wrong.

Tardieu, in the course of his skillful siege in Washington, had learned enough to know that Pershing had the confidence of Secretary Baker and President Wilson. So his last resort was to influence Pershing himself. After this interview he wrote, as a conclusion for his political chiefs, that the only way with the Americans was to "keep on working as we have begun: . . . Our real and only danger lies in the failure to make allowances for the spirit of the American people and for the idiosyncracies of American mentality." It could no more occur to M. Tardieu than to Premier Clemenceau that the French mentality had any idiosyncracies.

"Tiger" Clemenceau, who trumpeted his defiant "I will fight in front of Paris. I will fight in Paris. I will fight behind Paris," was at heart a frightened old man at the Versailles meeting. Again all the "black coats," as the statesmen were called, and their war ministers and foreign ministers, were summoned to this meeting along with Foch and Pershing in addition to the permanent military representatives on the Supreme War Council. It was a most august gathering of official and military importance in a high state of alarm.

The distant roar of the guns was in their ears. They listened to hear if it grew louder, signifying the nearer approach of the enemy. They were aware of the portent that the polished floors of the Palace of Versailles, where, in the Hall of Mirrors, Bismarck had proclaimed the German Empire, might again know the footsteps of another kaiser with the triumphant jingling of spurs.

But one American division was across the Paris road facing the Germans. Another American division was holding the banks of the Marne to prevent the Germans crossing. This much was known to the "black coats" and the generals who, after having parted in such good humor at Abbeville, were now to renew irritably in their suspense the controversies which seemed to be the ruling passion. The French had no scapegoat unless it was the Americans. The British did have one in the mistake of the French staff about the location of the offensive which they did not neglect to mention.

When Pershing preferred to be organizing his divisions for action at the front he had to face another offensive in council. He would proceed on the premise that the Supreme Council, that is, the Allied statesmen, had no authority over him as a soldier. He was under Marshal Foch.

The statesmen went into closed session where Clemenceau and Lloyd George twitted Premier Orlando of Italy with the discretion of the Italian navy in remaining in port, which led General Bliss to remark, when someone asked him how the discussions were going, that "they are all at sea except the Italian navy." Meanwhile the soldiers were left together to consider the necessary military action in the crisis.

J.J.P. was in a receptive mood to Foch's suggestions. Foch wanted America to raise its limit of exclusive infantry and machine gun units in June and July to 250,000 a month. J.J.P. explained to him that some allowance must be made with the broken down conditions of the railroads in France for material and personnel for inland and sea transport and supply. Foch was far from being a serene Generalissimo. His moustache trembled the while he beat the air with gestures and kept repeating, "The battle, nothing else counts." Both he and Weygand, his inseparable adjutant, who was sometimes called his brain, were impatient about the matter of supplies.

There were intervals when both seemed to think that an army lived not on its belly but on air. Their concern was combat, strategy and tactics and not preparation. When Pershing made the point that if we brought over troops at this rate we should soon empty our cantonments of men with the necessary training, Foch voiced his criticism of the American organization as a whole. We had failed to provide enough infantry in proportion to other troops.

Lloyd George and Clemenceau, having had it out with Orlando, now joined the soldier conference. Since President Wilson was not present, Lloyd George thought the question should be brought before the whole council in order that the President might have General Foch's views. If Pershing yielded this at the outset it would provide a leverage for further pressure. He proposed that the meeting should adjourn until the following day to allow a little time for further discussion and reflection.

By the morning of the next day it was known that not only was the German advance on the Paris road stopped and the Germans held from crossing the Marne by the American divisions, but that the American division along the Paris road had attacked and gained ground. The "black coats" and the generals of the Allies could take a long breath in relief, but the initiative that these two divisions had shown naturally only made them more greedy for more American soldiers. Lloyd George and Clemenceau, who disagreed so frequently, were now in complete agreement that we should send over 250,000 and even 300,000 troops in both June and July.

Pershing held that at least the troops should have three months' training before they came. Clemenceau argued that they were trained faster in the atmosphere of war. Pershing again turned to Foch and Weygand with the plea that they should understand as soldiers the importance of replacements in our trained divisions and of transport and supply and that we were operating three thousand miles from home short of shipping and adequate rail and port facilities. But Foch and Weygand were quite indifferent, although Lord Milner, the British Secretary of War, out of the experience of forming a new army and supplying it across the English Channel, put in a word in Pershing's support.

Clemenceau was surprised to learn that our draft was drawing upon a man power already fully occupied under the tremendous strain on our natural resources and our industrial power in support of both our own and the Allied armies and navies. He said that he thought our resources were inexhaustible, and his attitude as well as that of Foch was really that we were not doing our share in the war. Foch continued to dwell on the danger that the Allies had only 150 divisions against 200 German divisions. He pointed out the heavy casualties the Allies had suffered in defense while taking it for granted that the Germans continued to grow stronger.

The unspoken palpable purpose, from an attitude which was little less than defeatism, was that once we had in France a host of untrained infantry and machine gun units they could not escape infiltration into the French army. Following the precedent of inter-Allied jousting in council, J.J.P. might well have let out a blast in something like these terms:

"Instead of the handful of troops which you first asked us for we now have more than 600,000 men in France. Taking for granted that the Germans do have 200 divisions, which is an over-estimate, as you know, against the Allies' 160, which is an under-estimate, you are in stark fear lest you shall be overwhelmed. Only bad generalship, general incompetence, and recognition that the enemy has a super staff and super soldiers, warrant your fear against such small odds in powerful defensive lines which admit of no flanking attack except by vastly superior numbers.

"Ours is the army that must win the war. You are fighting for your control of the sea, for the soil of France, for your very existence. We have come over here to help you for a world cause. I do not propose that we shall send untrained men into battle under your command which has failed in this war but ours shall be the final decision as to how our troops shall be employed.

"With or without your consent we propose to save you from a policy which can lead only to disaster. And suppose the American people were listening to what you said in the Abbeville conference and this conference. Suppose they knew all the inter-Allied bickering and quarreling. Far be it from you to tell us how to win a war when you have made such a bad job of winning this one with all the resources of the world at your back.

"Finally, you wasted lives on the Marne. Your defense of Verdun was more costly than the German offensive against forts in attack up steep slopes. We have learned all we could from you, and some of the lessons we do not mean to apply in sacrifice of our own troops in assuring the loss of the war which you seem to think is as good as lost without our enormous reinforcements."

At the time the American people, fighting to make the world safe for democracy, as they read the reports, thought that all the meetings of the "black coats" and the generals were a kind of love feast of unity. Word was circulated in inner circles at home that there were differences between Foch and Pershing, but this was accepted as insidious German propaganda. It could not be true.

However, those of us in uniform in France did not have to listen to one argument which Allied and our own propaganda continually made at home. This was in the simple phrase so often used, "You'll be next if the Germans conquer us." To say it across the council table in France to J.J.P. was not in order though it might be at a dinner party in Washington. If the United States could not defend itself as a last resort against the whole world with such divisions as the two now facing the German offensive, then it was time we became vassals of the Kaiser.

The calmest one of all in the conference, J.J.P. simply held fast to his conviction that we could not send over only machine gun units and infantry to the exclusion of personnel and material for supply. So often had he expressed his view that it seemed unnecessary for him to stress again, which he did, that he was ready to make any reasonable concessions to assure that the Allied lines held fast in defense before we could renew our preparations for the eventual, decisive American offensive.

At last, after Foch had somewhat exhausted himself with his objections, Weygand suggested that we be allowed to train our new drafts at home a month or two longer. Weygand knew his Foch and when to take the lead, which was now accepted. Ultimately Foch, Milner and Pershing signed an agreement by which we were to send over 250,000 troops a month. Of these, 140,000 were to be combat troops including replacements, but the balance were to be designated by the Commander-in-Chief of the AEF which allowed him to make sure that his men should not starve before they ever reached the front.

Now the statesmen had their turn in sending a message to the President of the United States, in which they made the most of Foch's great prestige with the American people. They made the odds in German numbers appear appalling, in Foch's name, though when it came to putting the numbers down on paper, they did increase Foch's conversational estimate of the Allied divisions from 150 to 162.

"Looking to the future," said the cablegram, "he (Foch) represents that it is impossible to foresee ultimate victory in the war unless America is able to provide such an army as will enable the Allies ultimately to establish numerical superiority. He places the total American force required for this at no less than 100 divisions, and urges the continuous raising of American levies which, in his opinion, should not be less than 300,000 a month with a view to establishing a total American force of 100 divisions at as early a date as this can possibly be done."

One hundred of our big divisions, with adequate personnel for the Services of Supply, would mean we should have more than four million men in France. Our actual combat force would outnumber any the Germans ever had in the field or the British and French had together. Foch wanted to be sure that he had enough. And they ought to be enough if they were all fighting the way the two divisions were now fighting the Germans in the Marne sector.

Since Foch had not escaped British twitting, first, over the failure of the French divisions to hold Memel Hill in the second German offensive and, next, over his error about the location of the third German offensive, it was in order that the statesmen should pay him a public tribute to make sure lest his prestige might be dimmed with the Allied publics. He might not be the perfect generalissimo, but now we had him we must support him. We might get a worse horse in any swap in crossing the present turbulent stream. In the cablegram the statesmen stated:

"That we are satisfied that General Foch, who is conducting the present campaign with consummate ability, and on whose military judgment we continue to place the most absolute reliance, is not over-estimating the needs of the case."

The third German offensive having now been definitely arrested, as the statesmen put their pens to paper in signature, they were all feeling much better. In that conference J.J.P. had risen a little higher in dignity in the course of his education, not to say in his canniness, as a negotiater, who had further learned the value of demanding more than he expected to get to give him a trading position at the outset. In his own cablegram to the War Office he said:

"It should be most fully realized at home that the time has come for us to take up the brunt of the war and that France and England are not going to be able to keep their armies at present strength very much longer . . . I can only add that our program should be laid out systematically and broadly and men called out as fast as they can be handled."

His original plan, which foresaw that our army must be of such force and numbers as to strike the decisive blow in 1919, had been confirmed. He recognized the value of the urgent cable signed by Clemenceau, Lloyd George and Orlando in stirring our people in their effort to be sufficiently strong at home and in France to insure victory in 1919.

26

Not "Too Proud to Fight"

WITH OUR CANTIGNY offensive and the action against the third German offensive we had inaugurated the one hundred and fifty days of fighting which were to continue to Armistice Day. When the third German offensive broke, our 2d Division (Major General Omar Bundy) was on its way to replace the 1st Division in holding the ground that it had gained. Rested, fresh, well trained, the 2d was turned back and hurried in buses and on foot along the Paris road, to take the place of the hollow-eyed, broken and exhausted French battalions who had fought in desperate delaying action in vain to hold the German tide.

Bent heads of refugees and soldiers raised and faces lighted at the sight of the firmly marching, vigorous reinforcements. The cry of *"les américains' "* had never meant so much to any human beings on the continent of Europe.

What a contrast they were to the slouchy recruits who arrived at St. Lazaire without the kinks out of their sea legs yet! They were made soldiers now. A professional glance at them carried professional conviction.

So men, guns and machine guns of the 2d went into position on either side of the Paris road with the practiced precision of a veteran football or baseball team going to their places in the field. They answered the enemy's fire with more accurate fire than he sent. Instead of losing ground they began gaining ground on both sides of the road.

The Division's 2d Brigade. under command of Harbord, composed of Marines, had a line to straighten out and took the village of Bouresches. The Germans had a commanding position in the possession of Belleau Wood for further advance or to harass the 2d Brigade with plunging fire. Harbord was not one to sit content under this threat. Under their resolute leader, the Marines proceeded as though the eye of the world was upon them, as it was at that moment. If it had not been their intrepidity would have drawn its attention.

They had been taught and drilled that they were to be masters of the enemy and here was their chance to prove it. So they began that long day after day siege of Belleau Wood, from fox hole to fox hole, in which, severe as were their own casualties, they inflicted more on the enemy, including the number of prisoners they took.

The Allied publics, famished for good news, conscious of their dependence upon the Americans, soon had the word not only through the official communiqués, but spreading from lip to lip all over France and through to England, of how the Americans had come to hand-to-hand grapple with the enemy. Tales spread describing them as fighting like devils, like American red skins, knocking German machine gunners down with their fists in their demoniac American energy. The effect of their gallantry was the more pronounced because there still stuck in the Allied public mind the "too proud to fight" phrase of President Wilson before our entry into the war.

But it is time to turn to the other American division's

part against the third German offensive. We had not had to go so far to serve against the third as against the first and second. The third offensive was nearer our sector in Lorraine. As the Germans swept down from the Chemin des Dames toward the Marne, Pershing had ordered the 3d Division (Major General Joseph T. Dickman) which was available and within the shortest distance, to Château-Thierry or wherever it would meet the enemy.

Its motorized machine gun units sped on ahead of the infantry and guns. A few got across the Marne for a brief, desperate resistance on the water front of Château-Thierry against the enemy pressing through the streets of the town and on its outskirts to surround them. They retreated across the bridge but no farther, and in their support the infantry and guns of the 3d were taking position, in the confidence of men who knew how to shoot. If the French infantry had been equally proficient with the rifle the Germans would have paid a higher price to have reached the Marne.

Our 3d Division had not had the long period of training, the trench experience, of our 2d. But its skill and celerity held promise of the dependability in a crisis of later arrivals, especially under so redoubtable a leader as General Dickman, whose thickly set figure at times suggested an immovable body and again an irresistible force.

Probably a factor saving the Allies from defeat in the war was Ludendorff's error in judgment about the British and French armies. The pedantic and academic strain in this vain, disagreeable, overbearing genius, influenced by tradition, convinced him, according to his own account, that the British, being a new and amateur army, was weaker than the French which had a long professional conscript background, and had led him to center his first and second offensives against the British. However, the British had now become a highly professional army, still near the peak

of its power while the French, which had borne the brunt
of the fighting in the first two years, was on the decline.

How brittle was the French mood, both of the army and
people, appeared among the soldiers and refugees and far
to the rear in the attitude after the fall of Château-Thierry!
One heard very frequently the view expressed that "It is
too much—France can no more," as the background to
enhance the moral effect of the way we had stood on the
Paris road and the bank of the Marne.

Ludendorff's easy progress against the French in the
third offensive would seem to warrant him striking his next
blow against the French in the region of the Marne salient.
J.J.P. proposed to Foch, and quickly received his assent,
that he should divert the 4th (Major General Mark L.
Hersey) and the 28th (Major General Charles H. Muir)—
on their way from the British front to further trench experience in our own sector—to the Château-Thierry sector
to meet any emergency. He also brought the veteran 42d
Division (Major General Charles T. Menoher) to aid
against any attack on Rheims when it was vital to hold
Rheims.

Just where toward Paris would the fourth offensive
break? It came on June 11 west of the Marne salient between Montdidier and the Oise. The first day's results
promised a repetition of previous deep gains in a closer
threat to Paris.

On that June 11 of unpleasant news J.J.P. had a talk
with Clemenceau. When J.J.P. asked him what the French
would do if Paris were to fall, the doughty "Tiger" said
that he and Lloyd George had agreed that they would fight
on. J.J.P. told him:

"Well, Mr. President, it may not look encouraging just
now but we are certain to win in the end."

He clung to J.J.P.'s hand saying:

"Do you really think that? I am glad to hear you say it."

Later, that day, Pershing talked with Foch who also said

that France would go on with the war. If the American general had heartened the French premier and the Allied generalissimo, they had also heartened him; for there was an over-shadowing fear that further disaster might mean the fall of the militant Clemenceau government to be succeeded by a government that would be open to peace terms. In that case either America must insist on continuing the war or yield in a compromise.

But against the fourth German offensive, under the brilliant leadership of General Mangin, the French were again the French of the Marne and of Verdun. They made the enemy pay for the ground they yielded under the initial impact, and then— in what might be taken as a warning to Ludendorff that the French was still a great army—with the skillful use of their tanks and gas, and not overlooking the value of their own rifles as well as machine guns, they retook more than a mile of depth of the ground lost, and the fourth German offensive was over. If it had not been stopped in its tracks its gains were not serious.

The people were returning to Paris which again seemed secure. We unpacked our papers in GHQ and restored them to their places.

27

Fifth and Last

IT WAS AFTER the fourth German offensive had been checked that J.J.P., glancing at the map on the wall, rose from his desk as if drawn to it as a magnet by the change in the old trench line wrought by the third offensive. Here was a deep semi-circle, which the fourth offensive had been unable to spread, projected into the Allied front. For five weeks it had been staring at J.J.P with its invitation to a wide open military opportunity. Those who had thought of him as too cautious, too insistent on the thorough slow process of preparation, would have found nothing Fabian in him in the face of this challenge. He was flushed with indignation.

"Look at what the German army has done to the Allies after nearly four years of war! It has blown a balloon into their lines.

"It is a great army," he added, in professional admiration of soldier for soldier. "I have some German blood in my veins and we will give them as good as they send, German against German, and better. We have some fully trained divisions but we have others not so well trained who will fight. It is time we no longer had to endure this insult. We can close that salient. I am ready when Foch says the word."

Two days later he was making the offer and the suggestion to Foch which was to be carried out five weeks afterward in the drive to Soissons which "turned the tide." But Foch was not ready at this time. He was waiting for the next blow, waiting for the enemy fully to exploit his offensive power before any Allied offensive. No risk must be taken of weakening the Allies in attack lest it might enable the enemy to win a decisive success.

Having tested our troops in battle Foch could afford to wait on the arrival of more from the reservoir of man power across the Atlantic. Time was on his side in relying not only on our increase of numbers but upon their moral effect upon the French and British troops. In a cable to Secretary Baker, June 21, J.J.P said:

". . . The morale of the lower grades of the French army is distinctly poor. Both the French and British people are extremely tired of the war and their troops are reflecting this attitude in their frequent inability to meet success with the German attacks. It is the American soldiers now in France upon whom they rely. It is the morale as well as the material aid given by the American soldier that is making continuation of the war possible."

Three days before this he had written in a letter to Secretary Baker that the situation was such among the Allies that unless we could end the war next year we were likely to be left practically alone in the fight. He thought it would be difficult in case of further serious reverses even to hold France in the war.

In the same letter he stressed the importance of being able to strike immediately the German offensives were checked for good. It was his judgment that the German divisions were growing weaker and their man power running low. A few very heavy blows would incline the German people to peace. We should be ready to strike them. The larger force we had the sooner we should end the war and avoid the large losses which the Allies had suffered.

When Premier Clemenceau and Foch and Weygand came to Chaumont late in June they were in a particularly amiable mood. Not only were our troops arriving in such large numbers, but we had received the first D. H. planes (later called "flying coffins" by our aviators) of our own manufacture from America a year after J.J.P.'s arrival in France. The initial lot of our Liberty motors had won such esteem that it was impossible, in spite of our mass production, to meet the demands of the Allies for them. The personnel of the SOS alone had increased in three months from 100,000 to 175,000 and now we were unloading supplies from ten piers which we had built. Our effort from port to front had earned the right to an independent army.

J.J.P. in his own account recalls, in the course of a talk about the future of the Allies after the peace, how Clemenceau thought that Great Britain's great days were over. She could no longer retain her commercial supremacy, and the experience of the Dominion troops in the war would make them more independent. He said the Germans were a great people but Germany would not regain her prestige and influence for generations. As for the future of France, the "Tiger" was in a more optimistic mood than he was before the American action in the Château-Thierry region and the fourth offensive had been stopped. France would again become the leading power in Europe. And America— it was a wonderful country with unlimited possibilities.

Clemenceau, in his most gracious and felicitous mood, knew how to make it appear, when the news was good, that it was a great honor for any ally to accept French leadership in direction in war. However, Foch now favored the creation of a great American Army in France at once. It served his purpose in appealing to our pride in winning us to do our utmost.

Although the fourth German offensive had been stopped Foch still insisted upon 100 divisions from America. Since they were equal to 200 European divisions, this would be 40 more than the French and British had altogether, requiring for supply at least 5,000,000 dead weight tons monthly when at present we had only 1,500,000.

Already our supply system had been dislocated owing to the necessity of diverting food and munitions from the main line to the Château-Thierry sector. But, as usual, Foch lost interest when supplies were mentioned. He needed 4,000,000 Americans in France to assure the victory and it was the business of others to make sure they were fed and armed and ready, as chessmen, to be moved on the board by the master tactician.

Pershing agreed to send a joint telegram to the War Department signed by himself and by Foch asking for 80 American divisions in France as early as April, 1919, and 100 divisions by July, 1919. As a matter of policy probably J.J.P. thought that if they asked for 100 they would surely get eighty. Moreover, it strengthened his argument for the recovery of his scattered divisions as soon as the emergency was over, his pressure for a counter-attack, and his proposal that the first objective of our army should be in our own sector to reduce the St. Mihiel salient in keeping with his plan.

Foch said that he was having a study made for a counter-attack on the Marne salient and seemed to accept the St. Mihiel salient as the next step once the Marne salient was reduced. Marne salient and then St. Mihiel salient—J.J.P.'s eye was ever on the goal of the great flanking movement by our army.

Meanwhile Foch continued to wait on the fifth German offensive. It came on July 14 between Rheims and Château-Thierry. Our 42d under General Gouraud, was ready in its part, with an elastic defense which did not permit the German infantry to advance far enough to displace our guns. Then, protected by the enormous volume of our artillery fire, the 42d joined in a successful counter-attack.

But there was action of a more picturesque and less conventional kind in the World War for the 3d Division which was holding the south bank of the Marne. There two American infantry regiments of the 3d wrote history of a kind that would have delighted Daniel Boone no less than Stonewall Jackson. It was vital to the Germans not only to cross the Marne but to advance up rising ground until they commanded positions which would give them the downhill advantage in what was Ludendorff's last desperate struggle for an envelopment.

Covered by a smoke screen and protected by their barrage, the Germans crossed in their little boats which they had carefully constructed and concealed and then advanced with their now established method of group infiltration. On the Americans' part it was a battle for colonels and not generals, for reserve officer captains and lieutenants, and for privates, in field generalship and the accuracy of sweeping machine gun fire and individual rifle fire. Both sides suffered heavy casualties, but the Germans the heavier, and the next day the south bank of the Marne was clear of any Germans who were not wounded, dead or prisoners. The fifth and last German offensive was over in practically complete failure.

28
Turning the Tide

Now J. J. P. COULD look up in a more cheerful mood at the map on the wall of his office. He could visualize two arrows pointing toward the base of the salient. The two arrows were his two pioneer divisions, the 1st and 2d, about to prick the balloon, as he had called the salient.

Before the fifth German offensive had begun Foch had completed his study for a counter-offensive. The plan was already made and its execution hastened instantly the fifth German offensive had failed. Both the 1st Division (under command of Major General Charles F. Summerall) and the 2d (under command of Major General James G. Harbord) had had a period of rest. Replacements had filled the gaps in their ranks. They were fresh for the attack when the word came that sped them north to Villers-Cotterêt and the Retz Forest. The forest covered their mobilization from the enemy.

The 1st was already in position the night of July 17. But the 2d, arriving later with the infantry working its way along the traffic-gorged road, had to sprint in order to be at the front in time for the zero hour of 4:35 A. M. Heavy rain intensified the darkness and soaked officers' maps as they tried to identify their directives in the dense darkness of the thick forest. All the units were at the jumping off line on time, although for some the charge was a continuation of the march into position.

Between the 1st and 2d was the veteran Moroccan division which included the Foreign Legion operating in the 20th French Corps and under the redoubtable General Mangin as army commander. Mangin was the true disciple of *"toujours l'attaque."* Once when I remarked to him that soldiers on occasion might be too brave (which had been a French criticism of the British gallantry in their lack of skill in the early days of the war), he thrust out his heavy jaw with the reply, "Rarely." There was no being too brave or too skillful on July 18 in the jealous race in martial pride and zeal between our two pioneer divisions and the French.

So far we had done the conventional local offensive at Cantigny. We had held the Marne bank in the third German offensive and thrown the German attack back across the Marne in the fifth. We had held our lines in the cruelly exasperating Toul sector, held the Paris road, and conquered the Bois de Belleau in grim progress foot by foot. This time the hounds were off the leash in the open field operations which had been the ultimate aim of J.J.P.'s training.

The Germans were taken completely by surprise. Confident of their ground and weary of body and spirit after the gruelling weeks of labor and fighting in Ludendorff's offensive campaign, they had dug only shallow trenches. Their front line was so quickly overwhelmed that they did not have time to get their reserves into action. It was now their part to know something of the demoralization which they had inflicted upon the Allied fronts in their first three offensives. We were taking machine guns and guns and prisoners, including officers, in bunches. Success made us oblivious of fatigue and casualties. One veteran German officer expressed his feelings thus:

"I did not ever think this would happen to us in this way and from you, but you caught us napping and we're tired. It has been a long war and you're fresh as we were in 1914. And how many more soldiers like these have you coming?"

Ahead of us was Soissons. If we could reach Soissons or the heights above it, then the base of the salient would be very seriously threatened by another equally strong attack by fresh divisions which would take our place. The thing was to go as far as we could after the Germans, banking their reserves up against us, and reorganized and aware of their danger, were showing again their veteran efficiency.

In the forty-eight hours of day and night fighting seven German divisions had been mustered against the 1st Division before it was withdrawn on the fourth day after having taken 3500 prisoners, 68 guns and suffered 7000 casualties. The 2d Division, withdrawn at the end of the second day, had taken 75 guns and 3000 prisoners and suffered 5000 casualties in turn as the price it paid for a victory which was thereafter called "the turn of the tide." Never again was the German army to undertake an offensive except in local counter-attacks.

If our Allies had had reason to ask the previous fall and winter where the American divisions in France were and what they were doing, they had less reason now than after Château-Thierry. We were established not as a waiting and drilling army but as an offensive army.

Before his death Chancellor von Hertling of Germany wrote:

"We expected grave events in Paris for the end of July. That was on the 15th. On the 18th even the most optimistic among us understood that all was lost. The history of the world was played out in three days."

Field Marshal von Hindenburg wrote in *Out Of My Life:*

"From the purely military point of view it was of the greatest and most fateful importance that we had lost the initiative to the enemy . . . The effect on the country and our Allies was even greater judging by our first impressions. How many hopes, cherished during the last few months, had probably collapsed at one blow! How many calculations had been scattered to the winds!"

General Mangin thus congratulated our 3d Army Corps (Major General Robert L. Bullard) which comprised the 1st and 2d Divisions:

"You rushed into the fight as to a fête . . . Your magnificent courage completely routed a surprised enemy . . . You have shown yourselves worthy sons of your great country and you were admired by your brothers-in-arms."

If there was any doubt that the tide had been turned it was dispelled on August 8th by the offensive of the British and the Canadian Corps when the enemy broke under their attack in much the same fashion as on July 18. It was then that Ludendorff referred to the sword as having broken in his hand. His hope had been that he could win a decisive victory before American reinforcements arrived in sufficient numbers to be a considerable weight in the balance against him. Now the most skeptical Allied statesman or staff officer could not question that with the Americans we had an American superiority in France. Our total in France was now 1,200,000 men.

It was no longer a question of "all we have" in an emergency to insure the protecting wall of our drill ground, but a time to strike the heavy blows against the weakening enemy which J.J.P. had in mind.

All matters must wait while his car, fluttering its four-star flag, bore him toward the front. But even his car could not always immediately get the right of way through the heavy traffic behind the battle lines. The headquarters of the 1st and 2d had his congratulations in person. He saw how their wounded necessarily, in so swift a change of position, had been left to French hospitalization which was quite inadequate. They waited long for their second dressings, some of them in agony.

This had been a part of the cost for such a victory, but it was a reminder that we should have sufficient hospitalization of our own back of our own army and that he had not been in error in the building of our immense hospitals and immense requisitions for ambulances and medical corps personnel. He saw for himself our other divisions in a cluster around the Marne salient. They were ready in spirit, if they had not as long training as the 1st and 2d, to follow their example in pressing on in their part of the operations for the reduction of the salient.

He was in council with Major General Hunter Liggett whom he had chosen to command our 1st Corps and the plans completed which would give that accomplished soldier and his staff their first offensive battle experience. Convinced he could rely upon Liggett and rely upon the divisions, he might look away from the salient on the map again toward the Lorraine goal.

He was off to a conference with Sir Douglas Haig and then to one of the Allied commanders-in-chief with Foch. What a reversal in the fortunes of war since the gap had been broken on March 26 between the British and French armies and since only seven weeks ago the people were evacuating Paris! They met with genuine instead of forced smiles to cover their alarm. The Allies had not yet won the war, but the danger that the Germans could win it by any master stroke on the western front was past.

Haig, after having borne the burden of the years of stonewalling and heavy attrition, was as forthright as Pershing for offensive action. Foch was in the serene mood of the Generalissimo whose tactics had been justified but not so optimistic, though he considered it vital that the Americans should continue to send over troops at the rate of 300,000 a month the while he favored his series of alternating attacks. He was ready to listen to the plans of the other commanders.

J.J.P.'s best trained divisions had been diverted to the Château-Thierry sector which had prevented him forming our army in Lorraine. He forestalled any request from Haig that the divisions which were with the British should remain permanently there to serve in British offensives. He recalled to Foch and to Pétain the agreement of the Abbeville conference. Once his divisions had finished their part in the reduction of the Marne salient they should be moved back to their own sector. He looked forward definitely to the next step being the reduction of the St. Mihiel salient with his own army under his command. His feet firmly planted on sure ground, he was not so much making a request as he was carrying out a program which they had already accepted. Foch did not commit himself except to say that he would take this under consideration. Foch was friendly but somewhat evasive.

Having already established corps commands as the larger unit of direction over divisions J.J.P. now created the still larger one, of the First Army, with its staff under his command for the coming operation against the St. Mihiel salient. This, too, was check if not checkmate to prevent the continued scattering of his divisions. His indomitable canny watchfulness in all conferences was backed by the fact that he had always kept his word and that he expected others to keep their word.

29

A Crisis in the SOS

It Was a Jubilant J.J.P. who looked at the wall map.

"The 3d and 28th are across the Marne. They have retaken Château-Thierry. Our other divisions are moving according to plan. Not all have had enough training, but, as I told Foch, all will fight. All have been grounded in sound principles."

He need not worry now about the security of the trench wall to protect the forming of his army. The wall was moving forward under the impact of our divisions in coöperation with the French in closing the Marne salient.

Confident of their competence, J.J.P. had seen them started on their mission. Then he had to deal with another emergency. He had to look away from the front to the lines of the SOS across France, the ports of southern France and the ports and cantonments across the Atlantic in the homeland.

Ten thousand American soldiers were arriving every twenty-four hours in France. All must be provided with munitions and supplies. At home we were on the way to the "Work or Fight" order and about to draft all men up to the age of forty-five. Those unfit for the armed services must labor.

Under the Overman Act, in response to the alarm of the German offensives, Congress had vested in President Wilson authority far beyond that Lincoln had ever received and not to be equalled until that conferred upon Franklin Roosevelt during the depression of the nineteen-thirties. The War Department had not yet completed a study for the 80-division program, which had been called for in the Château-Thierry crisis before it received the Foch-Pershing appeal for 100 divisions. This meant two millions more men drawn from civil life for combat training when all the war industries were crying for more labor.

The Department continued its study of the 80-100 division program to ascertain whether or not it was possible for the United States, which Clemenceau and Foch thought had inexhaustible resources, to maintain more than four millions of soldiers across three thousand miles of ocean and then three hundred miles or more to eastern France.

As the daily pile of requisitions from France continued to increase with the increase of the AEF, Washington was disturbed about the slow turn-around of ships between our own ports and French ports. In some instances it had taken as many as seventy-two days. Supplies were piled up on our home piers owing to apparently unnecessary delay in unloading our ships on the French side, which was in turn owing to a shortage of labor.

Already some ships were building in the new shipyards at home, but few would be completed until well into the winter. Pershing had been justified not only in his view that the British had ships they could spare but that others were available. And war's demand, which becomes an irresistible command, had led us to scour the seas for more ships, and, in the practice of war's pressure of the "right" of international eminent domain, we had impressed neutral ships in the Allied service. Literally, any ship anywhere in the world which was idle must carry Allied troops or freight. But still there were not enough to meet the needs of the AEF unless less time was lost in ports.

"I have a suggestion from Secretary Baker," said J.J.P., "which is based on a situation that must be remedied, but I think the plan proposed is wrong. General March has the room next to the Secretary's. He has the Secretary's ear. I have to communicate with him by cable and letter but I think I can convince him that the plan is wrong."

General Peyton C. March was the Chief of Staff of whom a subordinate once said, "His blood corpuscles are steel filings." He had preceded Pershing as the attaché with Kuroki's army in Manchuria. He had had the artillery command in France early in the war and Pershing had advised his choice as Chief of Staff in the spring of 1918 when a younger and more forceful hand was needed at the helm.

To March war was action and procrastination an unforgivable failing. He mercilessly drove the spurs into the army and industrial steeds, though the industrial were not under his authority. He flashed his decisions with a machine gun rapidity. Allowance for lame ducks was not in his philosophy of personal infallibility which wasted no time in the sympathetic touch to promote coördination. Secretary Baker recognized his value as a driver after our forces, army and industrial, which had been inexperienced in war, had been trained in harness.

When March, in a later lecture at the War College, spoke of his part in "the education of a secretary of war," Baker, who never forfeited his sense of humor or his poise, was understandingly amused. His own comment of March is worth quoting:

"I learned . . . from General March that when the moment comes to strike, a vigour and intolerance of position that amounts to ruthlessness may be necessary. I used to say to General March that he wasted a substantial part of my time, and he would ask how; and I would tell him that I had to go around with a cruse of oil and a bandage to fix up the wounds which he had made. These seemed unnecessary in the day's work, and if I could abandon the oil and bandage, I could probably devote more time to my own job; but he would go out and make more wounds."

Soon after March became Chief of Staff he heard that singing instruction was being given to the men in our camps and cantonments. March sent for Raymond Fosdick, in charge of soldier welfare and entertainment and recreation, and asked him what singing had to do with winning a war. It must be stopped. Fosdick inquired of Baker if this was to be taken as an order, and Baker smiled and said that he stood by a talk he had made on the first National Community Song Day:

"I do not know whether history records it, but I imagine that the Song of Deborah was sung by the people of Israel until the days of the Maccabees, for it not only embodied the highest inspiration of the military and moral ideals of a great people, but it was the top pitch of their enthusiasm . . . I remember that I once heard (these things come back like pages from a scrap-book) how some ancient king planned to send his army against an adversary, and in advance he sent an ambassador, or messenger; and the ambassador came back and said, 'Your Majesty, these people cannot be overcome. They sing as they fight!' Our Army in France will sing because of the helpfulness of song. There are emotions which find no other mode of expression. They will sing because their cause is just and they know it. They will sing because they are the sons of a free people."

March was charged with an ambition to succeed Pershing as Commander-in-Chief in the field. In warrant of this ambition it seemed not unlikely on precedent that Pershing's difficulties promised the same fate for him as all the other original field commanders in our wars with the exception of Washington. But, as Secretary Baker said to the author, he had informed March very directly that he would never be made Commander-in-Chief in France. His career was now entirely bound up in success or failure as Chief of Staff.

March did not forget that as Chief of Staff he was nominally Pershing's superior. However, his own superior was Secretary Baker, and Secretary Baker had told Pershing, upon his departure to France, that he would give him only two orders, one to go and one to return.

Pershing had admiration for March as a driver, but March seemed to have little for Pershing. March was not given to admirations. His tongue had no less sharp edge, with his stenographer at his elbow, writing a cable to the commander in France than it had when he had an officer on the carpet for castigation. His cables included irritating sharp stabs as well as pinpricks, which aroused a hot impulse on the part of staff officers of GHQ in France to reply in kind.

But J.J.P would not have this, even though his temper momentarily flamed. If he had signed all the stinging paragraphs in cables in answer to March, or letters and messages to our Allies which were placed on his desk, relations would have been far more difficult. Secretary Baker might have concluded that he had a Commander-in-Chief in France who was as fond of inflicting wounds as his Chief of Staff; and in those days, when there was no long distance telephone across the Atlantic, he could not have utilized his pacifying gift of well chosen ingratiating and disarming sentences in place of carrying a cruse of oil about GHQ.

Not once did Pershing ever reply in kind to March. He remained impersonal and objective as the Commander-in-Chief of the AEF to the Chief of Staff of the Army if at times he undoubtedly had the temptation to use some short and ugly words. Once he remarked: "I wish March were a little more human. He would be happier."

Naturally Pershing favored the soldiers singing and anything that would give them entertainment and relaxation off duty and out of the trenches. And even March, had he been in command at the front in a crisis, would not have found the arrival of reinforcements the less welcome if they were singing their rousing, confident, "Hail! Hail! The Gang's All Here!" In the suggestive letter written on July 6 to Pershing, Baker said:

"As the American troops in France become more and more numerous and the battle initiative on some parts of the front passes to you, the purely military part of your task will necessarily take more and more of your time, and both the President and I want to feel that the planning and the executing of military undertakings has your personal consideration and that your mind is free for that as far as possible.

"The American people think of you as their 'fighting General,' and I want them to have that idea more and more brought home to them. For these reasons, it seems to me that it would help if some plan were devised by which you would be free from any necessity of giving attention to Services of Supply; and one plan in that direction which suggested itself was to send General Goethals over to take charge of the Services of Supply, establishing a direct relationship between him and Washington . . .

"Such a plan would place General Goethals in a coördinate rather than a subordinate relation to you, but of course it would transfer all the supply responsibilities from you to him, and you could then forget about docks, railroads, storage houses, and all the other vast industrial undertakings to which up to now you have given a good deal of your time, and as you know, we all think with superb success. I would be very glad to know what you think about this suggestion . . . The President and I will consider your reply together, and you may rely upon our being guided only by confidence in your judgment and the deep desire to aid you.

"One other aspect of your burdens the President feels can be somewhat lightened by a larger use of General Bliss as diplomatic intermediary. The President is adopting as a definite rule of action an insistence that inter-Allied military questions be referred to the Permanent Military Representatives . . . As the President deals in matters of military diplomacy with General Bliss, it would seem that he could with propriety relieve you of some part of the conferences and consultations which in the early days you were obliged to have with the British War Office and the French War Office, thus simplifying the presentation of inter-Allied questions to the President."

Major General George W. Goethals, the builder of the Panama Canal, had been made Quartermaster General in the reorganization of the War Department. He was of a dominant nature and used to dictatorial authority. The suggestion was to make his position coördinate but not subordinate. This would really mean two commanders in France. The other commanders-in-chief of the Allies had control over their supply departments. Pershing had been insistent on the coördination of the Services of Supply under GHQ, since every bag of flour, every pair of shoes, every rifle and gun bullet and shell had but one purpose, and that was the military objective

In spite of his readiness to leave until tomorrow what could be better settled tomorrow, J.J.P could be as quick in decision as March himself. He wrote very vigorously on his pad a cable which was marked "RUSH RUSH RUSH RUSH" across the top:

". . . I very much appreciate your desire to relieve me of every burden that might interfere with the direction of military operations. However, there appears to be an exaggerated view concerning the personal attention required in handling the details of administration of this command . . . The whole must remain absolutely under one head. Any division of responsibility or coördinate control in any sense would be fatal. The man who fights the armies must control their supply through subordinates responsible to him alone. The responsibility is then fixed, and the possibility of conflicting authority avoided. This military principle is vital and cannot be violated without inviting failure . . . When it becomes necessary for me to be constantly at the front I shall retain general control through the General Staff . . . General Kernan has worked very hard but has not all the qualifications necessary for success."

For to J.J.P it was a revolutionary suggestion prejudicial to his plan and the progress to its goal. He stressed the views of the cable in a letter to Baker, in which he said that relations with General Bliss had been in harmonious understanding of their parts. His own inter-Allied relations now were with Foch and the British and French commanders-in-chief for the prosecution of the war and maintaining the independence of his army.

In his book, General Harbord, who went into the whole subject thoroughly, produces evidence to show that the idea of sending Goethals to France was March's and that Goethals had been actually informed he was to go and made preparations to go. Major General Francis J. Kernan, a scholarly officer with a most distinguished record, had had a long and tiring siege in the SOS. Undoubtedly J.J.P had been diverted by the German offensives from attention to the SOS with the mounting demands upon it by the rapid arrival of our troops. Organization and efficiency had not kept pace with the needs. Various departments, which included those with civil heads, had become compartments in time-wasting controversies.

Brigadier General W. W. Atterbury, in charge of railroad transportation, and other civil chiefs were impatient under General Kernan whom they saw as hidebound in Regular army forms and unappreciative of industrial organization in which they were experienced.

Strengthening his prestige, and in justification of his

judgment, Pershing now had the success of our troops, in their widely heralded advance in closing the Marne salient. His canniness was in full play. He had a strong card to play in the man who had commanded the 2d Division in its drive toward Soissons. When Baker was in France he had met Harbord and formed a high opinion of him. In the Secretary's canvass of a possible successor to Pershing in case "the General should be hit by a shell"—which included no thought of relieving Pershing—the choice was between Harbord and Major General Hunter Liggett, and it was Harbord, owing to his having been the AEF's pioneer Chief of Staff and therefore the best prepared to continue the organization.

J.J.P. sent a hurried message for Harbord to report to GHQ. After the usual greeting he went straight to the point in characteristic fashion. It took a good deal to depress the imperturbable Harbord, but he came out of J.J.P.'s office in the mood of one who had received a numbing blow and was gathering his faculties to stand up under it. As he dropped into a chair in my office, he said:

"Here I had a first-class fighting division. Now see what my General has done to me."

In old army terms, after "serving with troops," it was to the rear for him. He had the prospect of possibly a corps and even an army command, and his General had told him that he was the one to straighten out the Services of Supply, though more in the terms of a request than an order, since J.J.P. recognized the personal sacrifice it meant. He asked Harbord to consider the matter over night. There could be only one decision for Harbord in all loyalty to his chief.

So the fortunes of the two were still more closely linked together. No one understood the workings of Pershing's mind so well as Harbord, and both their minds were now centered on the Services of Supply. Together they would inspect it, length, breadth and depth. The next morning they were at Tours, the headquarters of the SOS. They were meeting all the chiefs of administration to learn the situation in their departments and their difficulties. Each was calling for more under the pressure of the rapid arrival of American troops and the additional demands from our divisions which were in action.

Brigadier General Harry L. Rogers, Chief Quartermaster, had forty-five million rations or ninety millions of tons of supplies in hand and his main trouble was how to get sufficient horses. Brigadier General Meriwether L. Walker, in charge of motor transport, lacked trucks and particularly trained chauffeurs and mechanics. While Brigadier General Charles B. Wheeler, the Chief of Ordnance, had enough powder and explosives, no guns of our own manufacture had yet arrived from America, and we must have more from the Allies if we were to do more extensive fighting this year.

The American saw mills which had been cutting lumber from French forests were working full capacity, said Brigadier General Edgar Jadwin, but production of lumber was insufficient for our construction program. Brigadier General Merritte W. Ireland, the Chief of the Medical Corps, already had 59,000 hospital beds but they would not be enough. Construction of new hospitals must be hastened.

J.J.P. visited a hospital at Tours. Wherever he went he did not miss a glimpse of the hospital administration and a talk with the sick and wounded. And he had time there at Tours for a call on the old *pension* where he and Mrs. Pershing had spent two months in 1908, and he kept on laboring with his French in the region of the château country which insists that it speaks the purest French. He had no time now to visit old châteaux or cathedrals of which he had only a glimpse as he flashed by in his car or train.

Back on his train he bent over the accumulation of important papers on his night desk. He was in telephonic touch with the Chief of Staff at GHQ; hearing from Fox

Conner, Chief of G-3 (operations), that our divisions in the Marne salient had met heavier resistance in the valley of the River Ourcq, but were across it and attacking the heights on the other side.

He refused to spread demands for material and labor by gratifying the Italian request for establishing training centers for our troops in Italy. The expedition to Murmansk in northern Russia, and particularly that to Siberia, had left him far from a receptive mood about further distant ventures. He, Foch, Baker and March had all opposed sending troops to Siberia, but President Wilson had consented to what proved to be an absurd and futile enterprise as a political objective to please Lloyd George.

The next morning he and Harbord were at Bordeaux. He was out on the piers of Bordeaux and Bassens from the railroad yards and the base depot at St. Sulpice. It was anything but a gentle J.J.P. who saw the confusion on the piers. He expressed himself in language as curt and incisive as he ever directed at any combatant commander of a slouchy combat battalion.

However, he was in better mood in his talk with the colored stevedores from Mississippi in their camp in this strange land. They were the most homesick of all the Americans in France and had not been over hurrying in their work. He reminded them that he had served with colored troops and charged with them up San Juan Hill. Later they might have their turn at the front. They spoke to him with the ingratiating candor of their race which is always disarming. Many of them said they would rather go home than any farther into the interior.

They were most important, these stalwart Negro laborers, if we were to shorten the time of ships' turn-around between American and French ports. It was vital to find a way to arouse their *esprit de corps*. Harbord hit upon one that was completely successful. They were organized in competitive teams. The team with the best record was to be the first to return home when the war was over and so on in sequence. Shipmasters became worried lest in the energetic attacks on their cargo the very stanchions in the hold should be torn out.

In a hospital at Bordeaux J.J.P. witnessed very vividly another cost of war than that of industrial strain. Here were the wounded who for the most part would never recover to fight again and were soon to be sent home. Many of those who still live are among the disabled in our hospitals at the time of writing. How much greater might have been their number if it had not been for the Pershing discipline and training and his insistence that our soldiers should not be merged as recruits into the British and French armies! The more efficient the fighting force and the SOS, the fewer disabled we should have.

Pershing proceeded on past the web of railroad tracks and installations we were spreading out over the sandy expanses whence came the Bordeaux wines the grapes ripening for harvest—on to the other port of La Rochelle, where Brigadier General Charles Gerhardt was in command. Here we received our coal and here we had our main storage depot for oil and gasoline and a cement plant nearby. Sixty railroad cars from home were being assembled every day, and all was going well. Then J.J.P. went on to Nantes, to the motor reception park and more base hospitals, and then the next day on to our base section at St. Lazaire. His cavalryman's eye was inspecting the remount station, noticing the condition of the horses and mules after their sea voyage.

Next he was in an American world of experts repairing locomotives and assembling the parts of those which had just arrived. Riding on a flat car he had a view of the two hundred miles of track in an area of two thousand acres with over four thousand square feet of storehouses which we had built. These railroad groups had all the civil efficiency of the troops of his Mexican expedition or his best trained divisions in France. There were no rough words of criticism for them.

Five thousand of the workers in the plant and stevedores gathered in the square and they must have a speech from the Commander-in-Chief. He made one, characteristic in its energy and brevity, which carried the conviction that there was no nonsense about the great boss and that he knew how to win a war.

He saw the training base for incoming engineer casuals, the aerial observation schools and the artillery school at Saumur, another locomotive terminal and repair shop at Rennes, and another coal port at Granville. He passed from the sphere of material transport to that of the troops when he reached Brest where most of them were being disembarked. Here there was gratifying coördination between Brigadier General George H. Harries and Rear Admiral Henry B. Wilson, commanding the naval district, who saw our troops safely through the submarine danger zone and on shore.

J.J.P. thrust his arm into that of Major John J. O'Neil, the chief stevedore, who was a little shy about meeting the Commander-in-Chief, if not as a two-fisted man with a two-fisted job. J.J.P. wanted to know how he had been able to land forty-two thousand troops all by lighters in one day. O'Neil pointed to two officers in shirt sleeves down at the bottom of a lighter. They had done just what he had done to set an example—taken off their Sam Brown belts and shown the men how. This appealed to the plower of Laclede, who, in his first brigade command in the Philippines, when an officer said that he could not cross a stream, had bidden the officer follow him, and he himself swam the stream. When O'Neil said this was how he won his right to wear the uniform, he expressed the secret of military command, which is not in the tabs on the shoulders but in the proven mastery which is the secret of leadership. J.J.P. told that shy captain of stevedores:

"You're just the man I've been looking for, and I'm going to send you to every port we use to show them your secret."

If J.J.P had not already earned the sobriquet of "Pershing, the thorough," he was entitled to it after this trip—entitled to it as the Commander-in-Chief of a great business enterprise. For it was the men of business, the experts, organizers and labor of all kinds from civil life who were the brain, bone and sinew of the SOS.

J.J.P. would miss nothing which would enable him and Harbord to understand the problem in full. He was on from the base sections, to the intermediate sections; to the storage depots of Gièvres; to more hospital centers; the air service training center at Issodun; the motor transport and other repair shops; the center of mobilization for hospital trains; the storehouses and shops for the repair of all ordnance and the relining of worn out guns from the seventy-fives to the one hundred and fifty-fives; and to Blois where officers were classified according to their records and qualifications in the effort to fit round pegs into the round holes.

And, finally, he saw the regulating stations in the front zone, thus connecting up in a pattern the whole supply system, set as clearly now in his mind as the trench wall on the map which was the object of the whole effort.

The principal criticism of the SOS administration up to this time, as Pershing wrote in his own account, "was its lack of coördinating direction, initiative, and driving force." He also wrote: "The real answer, however, was the assignment of Harbord to command the Services of Supply."

And he also wrote: "No further action was taken with reference to the proposed assignment of Goethals. I should have been glad to have him under other conditions."

Thus Secretary Baker achieved the object of his suggestion. J.J.P.'s confidence in Harbord established him in approximately a coördinate capacity strengthened by his understanding as the pioneer Chief of Staff in founding the organization of the whole in its coördination for military ends.

Probably no appointment was more important than this in the history of the AEF. Harbord had the driving force. He carried his own cruse of oil to keep the human machinery running smoothly and bandaged the wounds others had made instead of making more. As the dynamic and tersely direct Atterbury said after leaving Harbord's office on his first call, "Here is a man!"

30

Closing the Marne Salient

"KITTY," "JENNY," "MINNIE," and the others had been doing valiantly well. These were the secret code names by which our divisions in the Marne sector were known. Upon J.J.P.'s return from the SOS, July 29, the Second Battle of the Marne was all but concluded. By this is meant the second one in the World War. The unfordable little stream had many times run red in making French military history.

In 1914 it had been the recovery of the Marne which marked the turn of the German tide in their gigantic effort. In 1918 an American division had stayed the Germans' advance on the Paris road, short of the distance they had gained in 1914, and an American division had checked their crossing in their third and fifth offensives.

Before J.J.P. went south with Harbord he had seen the other divisions initiate the second stage of the Second Battle of the Marne to recover for the second time the ground that had been twice lost in the World War. All the while during his absence in the SOS they had been steadily fighting.

We had had 300,000 men, four times the number which either Meade or Lee had at Gettysburg, engaged in this operation, under our own corps organization commanded by Liggett.

Since the purpose of this narrative centers on the Commander-in-Chief in his direction of the whole, the temptation must be resisted for any detailed accounts of our combat divisions. Most of them have their divisional histories. The complicated tactics of the direction of even a single division of 25,000 men is of itself an intricate technical study. Throughout the one hundred fifty days of fighting to the conclusion of the Armistice. Inevitably some divisions saw more fighting than others. Some, owing to their experience, were bound to be more efficient than others.

In the sense that a chain may be only as strong as its weakest link, the object of the high command, as in all modern armies, was to assure so far as possible an even level of efficiency. To accomplish this a division that seemed to have had particularly sturdy troops might get along with a lower grade of field officers than one which had not quite so good material, or at least as well trained. So the difference was made up frequently by giving the weaker divisions the best available regimental and brigade commanders.

The essential element of competition encouraged each division to think it was the best division in the AEF. Divisional prides were bound to persist in veterans of the AEF as they had in veterans of the Civil War. It will be recalled that so exclusive was the pride of the regiments which answered the second call for the 300,000 volunteers by President Lincoln that they refused to admit any new members to their clubs. They fought on with their depreciated numbers until they were reduced to a quarter or even fewer of their original numbers.

Thus when a commander thought of a regiment as a

regiment in assigning it to the line of battle he had first
to consider just how much length of line it would occupy.
Permissible as this handicap might be in armies the size
of those which fought the battles of the Civil War it was
too great to be allowable in a huge modern army. In the
AEF, as in the French and British armies, we would fill the
gaps left by the dead, wounded and sick by replacements,
so each regiment and the whole division should return
to the front with a full complement of personnel.

If a division came from one part of the country, say New
England or Pennsylvania, Iowa and Kansas, eventually it
might include replacements from every state in the Union,
which was true later in the Battle of the Meuse-Argonne
if not in the Second Battle of the Marne. We can imagine
the outbursts of protests, for example, from the "Iron
Brigade" of Wisconsin in 1863, after it had fought for two
years, at the arrival of Yankees and New Yorkers to bring
it up to its original quota.

It was the whole of even-tempered blades in equally
skillful hands which J.J.P. had firmly in mind as a part of
his plan on the way to his goal; of an AEF which would be
the United States Army in a complete coalition of Regulars. National Guard and the new National Army of the
draft. We were all to be in the same family with no branches
except those of organization.

If there is no singling out of divisions, there is also no
singling out of division commanders, who varied in their
abilities; or if inevitably there is, this is without prejudice.
The name of the division commander in full is included
with the first mention of a division or when it has a new
commander.

We have already had an account of how the 1st Division
(Summerall) and the 2d (Harbord) turned the tide in
that immortal drive toward Soissons; and it is in order to
go back a little and refer to the skillful execution of the
taking of Vaux by the 1st Brigade (Brigadier General Paul

B. Malone) of the 2d Division on the right of the Paris road early in the Château-Thierry operations. We have already seen how the 3d (Dickman) had crossed to Château-Thierry on the north bank of the Marne after its defense of the south bank.

The 28th (Muir) passed through the town getting its first heavy baptism of shell fire and the 3d (Dickman) stormed the heights east of the town. Meanwhile the 26th (Major General Clarence R. Edwards) was off the leash moving across north of Château-Thierry in an enveloping movement to force the German retreat after it had finally taken the formidable Hill 190 beyond Belleau Wood. Twice its charges up the hill had been arrested because the advance was not timed with the tactical plan.

Now we were over the Marne watershed looking down into the valley of the little Ourcq River. At last the 3d, having taken Mont St. Père, Charteves, Jaulgonne and the edge of the Forest de Fère in a brilliant advance, was to have a rest after having had a record breaking two months in the line. The 42d (Menoher) took the place of the exhausted 26th.

After the 42d had conquered Red Cross Farm, its walls impenetrable by bullets, in a fierce little close quarters action and very clever strategy, it was downhill for the 42d to the bank of the Ourcq River,—downhill over open ground exposed to the enemy's machine gun and artillery fire.

There was a lone tree on the descending apron occupied by a German observer who signalled back our dispositions to headquarters. He had partly sawed the tree through with a view to finishing the job quickly for his escape. But he was a target for accurate fire which never allowed him to attend to this little detail of characteristic veteran provision. Such was one of the many instances which kept the reduction of the Marne salient from being anything but a dull, plodding affair.

It required four days of repeated charges to take the vitally strategic point of Meurcy Farm. The Ourcq River, normally little more than a brook, was flooded from heavy rains. That too held us up. But we crossed it, and the 28th bridged it with timbers from ruined villages.

All this was open warfare of the kind an Anthony Wayne would have relished in tactics familiar to our frontiersmen of revolutionary days with their Pennsylvania rifles. And it was against an enemy skillful in covering his forced retreat, making use of every vantage point of ground, of woods, hillocks, ravines, villages, church towers, in placing his machine guns to command deadly fields of fire. In simple language his message was: "We have to go. That's orders and also orders to make you pay a price for all the ground you gain." He made us pay for it with bursts of shell fire from hidden batteries when we were advancing in the open. But our men had the bits in their teeth. It was better to go forward than backward, and forward they went.

Forest de Fère, Grimpettes, Meunières, Planchette, Gomblets and Pelger Woods! The villages of Epieds, Roncheres, Trugny, and Cierges which was the toughest of the lot! We conquered them all.

In place of the 28th, when it had done its turn, had come the 32d (Major General William G. Haan). Originally the 32d was National Guard of Wisconsin and Michigan. It had had bad luck. After its arrival in March it had been made a replacement division, back of the front line drilling replacements for other divisions, sending no fewer than two thousand men to the 1st Division. One regiment had been entirely separated from the 32d for a while. Some of its men had been sent to the SOS as labor troops. Only half of its personnel remained when it was made a temporary combat division.

Sent into quiet trenches in Alsace, it held sixteen miles of front under Haan's sturdy leadership. Word was passed back to GHQ that it took more than the handicaps it had endured to discourage the 32d. It still had lumberjacks and many men of German birth or German descent in its ranks. Neither the lumberjacks nor the farmers' sons came to France for a holiday, but to make a kind of army that the enemy would respect. Since Milwaukee was supposed to have been a hotbed of pro-German sentiment, they were the more determined to teach the Kaiser that he was in the wrong and no friend of theirs.

No division had harder going against stronger positions or heavier fire. When the 32d advanced into Grimpettes Woods, beyond the French division on its right, the Germans struck out of the depths of the big Meunières Woods in flank on troops of the 32d in Grimpettes to be met with bayonets fixed in the dark. It was an affair of darting shadows in encounter in underbrush and around tree trunks. One man might be disclosed to another at only a pace's distance, and between two men meeting it was a question of which made the first thrust.

The outcries of the Germans in the midst of the breaking of twigs and the straining breaths of struggle were mixed with the hot, panting shouts of the Americans, some of whom were using powerful language in both English and German. For a half hour this ugly, terrible, primitive hand-to-hand fighting continued until there were no more of the enemy in Grimpettes Woods except his dead and wounded.

Ahead beyond the village of Sergy, of slight tactical importance itself, were a series of heights with farm buildings that became the ramparts of defense, and with sunken roads, folds, swales, and patches of screening woods, culminating in Hill 230, which gives a view west and north and south for many miles. Such a position might have been chosen for a castle by a feudal baron but it was equally serviceable for machine gun nests. It was for the 32d to take these heights in conjunction with the 42d on its left. At times the men of the two divisions became intermixed.

But what did that matter? They were all in khaki and the enemy was in green.

Often it was a sergeant's fight and again a private's fight in taking a machine gun nest. Individual groups met emergencies. On a little plateau on one of the summits after the fighting was over, ten men of the 32d were lying dead facing ten Germans. All the Americans had their bayonets fixed and one with his bayonet pointing towards the enemy was rigid in the very attitude of charging, his toe dug in the ground just as he had fallen in the assault. Hadn't J.J.P said that all his divisions would fight after they were formed in the right pattern?

Those of German blood had given their answer as Americans, and the tribute to the 32d is paid not only on their account but because if ever a division had to take the hurdles before it got a fair chance to fight, it was the 32d.

After the heights beyond Cierges were conquered it was up the slopes to the crest of the valley of the River Vesle for the 32d which still had the vigour to continue its advance. On its left was still the 42d, which had been longer in line but now, finding the enemy was weakening, sent its engineers in as infantry for its final effort in pursuit. In its place came the 4th (Major General George H. Cameron), which had had a rest after stiff fighting with the Fench as its part in the drive of July 18 toward Soissons.

The 4th and the 32d fought their way up the slopes in ceaseless attacks, under heavy artillery and machine gun fire, until they reached the crest and looked down on the Vesle River, and then fought fiercely for the possession of its south bank. The 32d, in hand-to-hand fighting, took Fismes, not a village but a town. The rested 28th, now of hardened veteran experience, took the place of the 32d, and the 77th (Major General George B. Duncan) that of the 4th. They were occupying hastily made trenches face to face with the Germans and looking ahead to the famous Aisne River with its four years of bloody memories.

But we had not all the north bank of the Vesle yet. A company of the 28th charged in the night across a broken bridge and took the village of Fismette. Isolated by day, well entrenched, it met machine gun fire and sniping in kind; and at night, it received reliefs and food across the broken bridge under incessant fire. Thus the men of the Pennsylvania National Guard were again making good.

On their left was the 77th, the first draft division to go into an active sector, largely composed of New York City men. It had been much advertised, not to say favored, as the "melting pot" division. It had excellent officers, many of them Plattsburg graduates. Now they were under the test of the fire that crucibles require—the old test of facing sudden death, of suffering pain from wounds, and of submitting self to superior orders and to the will of destiny.

There, below the heights in the "Hell's Kitchen" of the Château Diable, men who had known only city lives and city streets, many of them foreign born who spoke only a little English were knowing the battle test. If they had not the physique of a Michigan lumberjack or an Iowa farmer in carrying trench mortars up to the front, the Pershing pattern of training had bred the American spirit into them, and in many instances, good food and army exercise had developed puniness into robustness with surprising rapidity.

Both the 28th and the 77th, in their little outposts across the river and along the railroad tracks, and in the woods and ravines, had to wear their gas masks for ten and twelve hours on end. Their persistence served its part, in aiding the powerful offensive of the French under Mangin in retaking Soissons, conquering the heights beyond and compelling the Germans to retreat to the Aisne with both the 28th and 77th in pursuit.

The second battle of the Marne was over for the Americans who had paid the price of 50,000 casualties, of which the 3d Division alone suffered six thousand.

31

Now for St. Mihiel

THAT "BALLOON," in the Allied lines, as J.J.P. had called it in defiant indignation, had been pricked, and its "insult" avenged. The Marne salient was closed.

"We did it," he said as he looked at the wall map in his office. "I knew we would. We have seen the enemy's heels. We shall keep him moving."

He had another cause for rejoicing. The War Department had confirmed his proposal that the Regulars, National Guard, and the National Army of draft men should hereafter be known as the Army of the United States of America in France. It was amalgamated as a whole without distinction of the origin of divisional units.

With the arrival of 300,000 troops from America in a single month and the plans for following up the American successes in the Marne salient, J.J.P. was busier than ever, though authority had been more and more delegated in the rapid spread of his organization. Our divisions were scattered either in the front line or in training all the way from Flanders to Switzerland.

"J.J.P.'s here," the word was passed when he returned from one of his more frequent and still speedier trips. There were well-known signs signifying his presence. The car with the four-star pennant was in front of the main entrance.

An orderly was at the little table in the hall beside the door which bore the name, "General Pershing." In the ante-room were waiting major generals and brigadier generals and those of lesser rank for whom he had sent. We also knew of his presence by something electric that ran through the offices, the vitalizing impulse of the Commander-in-Chief.

"Another hectic day," the staff sections were saying on the evening after his return. He went about distributing hectic days. It was he who said, "Stop!" or "Full speed ahead!"

With "make good" the test for everyone, with ambition driving everyone to the utmost endeavor, with the desire for power and for approval always beseeching the straight figure at the desk between the two windows, who had the authority of making and unmaking careers, he could have only one thought, which was to find the best agents to carry out his plans by the continuing tests and processes of elimination.

J.J.P. was deciding on more than the matter in hand; he was keeping watch of the human element. Was this sub-ordinate getting stale? Was he beginning to show nerves? Was he becoming greedy for authority's sake? Sometimes J.J.P. reached down through the channels of administra-tion and took up a seemingly small problem which only he thought vital until later events proved its significance.

A telephone call might bring an officer in front of his desk to answer the question, "What about this? It hasn't been done yet." A section or departmental chief might bring him a carefully prepared paper for his signature which J.J.P. approved in its main features, but with the direction to rewrite it and possibly to have the amended version ready in an hour. Again a chief might emerge from the office saying, "J.J.P. does not understand. I couldn't get any action out of him at all." This eager officer saw the fate of the nation depending upon the immediate adoption of his suggestion, which J.J.P. had concluded could wait pending some other development related to it. At the next session the same chief might emerge saying, "J.J.P. was quick on the trigger today. Approved everything. Now we fly!"

J.J.P.'s "Make it brief and clear" became more mandatory. "Cut this down and we'll make it an order."—"A good idea! Work it up into an order and let me see it."—"Reads well in theory, but will not work out in practice."—"That will carry us on for the present."—"Use your judgment and plenty of it, quick!"—"You were right. We went ahead too strong on that."—"I was thinking along these lines last night. Mull it over yourself and tell me how it strikes you tomorrow."

"J.J.P. had called for his car," and he was gone in body from GHQ but not in spirit, for wherever he went in his car couriers followed him with important papers.

After the closing of the Marne salient and the immense success of the British attack on August 8, which advanced six miles in a single day, he was off to see Marshal Foch, August 9, to propose that the time was now ripe for the American Army's attack on the St. Mihiel salient. In the glow of the good news Foch was receiving he acquiesced at once. J.J.P. hastened on to confer with General Pétain who was equally receptive in his discussion of arrangements.

And the next day J.J.P. was consulting with Liggett, Commander of the First Corps, which had finished its task in the Marne sector, about the transfer from the Marne sector and establishing the newly organized First Army, as the superior of the corps, in our own Lorraine sector, to direct the coming St. Mihiel operation.

Next in order was a conference with Haig, the British commander, about the release of more of our divisions in training with the British for our own sector. But Haig, in his preparation for continuing his own offensive, was just as covetous as in an emergency against a German offensive; and the more so, since in the action, August 8, a regiment of our 33d Division (Major General George Bell, Jr.), attached to a British division, had fought most intrepidly, suffering many casualties in advancing three miles.

King George V, who was on a tour of the British front, decorated soldiers of the regiment who had shown particular gallantry and also knighted J.J.P with the Grand Cross of the Order of the Bath, which entitled him to be called Sir John. It was not for the King, in his constitutional limitations, to make any political suggestions, as he remarked, but the thought of two English speaking peoples fighting together appealed to him, and it did occur to him that the French port of Dunkerque might be placed at our disposal for the debarkation of our troops.

Haig made the point that just as our divisions were becoming useful he was expected to part with them. J.J.P. had to remind him again about the agreement that they should be restored to our army once the crises of the German offensives was over, and that the common end of fighting a common enemy was best served by an independent American army.

Haig was not the one to deny a pledged word. He said: "Of course you shall have them. There can never be any difference between us."

Clemenceau, when J.J.P. saw him, after Clemenceau had heard the result of the visit to British headquarters, was in a most agreeable mood. The old "Tiger" fairly purred, as he could on occasion, most ingratiatingly. He generously admitted that Pershing had been right, he himself had been wrong, and he was now in favor of the Americans henceforth operating separately as an American army.

However, up his sleeve, the French Premier had a dagger for one of those thrusts at Lloyd George which seemed to give him both personal and patriotic satisfaction. It was a message he had received from the British Prime Minister stressing his appeal that a few American divisions should be retained with the British. Lloyd George made the point that a large part of the American troops in France had been brought over by British shipping. They might be required in another crisis. He said: "We are informed that a serious attack on the British front is still probable now."

Where he received this information was not divulged, certainly not from Haig who was now on the offensive. But Lloyd George had a most resourceful facility in providing information which suited his purpose. He could exaggerate the number of enemy divisions and their aggressive power at will. Ever blissfully unconscious of his inconsistencies, the British prime minister, who had strongly criticized Haig for his caution, now became alarmed lest Haig should be over confident in his recent successes and expose himself to a disastrous powerful counter-attack. Haig himself, after his prolonged ordeal, was convinced that attrition had done its work in softening the enemy and he was determined to continue offensive action.

Even Foch was disturbed about Haig's daring until results proved Haig was right. Sharing Haig's view, J.J.P. pressed his preparation for the St. Mihiel offensive after its confirmation by Foch and Pétain. Having earned the right in battle for our independent army to fight a great battle as an army, it seemed that it would be only a question of weeks before all our scattered divisions should be in the fold.

On a flat map, without contours, the St. Mihiel salient might appear to the lay eye as another "balloon," which had remained for four years as an "insult" to the French army. Its right on the bank of the Moselle, its deepest point surrounding the town of St. Mihiel, it was protected by heights which had a plunging fire. The French high command had concluded that these were conquerable only by a powerful force and at a cost which it could ill afford in view of its responsibilities elsewhere. Sentiment for the possession of the old city had been outweighed by realities.

St. Mihiel was in our sector, and the closing of the salient was the first step on the way to the goal of the plan J.J.P. had made after our arrival in Paris. It was not tenable under strong pressure striking from either side. We were to drive with seven divisions resting on the bank of the Moselle River against the southern side of the salient and two of our divisions were to coöperate with the French on the western side. In numbers we were to have three to one compared to the French, all under Pershing as commander of our First Army.

In all more than 500,000 men in front line, reserve and supply were to be concentrated in the St. Mihiel sector which had been limited for nearly four years to the installations limited to the defensive. This meant stretching many miles of telephone and telegraph lines, providing material ready to build roads across No-Man's Land after the advance, the laying of light railways which were transported in sections, the leveling of fields for aviation and establishing dumps for 3,300,000 rounds of artillery ammunition.

And these items were only a few of the requirements after our line of communications had been switched from supplying our troops in the second battle of the Marne. The troops themselves must be moved by truck and train before they marched up to the front line trenches to take over for their "jump off." Billets must be provided and camouflage to screen them by day after their movement under the cover of darkness. Traffic control to avoid inevitable congestion and confusion must be carefully regulated.

Our divisions having proved how well they would fight, our First Corps having proved that it could handle a corps organization, now we had to prove that we were equal to an independent army organization in battle.

In a talk with Foch, August 24, Pershing found him still in a favorable mood, but Foch would be unable to keep the promise to supply us with heavy tanks which he had made a month ago. This meant we should need more artillery to cut the barbed wire, and Foch assured Pershing that we should have all the French could spare. But Foch had decided that since Haig needed them in the attacks he had in view, our 27th (Major General John F. O'Ryan) and the 30th (Major General Edward M. Lewis), in our Second Corps (Major General George W. Read), were to remain with the British.

Haig's request to Foch, if not to Pershing, had succeeded. Foch was disappointed to learn that our War Department had confirmed the 80- but not the 100-division program. After extensive studies it had concluded that all the power of America, now in the full tide of its possible energy, would be incapable of maintaining more than four million men across three thousand miles of sea. Marshal Foch, who had received his Marshal's baton for the closing of the Marne salient, said the British were tired and the French exhausted and only by hastening the larger program could we be sure of winning the war in 1919. Neither he nor Pershing yet envisioned the possibility of victory in 1918.

Pershing looked forward to St. Mihiel as a battle with his own army in the autumn which would supply valuable lessons for training and reorganization in preparation for the decisive blows he should initiate in the spring. He and Foch were agreed in pressing for eighty divisions by April, 1919, and one hundred by July. Pershing hardly expected that he should ever have one hundred divisions, but he followed the precedent of commanders in the field that the more he asked for the more he would get. Secretary

Baker would soon arrive on a second visit to France, and J.J.P. suggested it would be best to let the subject wait for his consideration.

Convinced that he was all set with Foch's approval, J.J.P. concluded the final arrangements with Pétain for French coöperation in the attack. Now when he called for his car at Chaumont it was to go to his battle headquarters in the little town of Ligny-en-Barrois. There the old French general, in formally turning over the command of the St. Mihiel sector, presented him with two large volumes of a total of three hundred pages on his offensive and defensive plans. Pershing's own plan consisted of fourteen pages. At that he was concerned, in his devotion to brevity, lest it was unnecessarily long.

32

His Answer to Foch

Now, FREE from interruptions, J.J.P. thought he could devote all of his time and energy to the preparations for the St. Mihiel battle and its conduct, only to receive a call August 30, from Marshal Foch and Weygand who burst a bombshell out of the blue. Foch had quite changed his plans. By this time the actions of the last few days had convinced him of the wisdom of allowing the British to continue their attack toward Cambrai and St. Quentin and the French toward Mesnil.

He had found the enemy was more disorganized than he had realized and therefore he would restrict the St. Mihiel operation and turn the Americans westward to have a part in two other operations. The French Second Army, with a few American divisions, would attack between the Meuse River and the Argonne Forest. Beyond that from the Argonne to the Souain Road, an American Army would advance on either side of the Aisne under the French Fourth Army. The sum of this was that our army would lose its independence by being divided under French command. J.J.P. should have to give up his original plan and his goal.

Foch tried to be tactful at the start, asking for his impressions. J.J.P. protested, after all his preparations, that for him to strike for only a limited objective, once he was through the trench lines of the St. Mihiel salient and had the Germans on the move, would entail little more cost than to proceed according to the original plan.

"Marshal Foch," he said, "on the very day that you turn over a sector to the American Army, and almost on the eve of the offensive, you ask me to reduce the operation so that you can take away several of my divisions and assign some to the French Second Army and use others to form an American Army to operate on the Aisne in conjunction with the French Fourth Army, leaving me with little to do except hold what will become a quiet sector after the St. Mihiel offensive. This virtually destroys the American Army that we have been trying so long to form."

Foch persisted that he had sought in vain how not to divide the American Army, but found no other way. Pershing inquired why he should not bring together his scattered divisions and put them with their right on the River Meuse? Foch preferred to relieve our divisions after the St. Mihiel battle by tired French troops and send these divisions into an offensive elsewhere, and possibly another American Army might be formed of which Pershing could take command.

Moreover, Foch wanted American divisions sent to the Aisne sector from which we had been withdrawing while the St. Mihiel preparations were proceeding. He would attack at St. Mihiel only on one side of the salient, which might have meant an unsuccessful sacrifice, forgetting that only a month ago he had favored the clearing of the salient to enable us to reach the Briey Basin and spread our action between the Meuse and the Moselle Rivers.

Foch further argued that on the Aisne our troops would be under our old companion in arms, General Degoutte. We had had previous experiences with Degoutte in the Château-Thierry operations. There was no objection to his vanity and his ambition, but he had subjected our troops to unnecessary sacrifice by some pretty bad generalship which we did not care to repeat. Moreover, the position assigned us on the Aisne put the brunt of the action on us in impracticable terrain, as J.J.P. recognized at once. If Foch always had his Weygand at his elbow, with the picture of the map thoroughly in mind, J.J.P. had his Fox Conner.

As it was impossible for so convinced a Frenchman as Foch to cease to be a Frenchman even for a moment, the Generalissimo was possibly unconscious of two motives in this extraordinary reversal of his plans.

One was not only the morale value but the fighting value of the association of our divisions with the French. French commanders were competing with Haig for American divisions. There were even requests that a single regiment might be seen on the march back of the French lines even if it might not be put in the trenches. And already while this conference was proceeding between Foch and Pershing, the 32d Division (Haan), that doughty former replacement division, after it had a little rest for its part in closing the Marne salient, was with Mangin's army attacking fiercely in the capture of the town of Juvigny in an advance of more than three miles.

The other motive was a political one. There was evidence that Foch and the French government both disliked the prospect of a huge integral American Army actually outnumbering the French under American command on French soil. Finally, all the dispositions Foch proposed placed the main burden on the British and American Armies.

When he pressed the importance of the time factor to

make the most of the enemy's present discomfiture, the obvious answer was that very much more time would be lost by moving our divisions in concert with the new plan than holding them where they were as they were about to go into battle position. For more than a month our Services of Supply had been directing their operations toward the St. Mihiel sector. Harbord had so speeded up action in the SOS that now we were able to clear twenty-five thousand tons of freight a day from the piers, but we were only receiving sixteen thousand. This was not enough to meet the demand when we already had 1,300,000 men in France. Twenty of our base hospitals had arrived without their equipment. We lacked sufficient motor trucks and all manner of material in addition to the fact that we were barely keeping up with the food demands, and in danger of dipping into our reserves.

However, it might be taken for granted out of previous experience that supply did not interest Foch. He was ever thinking only in terms of the movement of divisions on the battle map, without much consideration not only as to how they were to be supplied but how they were actually to reach the front. Yet he was not quite so oblivious of this essential in war that he did not remind Pershing of our lack of artillery except that supplied by the French, which was owing to his importunate insistence that we send over only infantry and machine gunners.

Beyond all these considerations his proposal was in conflict with all the immemorial principles of strategy. After four years' talk by pessimists that the solid trench line from Switzerland to the North Sea allowed no opportunity for a flanking movement, since every offensive must be a frontal attack, he was actually proposing practically a frontal attack when at last the American Army was in position for the very flanking operation of Pershing's original plan.

While Foch would concentrate his pressure in western France we would concentrate to cut the railroad lines which supplied the German armies in western France. Possibly it has been the history of war that generals are inclined to follow the precedents of the successes which won their renown. Foch's had been won in his brilliant operations in Champagne in the first Battle of the Marne in 1914. He would follow the same tactics now as then in a frontal grapple when his divisions were at hand for his tactical dispositions in open warfare of pitched battle, before the trench systems were established.

Pershing told Foch, and very stiffly, that every time we were started to complete our army organization we had been interrupted by a new proposal. Once more he reminded Foch that the American people and government, more than ever, now that the Allies had the Germans on the move, would not want their army dispersed. However, J.J.P. might be considered as only crying "wolf" again, when the censorship must inevitably preserve secrecy until the war was won.

"Do you wish to take part in the battle?" Foch asked.

"Most assuredly," J.J.P. said, "but as an American Army and in no other way."

"There will not be time," Foch countered.

"If you will assign me a sector I will take it at once," Pershing agreed.

"Where would it be?" Foch asked.

"Wherever you say," Pershing replied.

Pershing was ready to operate east of the Meuse River or to have two American Armies, one east and one west of the Argonne Forest, or he would extend his present front to include the sector between the Meuse and the Argonne as Foch had suggested. But Foch now repudiated his own idea on the plea of lack of time. He still insisted upon dividing the American Army under French command. Never had the Generalissimo and Pershing been nearer at swords' points. Pershing was thoroughly aroused, his jaw hard set,

"Marshal Foch," he said, "you have no authority as an

Allied Commander-in-Chief to call upon me to yield up my command of the American Army and have it scattered among the Allied forces where it will not be an American Army at all."

"I must insist upon the arrangement," Foch concluded. They both rose to their feet as Pershing concluded:

'Marshal Foch, you may insist all you please, but I decline absolutely to agree to your plan. While our army will fight wherever you may decide it will not fight except as an independent American Army."

Finally, he reminded Foch of his promises and of President Wilson's decision. And Foch, before picking up his map and papers and retiring, "very pale and apparently exhausted," said in the doorway, as he handed Pershing his proposal, that he thought that further study would lead Pershing to agree with his conclusion.

There was another reason why Pershing did not want his troops to pass under French command. He had seen the neglect of the wounded under French hospitalization. This he mentioned very definitely in his formal answer to Foch written the next day, in which his opinion was unchanged and fortified. In that very masterful presentation he expressed his determination, after all the preparations had been made, to hold his divisions for the St. Mihiel operation. He concluded:

"In your capacity as Allied Commander-in-Chief it is your province to decide as to the strategy of operations and I abide by your decisions." But the American divisions must not be dispersed among the Allied armies. "If you decide to utilize American forces in attacking in the direction of Mézières I accept that decision even though it complicates my supply system and the care of the sick and wounded, but I do insist that the American Army must be employed as a whole either east of the Argonne or west of the Argonne and not four or five divisions here and six or seven there."

Pershing then discussed the situation with Pétain, the French commander, who agreed with his view. After receiving Pershing's letter Foch asked both Pershing and Pétain to join him in council. Again J.J.P. said he would restrict or even give up the St. Mihiel operation, mistaken as this was, and transfer his army to any sector Foch chose, but it must be as a separate army under his command.

Pétain favored striking on both sides of the salient, both as an important military objective and for the lift of the morale of both the American and French armies. Foch's conclusion was for the St. Mihiel offensive, striking at both sides of the salient, with the limited objective, and that meanwhile another American Army should be immediately mobilized to strike between the Meuse and the Argonne Forest, and this by September 15th.

In other words, before the St. Mihiel operation was concluded by one American Army, another, which would be more extensive, was to be launched. Therefore Pershing would be unable to utilize any division which was in the St. Mihiel to initiate the Meuse-Argonne drives. Available railroads, roads, rolling stock and trucks did not permit two such immense mobilizations at the same time, not to mention the handicap of divisions with no combat experience, and in some instances without even quiet trench experience, being sent against strong defenses in the Meuse-Argonne.

However, Pershing's objection was related only to the time factor. He agreed to have his divisions in line from the Argonne Forest to the Meuse River to attack on September 25. In twenty-four days beginning fourteen days before the St. Mihiel battle began he must concentrate 600,000 men and 2700 guns with 1,000,000 tons of supplies for a still greater operation. He had accepted a mighty challenge, but, as he wrote, it was a relief to have a decision.

33

St. Mihiel

FORTUNATELY HE HAD not allowed Foch's change of mind to interfere with the progress of the St. Mihiel mobilization plans. Previously no more than two of our divisions had ever fought side by side in any operation. A single division, or two divisions, had been in line between French divisions.

Now seven American divisions were to form line on the southern side of the salient. We were thinking not only in terms of divisions and corps, with corps reserves, but of an army over the corps, with army reserves. Major General Hunter Liggett commanded the First Corps and Major General Joseph D. Dickman commanded the Fourth Corps under Pershing as commander of the First Army.

Our original training area had been expanded over a far larger area where now one saw only American troops. Our veteran divisions as well as our young divisions were being trained for the new task. Divisions and their transport, with their guns, ambulances, motor trucks, and wagons, which had been streams in the French army, were flowing into a common reservoir. The throbbing pulse of the Services of Supply was felt running along the railroads from the ports to the rail heads and on up to the front.

Had we really grown this great from that little start in the Rue Constantine, Paris, fourteen months ago? Had our own and Allied shipping been able to bring all this force, human, mechanical and material, across the Atlantic in face of the submarine?

All that our officers had learned in the schools for staff organization, which J.J.P. had established, were now to be applied in practice in a huge organization. The preliminary studies of the staffs, from brigade and division on through corps and to Brigadier General Hugh A. Drum, the Chief of Staff of the First Army, were to have their real test.

In this impressive assembly of men and material we had a family reunion of members who had been separated. Responsibility for the immense enterprise, ambition, patriotism and the magnetic influence of being a part of this American whole, all gave impetus to our industry. Where old armies, weary of fighting, might become stale and possibly careless about details, it was for us to neglect no detail in the book. Our shortcomings must not be due to negligence.

Every private, every non-commissioned officer, every young lieutenant who played errand boy for a colonel; every reserve officer who directed traffic at a rail head or an ambulance section; every engineer, military policeman, surgeon, sanitary corps man, aviator and balloonist, was trying to keep everything he ought to do in mind and do it exactly according to directions.

Sometimes the directions were confusing; sometimes they did not work out. When they did not, initiative and improvisation came into play. Sleep did not matter; nothing mattered except to perform your own little part as an atom of the First American Army which was about to go into its first action. And J.J.P. was seen passing in his car as he went from headquarters to headquarters in his own indefatigable rounds.

Our map printing establishment had supplied the map directives for each platoon's part on through companies, battalion, divisions and corps. Everyone in his objective earnestness became subjective in the fear that he might be responsible for some vital mistake. What if we should run short of ammunition? If the engineers failed to make roads for the artillery? If the planes did not do their part? If the tanks did not come up to expectation? But back of this professional questioning was the confidence that we should be master of the enemy.

Cantigny and the Marne salient had apprised the Germans of our quality and our system. "We must reckon with America's strength and numbers said an editorial in the German paper, *Taglische Rundschau.* "We shall see soon in what form they intend to participate . . . As Americans pay strict attention to clock-like working of their machine, we must expect them to take their time while making minute studies and preparations for their attack."

This was true. We were meeting German thoroughness with Pershing thoroughness. As an example of our preparations for prompt communication of information and orders, the central telephone switchboard at Ligny-en-Barrois had thirty-eight circuits; our medical corps had 65 evacuation trains ready to care for casualties. We had actually built 250 miles of light railways behind the front, built a bridge 200 feet long, used 100,000 tons of rock in the repair of roads, and insured 1,200,000 gallons of water a day for our forces in the operation.

Once Foch, and especially General Pétain, were committed to attack, they gave us all available backing in guns and in tanks. Haig sent a much-needed bombing squadron in addition to the French planes to reinforce our own. For the Allies were still skeptical of our effectiveness as an army in spite of the record of our divisions.

An American success was essentially vital to spur the Allies on when they were taking the offensive and to depress the Germans when they were breaking as a further example of what might be expected of the huge flow of our troops across the Atlantic. Moreover, for the first time Pershing could consider the possibility that if we could strike hard enough blows in the next two months we might end the war without having to pass through another winter to make sure of the decision in 1919.

No officer or man who was sent to the St. Mihiel sector was supposed to say where he was going, or if he were sent away from the sector to say where he had been. We were having our first mass lesson in military secrecy. On the eve of our mobilization at St. Mihiel, J.J.P., as a diversion, had sent Major General Omar Bundy, commander of the Sixth Corps, as yet not formed, with a limited staff and instructions to give the impression that we were about to attack toward Mulhouse.

Colonel A. L. Conger, the battle order expert of G-2, left a copy of actually formulated instructions for this offensive on his desk in a hotel, which disappeared, presumably into the hands of a German spy. Anyhow, the Germans sent a reserve division into the sector. But as the mobilization of such an immense force proceeded there was no keeping the secret from the Germans.

The French and American troops were under American command. It was J.J.P.'s army, responsibility, and operation. Facing the heights of the tip of the western face of the salient were the French divisions which were not expected to scale and conquer the heights by immediate direct assault, but to wait on our attack on the southern side to ease the French advance by forcing the withdrawal from the heights of the Germans in danger of being cut off if they delayed their withdrawal. Farther north our 26th (Edwards) was to drive toward Vigneulles in its part in pinching out the salient, with our 4th (Cameron) in reserve.

Our main force on the southern face had its right, the 82d Division (Major General William P. Burnham) on the Moselle River. Then in line were the 90th (Major General Henry T. Allen), the 5th (Major General John E. McMahon), the 2d (Major General John A. Lejeune), the 89th (Major General William M. Wright), the 42d (Major General Charles T. Menoher), and the 1st (Major General Charles P. Summerall), covering a distance of about sixteen miles. They were to swing to the left to meet the 26th in the pinching movement.

The 1st, 2d, 26th and 42d were veteran. But the 5th, 82d, 89th and 90th Divisions were to know their first serious combat action. However, the 90th was in command of Allen and the 89th of Wright, who were to lead them with wisdom and initiative to the end of the war.

Reserves were the 78th (Major General James H. Mc-Rae), the 3d (Major General Beaumont Buck), the 4th (Major General John L. Hines), the 35th (Major General Peter E. Traub), the 80th (Major General Adelbert Cronkhite) and the 91st (Major General John A. Johnston).

The seven attacking divisions on the southern face, including the inexperienced, had a difficult maneuver in having to make a change in direction of sixty degrees. J.J.P. delayed the eventual employment into the line as far as possible until the night before the attack to prevent the enemy taking prisoners for information. He had decided on the later practice of a brief artillery preparation instead of prolonged bombardment.

On the night of September 11 all was ready so far as he could make it. In common with the army and corps staffs he must wait for the results of the morrow which rested with the valor and skill of the troops before he could further direct the action. There was another detail which was most important, in assigning a place where Secretary Baker, who was in France again, might have such a view of the battle as it could afford.

The seven divisions on the southern face were to go over the top at five A. M. while the French and our 26th Division on the western face were to wait their attack for three hours. Fortuitously, as it turned out, the Germans were already preparing in face of our mobilization, to withdraw from the salient, and we caught them just before withdrawal was beginning.

J.J.P. himself was at Old Fort Gironville waiting for the zero hour as he looked out, in the midst of the deafening roar, on the sharp flashes from gun mouths and the spreading flashes of the line of bursting shells into the enemy trenches and fields of barbed wire in front of them. Those fields were very deep, long set for the protection of the salient. The dawn broke in a heavy mist blanketing observation but also screening the movement of our troops. J.J.P. could follow their advance, however, with that of the shell bursts of the protective wall of their barrage.

They were through the barbed wire and were proceeding according to plan when he started back to his battle headquarters. On the way he passed groups of German prisoners who were already being brought in. All the reports he received assured him that on the southern face we were up with our objectives on time or even beyond them. By the afternoon he had heard that the roads between the two attacks were congested with the retreating enemy, his artillery and trains, in haste to escape having their retreat cut off.

Now he was on the telephone himself in most urgent mood, bidding corps and division commanders to speed on beyond their first day's objectives. On the flank of the southern face our 26th Division, operating with the French, with a long distance to go, had been slowed up. J.J.P. ordered that the regiment in reserve should immediately be put in and that they must reach Vigneulles. At the same time he sent a regiment of our 80th Division in reserve to the aid of the French.

Before dawn of the next morning troops from the two flanks had met at Vigneulles and the salient was closed. In difficult maneuvers by the sheer persistence of their attacks most of the divisions on the southern face had already reached their second objectives. Two days more they continued their attacks in cooperation with the French until our line stretched from Haudiomont, where the 4th Division had been brought into action to straighten it, more than thirty miles to the Moselle River.

Not all of the Germans had escaped. We had taken 16,000 prisoners and 450 enemy guns, and recovered 200 square miles of French soil. The Paris-Nancy railroad was freed, and this would be an aid in our transport of troops and supplies to the Meuse-Argonne.

"We ought to have that mountain," J.J.P. had said in the Valley Forge winter of 1917-1918 when our pioneer divisions were under the plunging fire of Montsec in what had been called our "old home sector." Now Montsec was ours and all the other heights and ravines and forests and countless acres of barbed wire, the gun positions, the shell-torn areas and all the enemy's defenses. And our cost had been only seven thousand casualties, fewer than half of the number of prisoners we had taken.

It was a relatively easy and highly spectacular triumph that of our first offensive as an American Army, thrilling our people at home and all the Allies. In the old town of St. Mihiel there was an unforgettable scene, after its delivery on the 13th, around an American Commander-in-Chief and a Secretary of War. The happy people had flocked around the Hotel de Ville. They had brought their children.

All had heard of "Général Pershaing." Here he was himself. They had heard, too, of President "Voodrow Veelson," but not of the little man, the Secretary of War. However, they would know more about him the next day when for the first time in four years they should receive their Paris newspapers. And there were not only the emancipated French who had had to do manual labor in aiding the enemy to make war on them. There were also Belgian prisoners who had been transferred to this sector as laborers. Now they too were free.

Lafayette, we were very much here! Baker was with Colonel de Chambrun when their car drew up before the seat of Chambrun's ancestor, the young adventurer who had been Washington's aide in the Revolution. Baker paused at the door, thinking that, on an occasion so touching and intimate, his companion would prefer to be alone as he noted what damage had been done by the enemy's occupation.

Many things were missing and the interior furnishings in a good deal of confusion. When Chambrun came out he brought a steel engraving of the Marquis de Lafayette as a present for Baker, which was one of the few offered him during the war which he thought he was warranted in accepting.

President Poincaré, accompanied by Madame Poincaré, returned to their home town of St. Mihiel and crossed the threshold of their own house for the first time in four years. In his elation and eagerness. Poincaré managed to get Colonel Boyd to conduct him over the conquered ground as far as Thiaucourt, whereon Premier Clemenceau, who had also wanted to drive on to the front, but who had been dissuaded by J.J.P.'s objection that it was too risky and impracticable, became rather envious of the President of the Republic and thought that General Pershing had not played fair.

The people also saw Pétain of "they shall not pass" who came in person to offer his congratulations to the victorious J.J.P., while Haig and President Wilson sent theirs by wire among the flood that came to him.

"I note one from a specialist as a congratulator of win-ners," said J.J.P. with a knowing smile in referring to a certain courtier who never missed a chance to curry favor with the great. "He has spent a good deal of money on cables of congratulation since Château-Thierry. But I had no encouragement from him before that. Indeed, in the early days, I think he was in favor of leaving our troops to the expert command of the French."

America had risen very much in Allied estimation. De-spite the fact that the German withdrawal had favored the signal success of our operation, Pétain was most interested in the rapidity and ease with which our troops had passed through the barbed wire. We had not only depended upon the artillery and upon tanks, of which we had only sufficient light ones, to destroy the barbed wire, but teams of pioneers and engineers had opened gaps with wire cutters and axes and with bangalore torpedoes, which were long tin or sheet iron tubes containing high explosive.

Now, instead of our being entirely pupils of the French, Pétain sent French officers and non-commissioned officers to study our methods. Included in the report of one officer was a reference to the advantage of Americans over French-men in having long legs and large feet.

Meanwhile J.J.P.'s own concentration was concerned in not repeating any mistakes our staff had made at St. Mihiel and being able to apply all the lessons for better coördinate action in the battle before him. He was distributing praise and also criticism. He had not ceased to live up to the old description of him as being tough but fair. When one division commander had complained to him that his men were too tired to proceed, J.J.P. replied:

"I've had a look at your men. I think it is you that is tired and not the men."

This commander was to be relieved for a berth in which fatigue would enable them to sit in a softer seat. But, to another division commander, J.J.P. said:

"Great! Great! You kept on and used your head. It is time your men had a rest and I shall see they have it very soon."

From the rocky promontory of Hattonchâtel, with the congeries of conquered heights behind him, he could look out on the great plain of the Woëvre, almost as level as a calm sea, toward the fortress of Metz, whose approaches he had studied during his previous sojourn in France. There was the goal of his original plan, but he must hold his present line, stonewalling while his main striking force was to be concentrated on another objective.

34

Against Terrific Odds

J.J.P. Had a new battle headquarters at Souilly on the road from Bar-le-Duc to Verdun. His office was in the little corner room of the *Mairie* (town hall and school house) whence Pétain had directed his divisions to keep faith with his phrase, "They shall not pass," and later Nivelle had planned the recovery of Fort Douaumont. Here the man from Laclede was to direct that prolonged siege battle of the Meuse-Argonne into which we were to send more than a million men.

Through the succeeding years until the present writing there still lingers in some uninformed minds the idea that Pershing, by his ruthless driving, submitted our army to a needless sacrifice. This was a view which was circulated by the French, mostly by those in Paris, to be spread among Franco-Americans, and thence home on the sometimes fertile ground of officers and soldiers who had cruel memories of what they had had to endure. The truth, as recognized by experts, not only our own but Allied, was that the losses in ratio to the obstacles overcome, often with little-trained troops, was no less than an immortal achievement both in skill and gallantry.

To describe this siege battle in the action of units from platoons to divisions and corps which had their significant parts in the whole,—even to describe their high moments in the long, vast, evermoving panorama,—would be equivalent and more to describing all the battles of the Civil War in tactical detail. Modern warfare becomes so complex in the play of numbers and weapons that it is restricted as a study to staff schools and war colleges.

As the commander of our First Army, Pershing was forming his line for his offensive in a sector south of the heights of Verdun on the east to the western edge of the Argonne Forest in the west.

Let us look first at the Argonne Forest, with its trees and undergrowth, which invading armies had considered impracticable of attack through all history. In the days of small armies they passed around it on their way to the Marne and Paris. For modern war it was a great natural fortification. Below its irregular rocky slopes on the east side toward Verdun ran the irregular river Aire which was fordable only in places. Its valley, on account of its winding course, afforded perfect positions for direct fire around bends of the river bottom and plunging fire from the heights on both sides.

The main part of the battlefield extended between the Aire and the unfordable Meuse River at the base of the Verdun heights. Rising from the front of the four-year-old trench line, from which we were to attack, was a great whale back, insuring uphill labor against irregular ridges, ravines, hillocks and woods The French had never considered an offensive between the Meuse and the Argonne. The Verdun forts were their defense, and the object of the German drive against Verdun in February, 1916, was to conquer the Verdun heights, to open the way, by flanking the Meuse-Argonne sector, to the more favorable approach toward central France. Be it repeated that through four years, except during the Verdun battle when the Germans drove for *Mort Homme* hill, which the French in their mighty effort recovered, the French line between the Meuse and the Aire Rivers and through the Argonne Forest had been stationary.

In order to hold their own line with as few troops as possible, the Germans not only had unusually deep fields of barbed wire in front of their first line and reserve trenches. They had prepared a second position (the *Giselher Stellung*) in line with Montfaucon to the Meuse; a third (the *Krimhilde Stellung*) through the Romagne Heights; and still had a fourth (the *Freya Stellung*). From a succession of favorable positions for guns and observation, adapted to successive stages of defense, the enemy looked down upon us from the whale back itself and the Argonne Forest, and also Verdun heights across the Meuse.

Foch's plan was to press the Meuse-Argonne offensive in coöperation with an Anglo-French toward St. Quentin and Cambrai, between the Oise and Scarpe Rivers, and the Franco-American on the general line of Rheims-Verdun between the Suippe and the Meuse Rivers. All the Allied armies, including the Belgian, as the plan developed, would be attacking.

In our progress through the forest and up the valleys of the river and up the whale back, in what the ground required should be an essentially even advance, we should be threatening the German main line of communications from the German army to its front in face of the British and French in western France.

Breaking this line, that is the severing of the Sedan-Mézières railroad, would leave the enemy only the narrow avenue between the Ardennes Forest and the Dutch frontier for the transport of men and supplies for his armies in western France. Every blow we struck in the Meuse-Argonne battle must release pressure from the Allied forces in western France, since the enemy could not afford to allow the American Army to conquer the heights above Romagne in the fourth German position on the whale back. Then it would be a downhill rush for us to the railroad, to cut off the German armies in western France in a decisive victory.

At any cost, therefore, while Ludendorff had reserves, or he could bring divisions from western France to defend this critical point, he must hold fast against us. Indeed, he must stonewall to the death to insure his retreat from western France in order to reform on the shorter line during the winter for final defense. It was a race against time and the closing in of winter for both the Germans and the Allies.

Foch, encouraged by the rising hope that the Allies might win a decision before he had to fight General Mud and Marshal Winter, was given to expecting the "impossible," at least of the American Army, and he assigned us an "impossible" in an offensive which might be blocked in a futile shambles.

Visible from our line of attack was the tower of the village of Montfaucon with its challenge in the center of the second German line of defense. This we were to have on the second day of our first operation. In the second operation we were to conquer the Romagne Heights of the third position and then, in the third operation, sweep on down to the railroad, the Fourth French Army on the west of the Argonne Forest coöperating with our advance.

If we could have done this with the speed which Foch seemed to expect of us, why then we should have bagged several German army corps. Pétain, that practical soldier who knew the heights around the Meuse River in the "They shall not pass" days, said that we should do very well if we got Montfaucon during the winter.

In a sense, in view of Pétain's judgment and his realization of the obstacles and the tactical miracle which looked so attractive on a flat map, it might be said that the story of the long siege battle is already told; for we kept hammering on with all the strength America could bring to bear until we did reach the railroad.

It is asked why Pershing committed himself to this seemingly hopeless task. He had given his word that he would fight his army as an independent army wherever it was placed by the Generalissimo. Such was his faith in his troops that he was ready to take the bold chance of our swifter success for so great a prize as possibly the capture of German forces unable to retreat from western France.

Not only this but, as J.J.P. wrote in his account, he felt that his army was the freshest and strongest of the Allied armies to make this impossible a reality. That line of communications had been his original goal. His terse feeling, "If we strike hard enough we may end this war this fall," was the most compelling reason. "It's altogether for all the Allied armies with all they've got while fighting weather lasts."

The sheer concentration, over roads that were out of repair, of so immense a force of men and material for a major offensive in twenty-four days from the time the order was given, and really only eleven days after the conclusion of the St. Mihiel operation, represented an undertaking for which the French or German army should have wanted at least a month.

It is further worth while repeating that while Conner, as Chief of Operations of the AEF, and Drum, as Chief of Staff of the First Army, were preparing for and conducting the St. Mihiel battle, they had to prepare for a second great battle on a front of twenty-four miles of greater magnitude and requiring more difficult mobilization than St. Mihiel.

Forty thousand tons of ammunition must be ready by September 25 with a daily supply of 3000 tons, or 12 to 14 train loads. There must be 19 rail heads; and 12 depots for ordnance, 24 for ammunition, 9 for gas and oil, 9 for quartermaster supplies, 12 for engineers' supplies, 8 for water supply, 6 for chemical warfare, and others for medical, signal, motor and tank supplies, in addition to 34 evacuation hospitals. All this must be on a front the requirements of which had been limited to stalemate warfare. We had to hurriedly enlarge and take over the regulating station at St. Dizier.

Two hundred thousand French soldiers must be moved out of the sector and 600,000 Americans replace them. Our nine big American divisions, for the attack and divisions in reserve, each one with its trains covering a distance of over twenty miles on a road, had to be placed in line in addition to the army and corps artillery and the immense amount of material mentioned.

Colonel George C. Marshall, Jr., the Assistant Chief of Staff of the First Army, was referred to as a "wizard" in troop movements and mobilization. At the time of our entry into the war he was a captain. He had been a graduate not of West Point, but of the Virginia Military Institute. In professional zeal he had been a star student at the Leavenworth Staff College who had never lost human contact with the private soldier.

When he was Chief of Staff of the 1st Division in the early training days at Gondrecourt he came under J.J.P.'s eye as an officer who could apply his knowledge in broadening practice. He and Drum in their cubicles in the barrack offices around the Mairie of Souilly were kept free from any unnecessary interruptions as they worked over their maps. Marshall was back and forth along the roads keeping personal touch. His system was simplified by his stationing of officers at given points to make sure that no division or other element should advance out of order and confuse the prescribed formations.

J.J.P.'s hand was on the plan checking its progress. He was not only back and forth to the headquarters of the corps, but to all the divisions, seeing for himself as usual without depending altogether on reports. Of course the divisions must take over from the French under the cover of darkness and not too soon lest the enemy be apprised that a heavy attack was coming.

In the requisite swiftness of our mobilization the mandatory consideration was to get our divisions in line on the time set, which meant that divisions could not all be placed opposite objectives which their experience best fitted them to attack. Nor was it in staff foresight to foresee which positions would be most strongly held by the enemy.

On the night of September 24 all were in position. From left to right (west to east) facing the Argonne Forest, were the 77th (now Major General Robert Alexander), the 28th (Muir) and the 35th (Traub) of the First Corps (Liggett); the 91st (Johnston), the 37th (Major General Charles S. Farnsworth) and the 79th (Major General Joseph E. Kuhn) of the Fifth Corps (Cameron); and the 4th (Hines), the 80th (Cronkhite) and the 33d (Major General George Bell, Jr.) of the Third Corps (Bullard). The reserve consisted of the colored 92d Division (Major General Charles C. Ballou), the 32d (Haan), the 3d (Buck), the 1st (Summerall), the 29th (Major General Charles G. Morton) and the 82d (Major General William P. Burnham).

Our four pioneer divisions which had been a year in France, and another which had conspicuous battle experience, were not in the initial attack. They had been engaged at St. Mihiel or were given other missions by Foch. Of the nine divisions some had had no experience except in quiet sectors and one had never been in the trenches. The nine had not worked together as divisions. They were unfamiliar with the requisites of liaison in a major offensive action.

J.J.P. knew that he must depend upon their ardor to make up for relative and inescapable lack of matured skill and upon superior numbers, making the most of the element of surprise. But surprise depended upon the concealment at least of the magnitude and purpose of our mobilization. In this we were extraordinarily successful.

J.J.P. himself and his staff had a full realization of the handicaps and the strength of the enemy's position, and while hoping he might gain the objectives of a ten-mile advance at the end of the second day and then to conquer all the heights beyond swiftly, his preparations, so far as he had the men and material available, looked to a prolonged operation.

The enemy had not expected a major attack. It had seemed impossible that the American Army could make one so soon after its large concentration at St. Mihiel. This was all in favor of our troops who, in some parts of the line, were not under heavy fire in working their way through the deep stretches of barbed wire, which was of itself a severe test for any young division in keeping its formations.

Looking directly toward the goal of the tower of Montfaucon in the center of the whale back, was the 79th Division (Major General Joseph E. Kuhn). Without trench experience, it had not even had time to get familiar with the trenches it occupied for the jump off. It had never even made a trench raid as a preparation for going over the top for that long rush to its goal. However, it did capture Montfaucon at the end of the second day.

The 77th was against the steep slopes at the edge of the Argonne Forest. The 28th had the ordeal of being astride the Aire River between heights. And the 35th, with little trench experience, sturdy men from Pershing's own state and from Kansas, were set to conquer most formidable natural positions. Badly directed by the division command the 35th kept on fighting and gaining ground until it had no reserves left. Half of its infantrymen were killed or wounded.

And we did have Montfaucon, which Pétain thought it would require the winter to take, and we had on the whole made an eight-mile advance at the end of the second day. By this time the German staff, fully aware of the threat to their line of communications, had rushed divisions in support. As we drove on we met vicious counter-attacks, more artillery fire, more machine gun nests with enfilade fire.

The most determined of our divisions had to yield advance positions in order to straighten their lines. A division, which had easier going or more dash and skill, had to halt because the division on its right or left was not up, thus leaving it within a pocket (salient). And the same was true for units within the divisions for brigades, regiments, battalions, companies, and even platoons.

Our men must have a breathing spell. Supplies must be brought up when they were fighting on without rations; and these, including ammunition for rifles and the advance of the artillery over roads which must be repaired after they had been under the blasts of shell fire for four years. Rain further mired transport.

In his round of division headquarters J.J.P. had word from Major General Muir of the 28th, in its wicked task astride the Aire, that he had need of some more skilled officers. J.J.P. had not to look beyond the barrack offices of the staff at Souilly to find two to whom the chance of a little action at the front was a release from school. Brigadier General Nolan, Chief of G-2 (Intelligence), and Colonel Conger, Chief of the Battle Order Division of G-2, applied their tactical skill to good effect in action. But J.J.P. allowed them only a short time to enjoy their holiday of being with troops and shot at. Somewhat sadly, but very grateful for their privilege, they were back to their desks.

With the first phase of the Meuse-Argonne battle over as we reformed for the second phase, two of our divisions with the British, under our Second Corps command of Major General George W. Read, the 27th, New York National Guard, and the 30th were in the attack on the powerful Hindenburg line. The 27th (Major General John F. O'Ryan) had most vicious fighting in the rabbit warrens on a more difficult front than the 30th (Major General Edward M. Lewis). The southern mountaineers of the 30th, who knew how to shoot without army target practice, took all of their objectives. They were extraordinarily homogeneous, efficient, disciplined soldiers and they had to their credit more Congressional Medals of Honor than any other division.

J.J.P. needed both those divisions in the Meuse-Argonne. He also needed the veteran 2d (Major General John A. Lejeune), which had made the stand on the Paris road against the third German offensive and later been in the drive to Soissons which turned the tide. But Foch had assigned the 2d, under the French, to conquer the Blanc Mont bridges, which it did on October 3, and then kept on for five days more until, exhausted, it proceeded on to St. Etienne to be succeeded in line by the 36th Division (Major General W. R. Smith). The 36th had no trench experience, but it could charge and keep on charging in the full flight of American initiative which is not at its worst in their home country of Texas.

Meanwhile, in the early days of October, as the Allies, all the way from Belgium to the Meuse River, were advancing or preparing to advance, according to Foch's plan, not only the military situation but the political should be considered in relation to the battle of the Meuse-Argonne. Ludendorff had confessed privately, September 30, to despair. The German Chancellor had resigned and the troubled Kaiser had appointed Prince Max of Baden, a liberal, as his successor.

Since the beginning of their offensives, July 18, the Allies had taken 3600 guns and 25,000 machine guns. Marshal von Hindenburg told the German statesmen, October 1, that a peace offer must be made immediately because the German army was breaking. Although this was as yet unknown to Foch, he realized the rich harvest his combinations were yielding when Secretary Baker called at his headquarters three days later. Having in mind Foch's insistence on the 100-division program, Baker asked the Marshal how many American divisions he wanted to win the war in 1919.

"Forty," Foch replied.

"I think I must have misunderstood the Marshal," Baker said to the interpreter. "Will you repeat the question and make sure he understands that I am referring to divisions to be in France for use in 1919."

When the interpreter repeated the question, Foch replied: "I understood the Secretary, and my answer is forty."

Baker reminded Foch that there were nearly that many divisions in France already.

"I win the war with forty," Foch replied.

Foch was out of touch with Pershing who had continued to support his 100-division program. In fact, Pershing was very much out of touch at the time with anything but his problem in the Meuse-Argonne.

Soon after Montfaucon was taken Clemenceau appeared at Pershing's headquarters. The gallant, if somewhat posturing, old "Tiger" wanted to go in person to Montfaucon. Since he had complained that Pershing had been disinclined to allow him to take any risk in a trip to Vigneulles after the St. Mihiel battle, J.J.P. assigned Colonel Bowditch to conduct him to the front this time. There was shell fire ahead, the traffic was extremely congested, and it was almost as impracticable to advance one French premier to his objective as it was yet for the American Army to conquer the Romagne heights which would open the way to cut off the German armies in western France.

The "Tiger" was not favorably impressed with our inability to make more than an eight-mile advance in two days in that sector where the French high command had considered an offensive impracticable. He was hardly appreciative of what the 79th Division, which had never been in the trenches before, had accomplished.

Nor would he quite have understood its handicap in that, before it sailed from America, at least a third of its trained soldiers had been drafted away from the division for different purposes, including those who had any technical training which in any way suited them for the building of ships to bring still more American troops to France. The gaps left were filled by recruits shortly before the division sailed.

Soon after Clemenceau's visit, which left him considerably peeved, General Weygand proposed, in speaking for Marshal Foch, that the French Second Army should be placed next to the French Fourth Army in the region of the Argonne Forest, limiting Pershing's command. This of itself would have been a confusing maneuver in the midst of preparations for an attack and placing still more "impossibles" on our men. J.J.P. refused to consider it for this reason if for no other. Afterward Weygand said he was quite right.

Lacking any documentary evidence in absolute proof, it seems only fair to draw the conclusion that the suggestion had come from Clemenceau. While Foch himself did not approve of it, he, nevertheless, though chosen as Generalissimo of the Allied armies, was actually a French general under the authority of Clemenceau as the Premier of France. So Clemenceau had the power to relieve him in the midst of the campaign. Only later was it known that the rift which later became an open break between Foch and Clemenceau, with ensuing post-war charges and counter charges, was already in the making.

Jealousy in sharing the honors of martial success has ever been more frequent than in sharing the responsibilities for martial defeat. And it was not human, particularly in Clemenceau, not to want to enjoy exclusively the title of the "Father of Victory," by which he was later acclaimed.

Events were moving fast in the councils of the Allied statesmen as well as in the offensives along the Allied fronts, which compelled Hindenburg, October 3, to insist on his previous demand "for the immediate forwarding of an offer of peace to our enemies."

"There is now no longer any possible hope of forcing peace on the enemy," he added. "The situation grows more desperate every day and may force the High Command to grave decisions."

Three days later the Chancellor appealed through the Swiss government to President Wilson to open peace negotiations on the acceptable program of his Fourteen Points. In the Chancellor's own words: "With a view to avoiding further bloodshed, the German Government requests the immediate conclusion of an armistice on land and water and in the air."

Pershing had no further information about this approach and the negotiations that followed except that the enemy was asking for an armistice. He did remark: "An armistice may give the German army a breathing spell in which to reorganize their defense. It is the more reason for us to press our attacks."

Not only was J.J.P. isolated from Allied councils in his intense preoccupation with his battle, but so was General Bliss, our permanent military representative with the Supreme War Council. It was not at a regular session of the Council but at a secret meeting, October 7, in Paris, that its statesmen members, Lloyd George, Clemenceau and Orlando, with their foreign ministers, began laying their plans with a view to undermining President Wilson's Fourteen Points.

Wilson, himself, as the fourth member of the inner governing circle of the Council, was neither consulted nor represented. Other Allied commanders were consulted about armistice terms, but not yet the American. His part was to continue his offensive when every blow he struck drew off German resistance against the French and British armies. The statesmen felt sure of their position in relation to American sentiment at a time when our people, in face of the mounting American casualty lists and the heavy strain on our energies, saw hope in the signal Allied successes for a speedy end of the war.

We had sent over 400,000 troops to France in a single month. Our total in France already was 1,700,000 on the way to two millions. But such was the prospect that soon the Allies would have no further need for an American Army. The revived Italian army was preparing for the offensive against the breaking Austrian army, all Turkish resistance was practically over, and the Allied offensive from Salonika promised an early capitulation by Bulgaria.

General Bliss found that ever since victory had been in sight political considerations had been predominant among his colleagues. In a letter to General March, our Chief of Staff in Washington, he wrote that it seemed to him "somewhat evident that the European Allies will attempt to minimize the American effort as much as possible. They think that they have got the Germans on the run and that they now do not need as much help as they were crying for a little while ago.

"I think I told you some time ago that I had heard a gentleman in high position here say that the United States was building a bridge for the Allies to pass over; that the time for the United States to secure acquiescence in its wishes was while the bridge was building; that after the Allies had crossed over the bridge they would have no further use for it or for its builders."

Before this, Baker, just preceding his return to the United States, had had a long conference with Lloyd George in which, as Baker wrote to Pershing, October 2, Lloyd George complained that as a result of all the British "pains and sacrifices for training American troops and equipping them they had gotten no good out of them whatever and that the American troops had not been of any service to the British.

"From this he (Lloyd George) went on to say," Baker

continued, "that he was earnestly desirous for opportunity for the American and British soldiers to fraternize. He felt that large issues to the future peace of the world depended upon the American and British peoples understanding one another and that much the best hope of such an understanding grew out of intermingling our soldiers so they could learn to know one another, but that it seemed to him that there was some influence at work to monopolize American soldiers for the assistance of the French and to keep them from the association of the British."

In answer, Baker's keen logic had all the facts in his favor for a lucid reply in which he had only to show how the contributions we had already made and were making were aiding to win the war.

On his part, Lloyd George made a point of their parting in a friendly mood, which had been Baker's all the while, but back of his complaint was his concern of American support, and that American interests should not become too closely allied with French interests, in the inevitable controversy between the British and French as to their share in the awards of the future peace conference.

35

Meuse-Argonne: Next Phases

BEFORE THE ATTACK in what might be called the second phase of the battle of the Meuse-Argonne, three divisions which had suffered very heavily, the 35th, 37th and 79th, must be relieved by divisions in reserve. Further reorganization, and readjustment and tactical plans must be hurried in order to make the most of our numbers before the enemy strengthened his own and his defenses.

But he too was on the alert. He already had twenty-seven divisions in line and seventeen in reserve. The volume of shell fire along our front indicated that he was bringing more and more guns into position. The German General Von der Marwitz, in command against us, in an order to his army, October 1, said in view of the coming attack:

"The objective is the cutting of the railroad line Longuyon-Sedan, which is the main line of communications of the Western Army. Furthermore, the enemy hopes to compel us to discontinue the exploitation of the iron mines of Briey, the possession of which is a great factor in our steel production . . . The fate of a large portion of the western front, perhaps of our nation, depends upon the firm holding of the Verdun front. The Fatherland believes that every commander and every soldier realizes the greatness of his task and that everyone will fulfill his duties to the utmost. If this is done, the enemy's attack will be shattered."

In line for the jump off, October 4, east to west, were the 33d Division (Bell), the 4th (Hines) and the 80th (Cronkhite) in the Third Corps (Bullard); then the 3d Division (Buck), and the 32d (Haan) in the 5th Corps (Cameron); the 1st Division (Summerall), the 28th (Muir), and the 77th (Alexander) in the First Corps (Liggett). The aim was to drive up the Aire River neutralizing the flanking fire from the Argonne Forest and by flanking movements to capture the forbidding Romagne and Cunel heights. Our young divisions fought with greater skill, our old with their veteran skill, but they were against immense odds in face of the sweep of artillery fire and cunningly placed machine guns commanding the slopes and ravines and blazing from the edges of patches of woods.

On the left (the west) the attack made the best progress. That first day the 1st Division (Summerall) hewed a wedge, stroke by stroke, over the rugged, uneven ground of the heights commanding the east bank of the River Aire. Undismayed by its losses, it kept on conquering machine gun nests until, on the evening of the 5th, in an heroic dash, it had scaled and captured hill 240, having made a gain of three miles.

The 28th (Muir), coöperating with the 1st, had braved the gusts of fire and taken the village of Chéhéry. This relieved the pressure on the 77th (Alexander) in the Argonne Forest and opened the way for it to advance and rescue Major Whittlesey's famous "lost battalion" which had become separated from the Division.

On the 77th's left the French Fourth Army, which had been held back in its offensive until our 2d Division under the French had taken Blanc Mont, was in turn relieved of pressure which enabled it to make a further advance. (Incidentally, Major General John A. Lejeune, of the Marines, in command of the 2d was so hotly indignant over the failure of French troops to keep pace with his men, leaving the 2d in a salient, that he telegraphed GHQ he would resign rather than ever fight again in liaison with the French; and J.J.P. had to send a diplomatic staff officer to restore amicable inter-Allied relations in that quarter.)

Hastening to press the advantages, the 82d Division (Major General George B. Duncan) marched up the valley of the Aire in the night, and, in a most difficult maneuver for all three divisions, established itself between the 28th and 1st. The 28th and the fresh 82d captured more important dominating hills; and the 28th, in a final dash which seemed to exhaust the last ounce of its reserve energy, captured Châtel-Chéhéry, and yet was able to press on until it was relieved by the 82d after it had been under continuous fire for twelve days.

The 82d entered Cornay as the next step, to be blasted out by shell fire, but again took Cornay, which it could not hold against a fresh German division brought up in reserve with more guns in support. While the 82d resisted further counter-attacks it was only getting up steam for further drives.

Against the heights of Romagne and Cunel of the whale back, progress was more difficult. It took the 4th Division (Hines) three days of persistent sleepless fighting to get the little Fays Wood and gain a mile and the 80th Division (Cronkhite) to get and hold a part of the little Ogons Wood against repeated counter-attacks. The 32d Division (Haan), fighting for every yard of ground, took the little village of Cierges and drove on until it had the village of Gesnes.

If one hillock or little patch of woods were taken in hand-to-hand fighting, it was only to meet equally stiff resistance from another hillock or patch of woods. But the honors on the whole were with us, though the German troops had resolutely responded to their commander's appeal "that everyone will fulfill his duties to the utmost."

In some instances our gains seemed out of keeping with the costs and yet, in view of the opposition, it was amazing that we made any. It was not only that the German artillery and machine guns had plunging fire from the Romagne and Cunel heights but they had what was still worse, artillery fire at right angle to our attack from still higher ground across the Meuse River where the enemy now had guns of larger calibre in position. Their shells were lashing our men whose ardor had carried them into salients against local counter-attacks, making it suicidal not to yield temporarily some hard won ground.

After four days of the most vicious fighting the American Army had known in France there must be a little breathing spell while we readjusted our lines and dug in for the next step. And the next step must wait until the divisions on the eastern slopes of Romagne and Cunel had some relief from the flanking artillery fire from the heights on the other side of the Meuse in the area of the old Verdun battlefield.

"Those German gunners are sitting there comfortably on top of the hills east of the Meuse without our being able to return their fire," J.J.P. said. "We must get at them."

This meant that we must extend our offensive to the east bank of the Meuse where French troops under his army command had been established as a protective flank, but not in enough strength for any forward movement.

The 33d Division (Bell) built bridges across the Meuse during the night, crossed in the morning, captured Consevoye, and with a brigade of the 29th Division (Major General Charles G. Morton) and two French divisions on their right, they conquered stretches of woods and slopes and some of the German battery positions. But they could get no farther under the guns from the heights above them, which were crowned by the Borne de Cornouiller whence came the enemy's most powerful flanking fire across the Meuse upon our troops on the whale back.

The 29th, fresh for the battle, was to continue in successive attacks. We had not only gained observation points and battery positions east of the Meuse, but we had established ourselves for further pressure, which drew more German divisions against us east of the Meuse, either away from our main battlefield or from the fronts of our Allies.

For our next general attack, October 14, we faced twenty-four German divisions not, of course, up to their full strength but veterans with veteran skill and with a large complement of machine gunners. In line east of the Meuse with the French we had the 29th (Morton) and 33d (Bell) divisions; west of the Meuse the 4th (Cameron), the 3d (Buck) and the 5th (MacMahon) in the Third Corps (Hines); then the 32d (Haan) and the 42d (Menoher) in the Fifth Corps (Summerall); then the 82d (Duncan) and the 77th (Alexander) in the First Corps.

From the outset all the way we met stubborn and persistent opposition. Everywhere we made progress, some that was very hard won across the Meuse. On the west bank of the Meuse, in the main battlefield, the 3d and 5th Divisions, still under the flanking fire from the Borne de Cornouiller, managed to get a hold in the eastern edge of the wood north of Cunel and then finally to clear it and to reach the top of the slopes northeast of Romagne. The 5th (MacMahon), in for the first time, drove through the Rappes Wood but, with fire concentrated upon it from three directions, had to withdraw.

Over on the left in the Aire sector the 82d (Duncan), breaking away for the advance of the 77th (Alexander) wrested the vital St. Juvin-St. Georges road from the enemy, and then, in attack and counter-attack for two days of unremitting action, was able only to hold its ground. At last the 77th with the French pushing on its left and the 82d on its right crossed the bend in the Aire, took St. Juvin itself, fought all day to gain the little island south of Grand Pré, and the next day had its outposts on the edge of the town. But it could go no farther under the plunging fire from the bluffs above the town.

After its long ordeal in the forest, which had known monotonous waiting before the release of the pressure on its flanks permitted another advance, the 77th (Alexander) might have its turn in rest billets, having been relieved by the 78th (Major General James H. McRae).

It was up the main height of the whale back itself that we won most vital positions. Pershing says in his account that unstinted praise must be given the 32d Division (Haan). Its 64th Brigade, under Brigadier General Edwin B. Winans, stormed the Côte Dame Marie, one of the strongest points of the formidable Romagne heights. Then the 32d took the town of Romagne and the eastern half of the Romagne woods and pressed on until it had advanced a mile into the big Rantheville Wood.

Nor was the "Rainbow" 42d (Menoher) to be denied. It had faced severe resistance in the Rheims sector and in the closing of the Marne salient, but nothing equal to this it met from the moment of its jump off. It drove through the western half of the Romagne woods. The 84th Brigade, under Brigadier General Douglas MacArthur, worked its way up the stiff heights of the Côte de Châtillon and, taking on machine guns nests hand-to-hand when rifle fire failed, pressed on. But there was a limit, and that was set by the ever-recurring danger of getting into a salient with cross fire from both flanks.

This is not saying that the 32d or 42d were fighting any better than the 82d which was doing its part assigned in the plan. The 4th Division might be inactive in its part in the plan, but must be ready to make an equal sacrifice when the command came.

In those three mortal days, October 14-16, we had finally gained the enemy's third line of defense, the Romagne

Heights and their most formidable point, the Côte Dame Marie. The fourth German position and more heights were beyond us, with the enemy crowding in more reinforcements in full realization that our next attack might take us over the crest and down hill to the vital line of communications with the German army in western France.

Thus the third phase of the greatest battle in our history was over. Now we had to resist the enemy's counter-attacks. We had to gird our loins and reorganize for what we hoped would be the final attack.

But during the three weeks we had been persistently fighting in the Meuse-Argonne we were also maintaining the front we had won at St. Mihiel, and with the spread of our command across into the Verdun area, we should soon hold a line stretching all the way from the Argonne Forest to the Moselle River. J.J.P. had not forgotten how the objective of the St. Mihiel operation had been restricted.

If he had gone on with the St. Mihiel offensive he might have had Conflans and cut the Metz-Sedan railroad. He looked forward to extending his offensive between the Meuse and Moselle across the plain of the Woëvre. To prepare for this Major General Robert L. Bullard was set to organizing a staff to form another army, the Second Army. And Major General Hunter Liggett was given command of the First Army in conduct of the Meuse-Argonne operation with Pershing in supreme command of the two armies.

36

Grim Mud Bound Fighting

DURING THE BATTLE, which was not yet half over, J.J.P. lived on his train. When he was not there he was in the little corner room in the *Mairie* of Souilly with his maps or at the front. This did not mean the trenches, where, as the commander of the whole, he would have seen only soldiers in fox holes, or screened machine gun and battery positions, and battalion, company and platoon commands.

The front for him was a division or brigade headquarters, which was often in timbered dugouts as a protected center of wire communication and under long-range shell fire. Here he had intimate touch with the local problems and the atmosphere of the battle. Here he brought to bear personal force, encouragement, counsel and imparted his indomitable will and driving energy to subordinates to carry out his tactical plans.

Only occasionally did a weak sun faintly lighten the mists which hung over the battlefield as a relief from the persistent rains. Practically all days were grey days.

This was no tanned army. It was an army of faces which

became grey as the mist itself. The tanned face of the Pershing who arrived in Washington from the Mexican border was also grey. I saw him grey from lack of sleep and the unceasing strain. For him, as for the army, this long uninterrupted siege was in grim contrast with pitch battles of the past which might last only a few hours. Lost or won, these were soon over. They did not continue for weeks.

Once I recall him with his own shoulders a little bent, if not quite in a stoop, as evidence that he was having no exercise to keep his muscles firm. As though in sudden consciousness that he was letting down, he drew back his shoulders and drew in his waistline in West Point form, his will dominant over himself as over his army. Then, at the mention of how steadily the men were fighting, and more and more skillfully, there were dancing blue lights of pride in his eyes.

"They're great," he said. "This battle is an American triumph of their sheer courage and determination. It is not just that they are all willing to fight, but it's their readiness to stand the gaff, to keep on day after day. It's hard to keep on driving them in, but that is best. I would not consider sacrificing some of the young divisions with so little training if it were not that it may save still greater sacrifice. How fast the young divisions are learning! They exceed my confident expectation. It is all the sooner to get home and have this murderous war over."

We were on the way to spending a million dollars an hour and to having two millions of men in France to make the world safe for democracy, and the one thought of all the two millions from ports to fox holes was to get home. For this they were really fighting and laboring under the terrific pressure not only of command but in their own zeal to that end. If marching battalions in American uniform had seemed at first strange on the roads of France, how much greater the phenomenon now on the Meuse-Argonne battlefield!

What a picture, that of the boys from the tenements and the farms of America under that grey sky in eastern France! The foreign born and the first generation of Americans and the older generations were simply fighting for America and to be back in America. "Buddy" did have a meaning in the common fellowship of all classes of men, elbow to elbow, not in the training camps now, but under fire.

The influenza epidemic was taking its toll at home. It spread across Europe through all the armies. It was brought from home by our arriving troops in France. In all we had 70,000 cases in the AEF, 32 percent of whom died.

Horses after a sea voyage must be acclimatized, but there was no time for such a luxury for our soldiers and officers packed on the transports. The reconditioned *Leviathan,* the former German *Vaterland,* which the German Staff had estimated could not carry more than 8000 men, was bringing 12,000 each trip. They were crowded into the 40-and-8 cars across France. Frequently they had had only a month's training at home. Divisions which had developed cantonment *esprit de corps* were broken up for replacements in order to keep the combat divisions up to strength.

The arriving man found himself at company muster in the place of a dead or wounded man of a division in rest billets. He was lucky if he slept in a comfortable haymow over a manure pile in a French village well back of the lines. But mainly the object was shelter whether in the ruins of a village or church or old dugouts back of the battle zone.

Only when the surgeon certified a man was not well enough was there any escape from going to the front. The Military Police picked up all the stray men and sent them to their "outfits." Those lynx-eyed "M.P.'s" formed a cordon back of the battlefield against slackers. No soldier could pass by them to the rear without being ticketed as wounded or too sick to fight.

Through the area of shell fire in the congested roads in the mist the fresh, rested men passed on in the night under cover of darkness to replace those who were fought out. "Okay, Buddy," and the newcomer was put next to the job in hand with warnings against the tricks of Heinie, as he took his place in the fox hole.

There were thousands of these little fox holes dug by individual soldiers. The incoming officers took over from the outgoing, studying their maps by flash light. It was a battle in the mud and rain with clothes never drying but always saturated as a sponge by the mist. When the word came to attack, the hope was that gun fire would help silence the enemy machine gun nests which now had their targets out of the fox holes. But the machine gun nests must be taken. Some advance must be won. It was a triumph to get a little ridge or hillock which was like gaining one more stair in the long flight of slippery stairs.

A captain down, a lieutenant took his place. The lieutenant down, and a sergeant succeeded him. Drive, drive and carry on! At least you must yield no ground. In some instances battalion and regimental commanders, who were called in by superior officers to report why they were not making more progress fell flat on their faces in exhaustion before their chiefs.

Men with coughs who entered the line came down with influenza or pneumonia. The wounded or sick who could walk plodded back through the darkness in the chill mist shivering as the weather grew colder with the advance of fall toward winter. It was astounding how cold it was lying in the mud of that battlefield when the thermometer was only at forty degrees Fahrenheit.

Roads torn by shell fire must be repaired. A little hole worn in the road, and in an hour our giant three-ton trucks had made it a slough that stalled the line of trucks. Sturdy Negroes from the levees and German prisoners stood by to fill the holes and build new roads to keep up with our advances.

Under fire the stretcher bearers brought the prostrate

wounded back from the front where the stretchers were slipped into the ambulances which ran on to the rail heads for the waiting railroad cars which bore them to the hospitals. There was a hurry call for 1500 more trained army nurses from home.

These women in uniform under army discipline who had taken the oath were the greatest soldiers of all. They had known now of the excitement of action. Their part was to welcome with a smile and professional efficiency the wounded, whether burned by gas or their flesh torn by shells, in their mud and filth and blood-soaked clothes, and make them clean and well again or make death easier for them.

The nurses worked eighteen and twenty hours a day, day after day. Theirs was an indispensable service while that of some—by no means all—of the young women, untrained in anything, who were brought over by the Red Cross through social or political influence, was quite dispensable. Some of the nurses were never to recover from the strain.

We had provided 479,491 normal and emergency hospital beds in 153 base hospitals, 66 camp hospitals and 12 convalescent camps. Meanwhile the Services of Supply must keep up with the demands which were magnified out of proportion even to generous calculations. The guns and the machine guns in their steady outpouring of fire must never want for ammunition. The men must have food if it could reach them.

Here is an example of an incident of what Secretary Baker called writing America on a piece of white paper in France. At 8:15 A. M. the following order was received at Gièvres: 1,250,000 cans of tomatoes, 1,000,000 tons of sugar, 600,000 cans of corned-beef, 756,000 pounds of tinned hash, 156,000 pounds of dried beans. This meant 4596 tons requiring 457 railroad cars for transport, and all was on the way at 6:15 in the evening. But those figures were for a day in August when we were only well started on the one hundred and fifty days of fighting in France.

The SOS was driving as hard as the men at the front. The personnel of the greatest industrial organization in our history had a spur for desperate effort as the word spread that the war "may be won this fall and we shall get home before spring." Thus the mill of war kept on grinding its mighty grist five thousand miles from the Mississippi valley.

It was forward to the front for the troops until they were fought out, wounded or killed; and then, when they received the welcome word of relief, it was out of line, with prayers that they would not be hit by shells on the way to the nectar of hot coffee and doughnuts served by the Salvation Army lassies; then to hot meals from the rolling kitchens; and then to fresh clothes while the old were being deloused.

But best of all it was to sleep on even a floor if it were dry. After sleep and clean clothes and some square meals, the next question was, "Where is the "Y," or, "a K. of C. hut?" with its chocolate, cigarettes and chewing gum. The legends about café life in pleasant villages did not apply in billets for the soldiers who were in and out of the Meuse-Argonne ordeal.

37

Behind His Back

It Was a single sentence, an allusion, which told much when I had a minute with J.J.P. in his room at Souilly. "Clemenceau seems to be at it again." J.J.P's face was stone grey, but the flash in his eyes bore a "Come one, come all" challenge. Evidently he was not yet himself informed of the nature of the latest action behind his back, which a whisper or two about GHQ had interpreted as nothing less than an effort to have him relieved of command in the midst of the Meuse-Argonne operation.

The progress of his greatest of our battles was relatively unsung after our praises had been so widely heralded in Château-Thierry days and the closing of the Marne salient. Our thankless and indispensable part in the final joint Allied offensives was little realized even by our people at home.

In common with the rest of the world they were looking at the map under the spell of the rapidly advancing British and French armies. Ours appeared a comparatively stalled army the while we drew German divisions away from their fronts. This is not implying that Haig and Pétain were not driving hard in the common hope of victory before fighting weather was over. Haig was bearing the brunt, at the cost of immense losses, in unremitting aggressiveness.

Old "Tiger" Clemenceau became hotly impatient with the slow progress we were making, while apparently it did not occur to him that the French Fourth army, on our left, was being held up by the same strong resistance when its objective was the same as our own. With victory in sight the French premier naturally was not disinclined to eliminate the stubborn American commander as a possible influence at the peace conference.

On October 21 he wrote a letter to Foch, which Foch said had "nothing less in view than to effect a change in Chief of Command of the American Army." Clemenceau said that he would not waste time in reviewing the "development of General Pershing's exactions" and "invincible obstinacy."

"I am the head of the French Army," Clemenceau wrote. "I would be a criminal if I allowed the French Army to wear itself out indefinitely in battle, without doing everything in my power to ensure that an Allied army, which had been hurried to its aid, was rendered capable of fulfilling the military rôle for which it is destined."

He complained that the American troops, "who are unanimously acknowledged to be great soldiers," had been "marking time" and "failed to conquer the ground assigned to them as an objective . . . "Nobody can maintain that these fine troops are unusable; they are merely not being used."

The rift between Clemenceau and Foch had reached the breaking point. It was hopeless now for Clemenceau to have exclusive rights as "The Father of Victory." Foch promptly refused to comply with his demand. Though Clemenceau had the power, as the French premier over a French general to relieve Foch, he could hardly afford to thwart the Generalissimo who was being hailed as the military genius of victory.

So the matter was settled between the two without troubling Pershing. Later, when it was brought to Secretary Baker's attention, he remarked that it would be a long time before an American commander would be relieved by any European premier. When Pershing saw Clemenceau, after Foch's reply to the note, the meeting was most pleasant. The "Tiger" was purringly congratulatory on Pershing's conduct of the battle.

Meanwhile the mill continued to grind on in the Meuse-Argonne. By a series of local operations J.J.P. sought to conquer certain positions for a final general attack.

The enemy was perfectly aware that he now had to make his last stand to protect his lines of communications for his retreating army in the west. He depended not only upon numbers but on their selective character for the task. There was a still larger proportion of selected machine gunners who not only knew how to make the most of every advantage of ground, but who had a veteran fatalism.

For four long, hard years they had been fighting. What was ahead of them? What mattered now? They had met the challenge of death many times. They rejoiced in the professional skill with which they could make every shot count to the last. Again, in a burst of despair, groups might suddenly yield. But this was not often true.

"They're making us earn every yard we gain and every prisoner we take," best expressed our situation in the second, third and fourth weeks of October.

The 78th Division (McRae) had ten days of incessant battle on the left next to the Fourth French army. Its advance units had started in on the river bottom at the edge of the little town of Grandpré looking up to the plunging machine gun fire from the houses on the steep streets and the wooded heights beyond. Attacks were met by counter-attacks which drove our men back, only to attack again and again until at last, October 28, they had driven the enemy from the town and the heights above it and now could come to the grapple in the Loges Wood.

Two divisions against the heights of the whale back, the veteran 3d and the 5th of the Third Corps, had been assigned more vigorous commanders after the costly misdirections under their predecessors in the terrific fighting of the general attack of October 14.

To the 3d came Brigadier General Preston Brown of the younger school of officers trained in tactics. He had been Chief of Staff of the 2d on the Paris road, in Belleau Wood, and in the drive toward Soissons.

To the 5th came the giant Major General Hanson E. Ely who had won his promotion as a regimental commander and then as brigade commander of the veteran 1st. He looked the invincible soldier he was to his men. The 5th soon felt his presence just as the 3d felt that of Brown.

The very "feel" of serving under a leader who led boldly and skillfully spread from headquarters to fox holes. And the two divisions could not have too much craft, determination and hardihood to win the hills and woods on the center of the whale back, requisite for a favorable jump off for the next general attack if it were to be successful.

On October 20 the 3d took Clairs Chênes Wood only to be driven out by a counter-attack, but attacked again and had the wood for good by nightfall. Two days later it made equally sure of the Forêt Wood. For three days it drove at the Rappes Wood, and on the fourth day had it finally, not to be dislodged by successive counter-attacks.

The 32d Division (Haan), still in line, was not yet so worn it could not keep faith with its prestige on the Vesle and at Juvigny by advancing into Bantheville Wood. The 89th, under its own well-loved Major General William M. Wright, took its place and made sure in vicious fighting that the rest of the Bantheville Wood was ours for keeps.

Across the Meuse River the enduring 29th (Morton), still whittling its way, took the important ridge north of Molleville Farm. The 26th was also now in line east of the Meuse. It too had a new commander, Brigadier General Frank E. Bamford, in place of Major General Clarence R. Edwards. The relief of Edwards caused the most comment of that of any division commander.

Of a dashing, winning personality Edwards had been a favorite of William H. Taft as Secretary of War and at the head of the Bureau of Insular Affairs. "We all know Clarence," as Taft and all the Regular army said. He went much into society and his flare for being well dressed made him something of the mould of fashion and glass of form. In his house in Washington he displayed his campaign hat, which he wore as General Lawton's chief of staff, with the names of his many "battles" under Lawton in the Philippine rebellion.

He had come to France in command of the 26th, New England National Guard, one of the first four divisions to arrive in France. J.J.P.'s "What am I going to do about ——?" had included Edwards very early in the Valley Forge days. The author's own answer had been:

"He is a good front, but not abreast of modern tactics. Shift him soon, unless he will follow the directions of an able division Chief of Staff assigned to him."—which it was not his inclination to do.

Edwards was no silent soldier. When General Liggett was told of some hardly complimentary remarks Edwards had passed about him, that very able and tolerant leader who commanded our First Army, replied: "Nobody could ever stop Clarence from talking."

Edwards was given to spreading gloom in the Valley Forge days when J.J.P. was so set against anything that held a hint of a defeatist attitude. To listen to him you might conclude Ludendorff's forthcoming offensive would end the war in a German victory.

He had a bent for self-pity which he imparted to his division as the object of unfairness in always being given the rough end of the stick. As a result other division staffs and their field commanders did develop a certain edge against the 26th as grouchy and complaining, which was bound to lead to its not receiving the credit it deserved. A Wright or an Allen, for example, would have imbued it with a more cheery spirit and better employed its gallantry.

J.J.P. retained Edwards, owing to the general fondness for Clarence, and possibly also owing to his powerful political friends in Washington who, if he had been relieved, would have borne down on Secretary Baker in their indignant protests, while other division commanders who were relieved took their soldier medicine.

It was cumulative dissatisfaction with Edwards' conduct of his division which finally brought decisive action in his case in the crisis of the Meuse-Argonne. His division did make better progress under Bamford. But Edwards had been ordered home in face of the enemy, which gave the effect of disgrace which was lacking in the case of relieved commanders who were transferred to other posts in France. This was the more unfortunate owing to his personal popularity with the division as its defender against unfair play.

New England sentiment saw him as an outraged hero and a victim of Pershing's grudge against him and the division. After the war there was local talk of demanding an inquiry by Congress for his vindication; but the proposal was dropped in view of all the evidence in the records of the indecisiveness of his orders and his general vacillation as early as the German raid on Seicheprey when his men were in the cruel Toul sector under the guns of Montsec.

Later New Englanders who listened to Clarence talk were less inclined to see him as a wronged hero and in some instances to a better understanding of the division's handicaps as warranting a still higher opinion of its service.

The error was in not having transferred him before the

hundred and fifty days of fighting began. He was the subject of the harsh eliminations in war's cruel gamble and
tests. He would have had still more company in retirement
as younger and more vigorous men, who had earned their
way, took the place of elders if the war had lasted into 1919.

Another of the youngsters was Brigadier General Frank
Parker who succeeded Summerall as commander of the 1st
Division after Summerall, as the reward of his victorious
drives, was promoted to a corps command. Liggett and Bul-
lard to army commands and Dickman, Hines, Menoher and
Muir to corps commands were among the many promotions.

38

For Unconditional Surrender

J.J.P. HAD set October 28 as the date for the general attack, but it was postponed until November 1 at the request of the French Fourth Army, on our left, which was not yet ready. Meanwhile President Wilson, in answer to the German Chancellor's appeal for an armistice on the basis of the Fourteen Points, had continued his negotiations without having communicated with the commander of our army in the Meuse-Argonne battle on the military aspect of the situation.

After these negotiations had been proceeding for more than three weeks J.J.P. was summoned by Foch to attend a meeting of the Allied commanders-in-chief on October 25 to consider armistice terms. Since J.J.P. was somewhat in the dark as to the attitude of his own government he asked if the others were there by authority of their governments.

Foch replied in the affirmative, and that the object was "to render Germany powerless to recommence operations in case hostilities were resumed." He then asked for Pershing's views. Pershing said he preferred to hear from Pétain and Haig, since the French and British armies had been longest in the war and suffered most.

Foch turned to Haig who declared for the immediate evacuation of occupied territory in Belgium and France and also of Alsace-Lorraine, and the surrender of Allied rolling stock seized by the enemy or its equivalent. He said that if the Germans were back on their old frontier the Allied armies would be in a much better position to continue fighting.

Pétain was for stronger terms than Haig: the occupation of the east bank of the Rhine as well as Alsace-Lorraine, the immediate delivery to the Allies of 5000 railroad locomotives, 100,000 freight cars and such prompt withdrawal by the German troops from their present lines that they would leave behind them their heavy guns and ammunition.

Pershing was for unconditional surrender. General Bliss, that soldier champion of peace and disarmament, who was to give his last years to this cause, held the same view. Both thought the enemy would accept unconditional surrender. Both, as we shall see later, were unchanged in their conviction that an acknowledgment of complete military defeat would have been better for the future of Europe.

However, when it was his ideas about an armistice which were asked at the meeting on October 25, Pershing agreed with Pétain's terms, including the occupation of the east bank of the Rhine by the Allies. Also he wanted the surrender of all the German submarines to assure the unrestricted transport of our army home.

On October 30 he had an answer by cable from President Wilson about his proposed terms which he had transmitted to the President by cable. The President would not insist upon the right to continue to send American troops to France during the armistice, though continuing to send supplies. He thought it would be enough to intern the

German submarines in neutral ports. Since this would be an invasion of German soil, he would not occupy the German submarine bases, Alsace-Lorraine or the east bank of the Rhine.

He would have the terms rigid enough to prevent the resumption of hostilities by the German army, but not humiliating enough "to throw the advantage to the military party"—being unaware that both Hindenburg and Ludendorff had told the German Chancellor that the German army was in desperate straits. The President asked Pershing to consult with Colonel E. M. House, his right hand adviser who was now in Paris. On October 30 Pershing wrote a letter for House to present to the Supreme War Council. In this he reviewed the military situation.

Our army was constantly increasing in strength. The morale of the Allied armies was high. German man power was constantly diminishing. In three months the German armies had lost 300,000 prisoners and over one-third of their artillery, "in their effort to extricate themselves from a difficult situation and avoid disaster." The Allies had already 35 per cent superiority in guns and 37 per cent in combat forces over the enemy on the western front. An armistice might enable the German army to withdraw from a critical situation to a more favorable one. German morale might be restored.

"It is the experience of history that victorious armies are prone to overestimate the enemy's strength and too eagerly seek an opportunity for peace. This mistake is likely to be made now on account of the reputation Germany has gained through her victories in the last four years.

"Finally, I believe the complete victory can only be obtained by continuing the war until we force unconditional surrender from Germany, but if the Allied governments decide to grant an armistice, the terms should be so rigid that under no circumstances could Germany again take up arms."

This was all that Pershing had to do with the framing of the armistice terms. As the AEF's commander he had spoken his own frank opinion to his commander-in-chief. Foch, who was actually to be the framer of the armistice terms, had been largely a listener at the meeting of the Allied army chiefs on October 25. His most pregnant remark to them was that "it is not the time to stop, it is the time to redouble one's blows without paying any attention to those he himself receives."

Upon this, of course, all the commanders were agreed. The breaking enemy should be given no breathing spell in which to reform his hard pressed legions and thus prolong the war.

Two of our divisions, the 37th (Farnsworth) and the 91st (Johnston), which had been in the first phase of the Meuse-Argonne, had been assigned to the Belgian army which was now in step with the progress of the Allied offensive on a front of three hundred miles. The 27th (O'Ryan) and the 30th (Lewis) were still with the British army. These four divisions were sharing the more rapid advance as the reward of their effort, and that of their brother divisions in the Meuse-Argonne which was releasing enemy pressure in western France.

For the general attack on November 1 in the Meuse-Argonne we were thoroughly set. Our divisions knew their ground and their tactics. The later arrivals had been trained without the aid of Allied instructors in making the most of the natural American initiative and intelligence. Thus they more quickly adapted themselves to the practice of open warfare in actual battle.

39

On to "Cease Firing"

THE ENEMY still held strong positions above us of which he would make the most. On the west the 78th (McRae) now had Grandpré, and had stormed the heights on the edge of the Bourgogne forest, but the main body of the Bourgogne and the key point of the stubborn little Loges Wood which had resisted all local attacks were yet to be conquered.

Eastward on the whale back we had the Romagne, Cunel and Clairs Chênes heights and the Bantheville, Rappes, Fays, Peut de Faux and Brieulles woods. But ahead were yet the formidable Barricourt heights and woods and other ridges, hills and woods which would be a skillful machine gunner's delight for his nests.

On the other, the east side, of the Meuse we had behind us those irregular wooded heights we had gained, including the tough Richêne hill, but ahead were still more tricky wooded slopes and the Borne de Cornouiller from which the big German guns had lashed our troops on the whale back in flank with their plunging fire.

337

In the center the 89th (Wright) and the 2d (Lejeune) of the Fifth Corps (Summerall) were to drive as a wedge to turn the west flank of the Barricourt heights. In close reserve were the 1st (Parker) and the 42d (Menoher), ready to throw their weight into the attack.

On the right of the Fifth Corps, against the east flank of Barricourt were the 5th (Ely) and the 90th (Allen) in the Third Corps (Hines). The 80th (Cronkhite), the 77th (Alexander), and the 78th (McRae) of the First Corps (Dickman) were to protect the left flank of the Fifth Corps and then strike for Boult-aux-Bois.

With the break of dawn on November 1, under a mighty barrage, our troops began the movement in fine professional precision and zeal. Our gunners had become veteran in practice, the better to protect the infantry. Three batteries of 14-inch naval guns, with navy personnel, sent their shells far back on the enemy's line of communications. Our planes had mastery of the air; and the weather took a favorable turn. More tanks would have been welcome. In the air and on the land, on the background of the shell-torn battlefield and countless fox holes we had won, the terrific orchestra of battle was attuned, the colossal machine of destruction in action.

Nightfall showed success all along the line. At all points we had reached our objectives. Keep on and we should be over the hills and on the downhill side. Only powerful counter-attacks by the enemy could recover the important tactical positions he had lost. But that was not in him. He was now resisting step by step with frequent displays of fatalistic desperation. Here and there we were held up by concentrations of sweeping machine gun fire, but we conquered the nests from which it came.

The 78th had the Loges Wood and the eastern edge of the Bourgogne forest and kept on. The 77th had done its assigned part and the 80th broken through the last of the German prepared defenses on its front. The 89th and the

2d could not be halted by machine gun blasts and took Tailly and had the Barricourt heights and woods. A brigade of the 2d (Colonel James C. Rhea), with the bit in its teeth, broke through the enemy lines and took Germans in their billets.

On the right, the eastern slope of the whale back, the 5th had its objective in Viller-devant-Dun and the 90th reached Villefranche on the second day. Then the two divisions had the heights commanding the Meuse around Stenay, forcing the enemy across the Meuse. By the fifth day the 5th had established bridgeheads at Dun-sur-Meuse.

Across the Meuse our 79th (Kuhn), fighting in liaison with the French Second Colonial Corps, under our First Army command, kept on attacking up hill through the woods until at last it had the Borne de Cornouiller. This gave the 26th (Bamford) its opening to press the enemy into full retreat as its part. The 81st (Major General Charles J. Bailey) relieved the 35th (Traub) after its long trench siege.

It was the first serious battle action for the 81st. Handicapped by lack of animals it had to drag some of its guns by hand, but it overcame strong resistance and captured Moranville Woods and Abaucourt. Attacking again, after meeting a counter-attack it then gained and held Grimaucourt while the 26th had Ville-devant-Chaumont. (Mentioning the names of the many divisions makes detail, but vital detail for the men who fought in them, and strange detail for an American Army in taking these villages and woods with French names three thousand miles from home.)

The 81st formed the connecting link on our First Army's right, with the left of our Second Army now extending the American front past Verdun from the Bourgogne forest to the Moselle River. Our Second Army held the line where our St. Mihiel offensive had been halted to dig in by the diversion to the Meuse-Argonne operation.

Again J.J.P. could look across the plain of the Woëvre toward Metz, Conflans and the Briey iron fields as well as the Sedan-Mézières railroad line as the objectives of that plan he had made sixteen months ago. The First Army's success warranted action by our Second Army (Bullard),— the French Seventeenth Corps, our 33d Division (Bell), the 28th (now commanded by Major General William H. Hay), the 7th (Wittenmyer) and the 92d (Ballou) in the Fourth Corps (Muir) and Sixth Corps (Menoher), with the 35th (Traub) and the 4th (Hersey) in corps and the 88th (Major General William Weigel) in army reserve,—in broadening our offensive to include both armies on a front of nearly one hundred miles.

For J.J.P. had to wait on Foch's consent to our Second Army's attack. He not only had Foch's approval on November 8, but Foch would have him make ready with six divisions under our command to join with the French under General Mangin in an offensive against Château-Salins, November 14. This meant that we should now have a Third Army, Major General Joseph T. Dickman, to be promoted from corps to army command.

Accordingly, on the 8th, immediately after Foch's consent, our Second Army shook the trench mud off its feet on the plain in an offensive which continued until the armistice hour. With a single exception it took all its objectives.

This spread the Allied advance from the North Sea to the Moselle. In the west Ostend, Bruges, Ghent, Lille and Maubeuge had been recovered, German resistance everywhere weakening. Austria had now capitulated in an armistice. Turkey and Bulgaria were out of the war. The sands in the hour glass were running fast.

But Foch was not yet certain on November 9 of the acceptance of his armistice terms. He would have still more powerful arguments to insure their acceptance at his coming meeting with the German delegates. He bade all the commanders-in-chief to expedite and coördinate their movements. When the enemy, "disorganized by our repeated attacks, retreats along the entire front," he appealed for "energy and initiative to make decisive the results obtained."

On the Meuse-Argonne front the rested 42d (now commanded by Brigadier General Douglas McArthur) had relieved the 78th (McRae), after it had concluded its long service in the line, by taking Les Petites Armoises and then advancing more than a mile; and the rested 1st (Parker), which had also been in close reserve, drove ahead with its fresh vigor in place of the 80th (Cronkhite) which had cleared the way by its own sustained and successful attacks.

We had still to meet sporadic last ditch resistance, but the uphill work was over. It was downhill in a foot race of our divisions spreading their front fan-shaped as the enemy tried to reform on the other side of the Meuse. Make the most of fighting weather while it continued. Winter was drawing near. The nights were too cold to sleep on the ground. Never mind sleep in the intoxication of keeping on the heels of the enemy and allowing him no time to about face.

We would not let him hold the opposite bank of the Meuse, not there in the Pouilly bend which was in our favor. Heavy rains had flooded the river; but the 89th (Wright) had elements across on rafts, the 2d (Lejeune) put a regiment across over two bridges it built, and the 77th (Alexander) had patrols across farther on.

Meanwhile Brigadier General Fox Conner, Chief of Operations of the AEF, had given a message approximately as follows to Colonel George C. Marshall of the First Army staff:

"The Commander-in-Chief desires that the honor of entering Sedan will fall to the First Army. He hopes that the First Corps, assisted on its right by the Fifth Corps, will enable him to realize this desire."

341

Brigadier General Hugh A. Drum Chief of Staff of the First Army, passed the message on to the corps commanders with this addition:

"For this purpose boundaries will be disregarded."

By this Drum meant the boundaries between our own and the French Fourth Army according to an understanding which Pershing thought he had with the French.

The ever-driving Summerall of the Fifth Corps, when he received the message, was at the headquarters of the 1st Division. His bold action was contrary to tactical practice. J.J.P. knew nothing of it until later, but forgave it in the glad hour of victory and out of respect to the prestige of the offenders. Summerall ordered the dashing Frank Parker to march the 1st across the rear of the 42d and 77th, much to the confusion of their transport and communications. But neither the 42d nor 77th was to be delayed by such interference in their rush to reach the Meuse in its westward bend.

Young Douglas McArthur of the 42d, which had Sedan in the prescribed sector of its advance, did not propose to share the prize with any sprinting rival when his division was also fresh. At Sedan Napoleon III had surrendered with his army to von Moltke in 1870 in France's disastrous war with Prussia. The 42d reached the outskirts of the city, which was its for the taking, but was halted by French request in order that the French Fourth Army, which was not up with the 42d on its left, might for sentiment's sake have the honor of the occupation in triumphant retaliation for the sad memory of the past.

Meanwhile our 6th Division (Major General George H. Gordon) which had been in close reserve, and now saw the goal of action near, had dragged its guns forward in want of animals, but too late. The German delegates had signed on the dotted line Foch's terms for the thirty-six day armistice: and at 11 A. M., November 11, the "cease firing" brought the silence—a silence which could literally be heard—after more than four years of war's incessant thunder from Switzerland to the North Sea.

J.J.P.'s plan had been fulfilled. We had cut the Mézières railroad line. The Briey iron fields were ours for the taking. In the Battle of the Meuse-Argonne, fighting up hill, ever on the offensive, we had suffered 117,000 casualties out of the approximately 1,000,000 men engaged, compared to an estimate of 100,000 for the enemy, whose forty-two divisions employed had an estimated strength of 470,000. We had captured 26,000 prisoners and 874 cannon.

40

Reversing the Machine

IN THE LIGHT of history no remark of J.J.P.'s told more than the one he made the day of President Wilson's arrival in Paris.

"He has been a good President to us, backed the army well, but he has his hands full now."

J.J.P.'s tone was one of gratitude, personal relief and sympathetic understanding. Once Woodrow Wilson was at war had drawn on our man power and resources to the limit. He had been as stern a fighter as his North of Ireland ancestors in their grim conviction that theirs was the Almighty's battle for the right.

Soon after the armistice, when J.J.P.'s car stopped in the devastated regions, a group of refugees, who had returned to the ruins of their homes, recognized him. Their greeting of "Général Pershaing" was too heartfelt to be noisy.

"You will rebuild better than before," he said, "clear the shell fragments out of your fields, recover them to harvest." They would,—oui, oui, absoluement, certainment.

He warned them to look out for unexploded shells. They said they realized that danger. They would take care. Then, as he turned back into his car, he said:

"How long before their new homes will again be smashed in another war? But that is with the statesmen who make the peace."

The Peace Conference was distinctly the statemen's business, and the fact that he was to have no part in it accounted for J.J.P.'s personal relief. Out of his own experience he foresaw the President's difficulties in his dealings with Lloyd George, Clemenceau and Orlando and all the spokesmen of the other Allies and subject minorities for nationhood in keeping faith with the Presidential doctrine of self-determination.

To the rear also were all the experts of our army staffs, mostly drawn from civil life, who knew Europe beyond the Rhine as well as this side of the Rhine in all its complicated set-up racially, economically and geographically as no group of Americans had ever known it in practical living terms; and they, too, were personally glad they were not to be used at the Peace Conference. They had done their "bits" in uniform. They asked only to be home, back in civil life.

The "peace ship" experts, who had arrived with the President, were to the front now. It was only natural they should think that those who had been in the army were warriors for war's sake and limited strictly to a warrior view. In the noblest of good intentions and in a very ecstasy of anticipation, like that of the soldier who marches away to the front without knowing what war is like, they were to have their disillusioning baptism of fire in the conflict of ideologies and self interests.

The ovations for Pershing upon his arrival in France had carried a plea for the aid of our armed power which had now done its service. Those for President Wilson as he rode through the avenues of cheering throngs in Paris,

London and Rome, carried a plea for his prestige in behalf of their nationalistic aims in the Peace Conference.

But J.J.P.'s soldier pride was doubtless a little hurt that his commander-in-chief did not visit our battlefields. The President did not even see the fox holes in Belleau Wood in our first siege of attack, or go a little farther from Paris to see the additional thousands of fox holes and the machine gun nests up ridge after ridge which had been conquered in the Meuse-Argonne. This oversight also hurt the pride of the soldiers who had fought that he should have his hour of triumph on the threshold of his own battle for his League of Nations. He may have missed an opportunity for his most memorable address. That of Lincoln was made on the battlefield of Gettysburg.

President Wilson arrived in Paris when the thirty-four day period of the first Armistice was about to expire. Now the Allies occupied the east bank of the Rhine. The enemy had surrendered many arms and much material. The Armistice must be extended before the Peace Conference met.

Three times it was to be extended, each time after the previous one had left the enemy more helpless. In the consideration of the final military terms General Bliss, a member of our Peace Commission, represented us in conference with Foch and Haig. Foch favored allowing the Germans an army of 100,000; Haig of 250,000 with fortifications on the German eastern frontier.

Bliss, who had been for unconditional surrender, had worked out a study in which he concluded that on the basis of population the Germans were entitled to an army of 450,000, with fortifications on both frontiers. He said that either you had to kill all the Germans or else make their young republic, formed on the remains of the extinct Hohenzollern empire, a self-respecting nation which should be the bulwark against the threatening spread of Bolshevism from Russia. He would have general limitation of armaments by all the Powers and take Germany into the League of Nations subject to her paying a war indemnity for the damages she had done on Allied soil. And he was ever on the watch against our army being held in Europe as a police force.

Finally in that conference Haig said wearily, "Let them (the French) have their way." That set the German army limit of 100,000. Pershing's views had already been expressed at the end of October the only occasion he was asked for them. He was for unconditional surrender, for a complete military victory.

Afterward, on his way to Trèves, when the terms of the first Armistice were being carried out, his car had passed through the belt of devastation. Jagged walls threw their shadows over the débris of towns and villages. Slashed, ugly, blackened trunks of trees stood above the shell-torn areas of what had once been pleasant growing woods and forests. Then the signs of destruction diminished.

At length his car was out of the scarred lands of the victors into the unscarred lands of the vanquished. For it was the victors who had known war in all its horrors of invasion, of houses, schools, churches and cathedrals as targets, while the vanquished had fought on the victor's soil.

J.J.P. remarked the contrast between the unharmed Trèves and the wreckage of Ypres, Arras, Rheims and Verdun. Ahead his soldiers were marching on to the Rhine occupation through a peaceful land which had not known a single shell-burst.

The point was not that he thought the enemy should suffer equivalent destruction in eye-for-eye and tooth-for-tooth reprisal. It was that the enemy soldiers had marched back with colors flying, and bands playing, as though in a triumphant homecoming. There had been no public acknowledgment of military victory as soldier to soldier,—no "We surrender. You have beaten us. It is all over now." To that the victor might have replied in professional tribute, "You made a mighty fight. The world was against you and too strong for you." Thus the enemy could have had no future alibi. He was visibly, admittedly down in the ring from a knock out blow after the count of ten.

As it was, he could build up a false psychology that the German army had not been actually defeated, but tricked by successive armistices in gradually weakening it to impotence, the German people tricked by the false promises of President Wilson's "Peace Without Victory," only to be unrepresented at the Peace Conference until their delegates were summoned to sign the Versailles Treaty.

All this was bound to be helpful in forwarding the ambitions of Adolph Hitler. The old Austrian Empire of 115,000,000 people, which had been a counter balance to the German, was broken up into small nations which might be struck in detail by the body of 65,000,000 Germans who had been left in an intact nation.

Possibly if the basis for peace had been set in 1918 by the unconditional surrender of general to general the world would not have been worse off than it was in the late nineteen-thirties. Secretary Baker's tribute to Pershing's vision as a commander possibly might be broadened to include that of a statesman in this instance.

There in J.J.P.'s car at Trèves, on that November afternoon of 1918, after he had received a shower of congratulations from kings, presidents, premiers and generals of all the Allied world, mention was made of how military victory had opened the door to the White House for other generals as well as Washington, Jackson, Harrison, Taylor and Grant. His reply was that of one who already measured and discounted this prospect. He spoke with the detachment of a third person about himself.

"My country trained me as a soldier. I have had the fortune to lead its army to victory. That is enough."

The statesmen would frame the peace terms, but his own task was not yet finished. His soldiers were still under his command, he was responsible for their conduct and welfare until they went up the ships' gangways homeward bound. "They may feel I am still hard on them after the war is won. Not one who is sick or wounded should fail to recover, get sick, for want of proper care or foresight or lack of discipline. Not one who might carry back an infectious disease shall leave France until he is cured. That I owe to them for their future as citizens. I will send a clean army home."

On the way to Trèves when he saw some of his soldiers were still on the Meuse-Argonne battlefields his eyes flashed fire.

"Still in the lousy, stinking dug-outs to get influenza and pneumonia. I thought I had settled that with Foch. They must be moved at once."

Foch had commanded that our troops remain on the battlefield after the first Armistice. He wanted them ready in case the Germans should renew the war when it expired. Upon receiving the order from Foch there was rage at GHQ. A chief of staff section wrote a savage note for J.J.P. to sign, revised it into a more polite one which was only ugly in its indignation, to say the least.

Then the word was passed that J.J.P. had called for his car. He was going to see Foch. Perhaps Foch had misunderstood the situation. Perhaps someone on his staff had sent the order which he had not seen. Here was another one of those vital matters which had best be settled in personal conference. It was evident enough that with the Allies occupying the bridgeheads of the Rhine our army could be marched from billets in the rear of the battlefield in time to meet any possible German action.

Later word was passed that "Foch is trying it on us again." He requested that our soldiers should be put to work clearing up the débris of the devastated regions as laborers. J.J.P.

349

made this "statesmen's business." Secretary Baker's reply was a prompt negative. If it had not been, doubtless J.J.P. would have made an effective protest which would have brought reconsideration.

A group of admirers high in the AEF got together with the idea of giving The Pershing Presidential candidacy a start. His apparent initial receptiveness to any friendly suggestion, which was often deceptive, might be construed as indicating with becoming modesty that he was "in the hands of his friends."

To them Grant's misfortunes in the Presidency were no criterion in Pershing's case. Pershing had studied law, he had seen much of Washington politics, he knew men, he had been a great executive of a vast combined military and industrial organization, and he had had a statesman's part in his conduct of relations with the Allies. The promoters would have him leave others to see his army embarked for home. He should return to Laclede, mix with the home folks and establish a background for further grooming as a candidate.

There may have been moments then and later when the temptation appealed to him. He may even have been shown the water and smiled as though it looked fine to him, but he refused even to dip in his fingers. The truth was that at the time the people at home were weary of the war and all its associations. There was no glamor left in its wake. His soldiers still felt the galls from the iron harness of his discipline.

If he had curried popular favor by relaxing that discipline during the war it might have made him more popular in the terms of a Presidential candidacy, but more of them might have been sacrificed. If he had been really and adaptably receptive after the Armistice, the iron commander might have warmed in ingratiating talks to his soldiers and eased restrictions in giving everybody a good time. But that was not in his nature or his sense of duty.

One may wonder as to the result as one asks: "What if he and not Warren G. Harding had succeeded Woodrow Wilson as President?"

His real answer to the planners, who would have him return to Laclede, was in remaining with his army. In his address to his soldiers on November 12, he had said:

". . . Our armies, hurriedly raised and hastily trained, met a veteran army, and by courage, discipline and skill always defeated him. Without complaint you have endured incessant toil, privation and danger. You have seen many of your comrades make the supreme sacrifice in order that freedom may live. I thank you for the courage and patience with which you have endured . . .

"These things you have done. There remains now a harder task which will test your soldierly qualities to the utmost . . . You will meet this test as gallantly as you have met the tests on the battlefield . . . Whether you stand on hostile territory or the soil of France, you will so bear yourself in discipline, appearance and respect for civil rights that you will confirm for all time the pride and love which every American feels for your uniform and you."

The great military and industrial machine from ports to front had to be reversed. The organization of the SOS, with its now spare supplies, was ready to hand for Herbert Hoover for the succor of starving central Europe. Soldiers arriving on transports at Brest saw only the shore. Without landing, after all their drill looking toward being "over there," they made the return voyage. They were the first to arrive for the home welcome while home enthusiasm still ran high. It had quite died down by the time the veteran divisions of the Rhine occupation greeted the Statue of Liberty after their long absence.

Our Allies were not so interested in supplying ships for our second as they had been for the first crossing in the crisis of the war. Our soldiers had to endure the long winter nights in billets in barns or houses of French villages while they were enriching the stores in French stockings by spending their pay. They must have drill and entertainment to occupy them. J.J.P. was paternally watchful from the ports to the Rhine.

From the embarkation camp at Brest no man went aboard ship except in absolutely clean clothing and past rigid medical inspection. Those who might be tempted by brothels as a last fling in France were denied the privilege, in spite of the appeal of the Mayor of Brest, who said that among his constituents now were many charming and perfectly healthy ladies of pleasure who had come from Paris in expectation of a flourishing business.

The French Government would distribute a shower of ribbons of the Legion of Honor among officers of its own selection. But J.J.P. objected to this. Experience had shown that the selection might be based on political or propagandic favoritism. We should be consulted as to the recipients. The choices should rest with our own boards as in the case of our own medals.

One day an expert statistician brought J.J.P. the record of all our divisions in miles marched, in losses, in prisoners and material taken and miles gained. J.J.P. glanced through the paper, and then pushed it aside in the characteristic fashion which we all knew meant positive rejection out of his knowledge and experience. How could all the human and other imponderables be included in such a listing? How express the nature of the obstacles overcome? One division might have gained little ground and fought better than another which gained more. It might have had better leadership.

He held no malice over past disagreements with Allied statesmen and generals. Each had been acting in his own

352

country's and army's interest as he saw it. There were amiable exchanges of good will in which the Pershing smile was not thin-lipped.

Majestic martial display had its part in the victory parades. Alphabetically as America, and not as the United States, our picked regiment, with its massed flags, led the way under the Arch of Triumph in Paris. The memory of the West Point precision combined with a veteran conviction with which it marched is one that may well remain in Europe as an example of what the United States could do in making a great army if it must. And J.J.P. himself, who had received all the high decorations the Allies could bestow upon him as commander-in-chief, wore only the ribbon of our Distinguished Service Medal upon his reception at home.

Congress conferred upon him the rank of General of the Armies. More than a possibility is envisioned in saying that if the war had lasted into the summer of 1919 he would have been the Allied generalissimo. I recall that the first suggestion of this came from Colonel Adalbert de Chambrun soon after Pershing had won his point in the Abbeville Conference.

"That General of yours has a very masterly way with him," said de Chambrun. "At the rate he is going as his army gets stronger his position will be stronger. There will be no resisting his will or the trend of the situation."

Through the winter of 1918-19, if the war had continued, J.J.P. would have been further training and reorganizing his army. There would have been promotion for officers and privates who had proven themselves in the test of the Meuse-Argonne. We should have had more young division commanders. Some reserve officers would have become regimental commanders with general's stars beckoning to them.

Our program at home and abroad had looked forward to 1919 as the year in which we should be able to make our full power felt in France. This was Pershing's outlook in July, 1917, in his cable to the War Department after he learned what we had to do to win the war. The urgent appeal of Foch and the Allied statesmen in the Château-Thierry crisis to President Wilson stressed sufficient American reinforcements to hold the Allied front in 1918 and then to gain the victory in 1919.

At home our new shipyards would be launching ships for transport. We should have the flow of the mass production of planes, Liberty motors, guns, machine guns, gas, all the weapons and material from our new plants. The 80-division program would have given us an army almost equal to the combined British and French armies with their weakened man power.

J.J.P's original plan was based on our striking the decisive blows in 1919. President Wilson, who lost his patience in his "If we were only dealing with reasonable people," would have insisted that more authority accompany graver responsibilities. The futile Archangel and Siberian expeditions were specific examples of waste effort in political adventures.

Secretary Baker had had the truth from Pershing on his visits to France and in Bliss' confidential letters about bickerings among the Allies and within the councils of each Ally. These were in contrast with our unity of purpose and the one-two-three delegation of authority from the White House to the headquarters in France.

Under the inevitably heavy casualty lists, once we were bearing the brunt of the fighting, our people might not have rested content that our men remain under Allied command. Secretary Baker's confidence in Pershing was established. Baker was not given to swapping a tried for an untried horse in crossing a stream. Pershing had detachment from European nationalistic aims. He was straight. He kept his word. He would have been more acceptable than a Frenchman to the British and their Dominions, and more acceptable than a Briton to the French, as supreme commander.

When this prospect was broached to him, apparently it had not occurred to him. He said:

"That is speculating very far ahead. Foch was an able commander. There would have been cooperation."

41

Quiet Days

GENERAL OF THE ARMIES over the door way identi-
fied the occupant of a suite of offices on the second floor of
the old State, War and Navy Building after his return to
Washington. At one end of a great high-ceilinged room
he placed his desk under the light of the tall windows,
with pictures of scenes from the AEF on the walls.

In his fifty-ninth year, still erect and vigorous, he should
have many years before old age was upon him. His fame and
prestige inevitably made him much sought after and en-
tailed certain responsibilities. There were engaging widows
who thought it was a pity he remained single and would
not be indifferent if asked to relieve him of his loneliness.

In order that he should better be able to maintain his
position, Secretary Baker had taken care that he should
receive all the pay and allowances of a four-star general for
life. The young lieutenant who had spent all his accumu-
lated pay on leave after an Indian campaign, had never
been much concerned about money. It was in the ethics
of the service to live simply as it was to keep fit.

He was bound to be subject to many appeals and offers to capitalize his name. It would carry weight as an honorary chairman or on any board of directors. As the president of a great corporation he could be assured of a large salary leaving active management to others. But it was not in the nature (or inclination) of one so used to command to serve in the rôle of a figurehead of that kind. Destiny had placed him under a continuing obligation. He had an unwritten contract to be worthy of the honor that had come to him, an unwritten contract with the soldiers who had served under him and with his country to fulfill in dignity before the army and the country. Lee's quiet conduct after defeat had set an example for him after victory. He was to remain the somewhat remote figure to the American people, popularly known as the iron commander, but to be held in increasing respect.

When he accepted President Coolidge's appointment as a delegate to the Tacna-Arica conference, his friends were surprised and regretful that he should be drawn into any arbitral part in the old ticklish and bitter territorial dispute between Chile and Peru. Surely there was nothing to be gained for him. He would be the subject of pinpricking irritations to try his patience when success seemed hopeless.

"The President asked me to go," he said. The President was his commander-in-chief.

A young professional diplomat, who was attached to the mission, was alarmed at the prospect. He foresaw the stiff-necked soldier, seeking to dominate the highly sensitive Latin-Americans by his military manner. On the contrary, he had the revelation of J.J.P. as a most courteous listener, painstaking in informing himself of all angles of the dispute and most considerate of all amenities. The conferees all liked him though they could not come to an agreement then; but he had done much to prepare the way in a better feeling which later brought a settlement.

357

And J.J.P. had not yet finished his task in France. He had in mind the heterogeneous array of monuments erected on the battlefield of Gettysburg by Northern States and veteran associations, which ruin the impressive effect to the eye. It would even seem that the size if not the ugliness of a monument to a regiment was a measure of its part in the battle.

We were on the way to spatter monuments in the same fashion in France. J.J.P was far from agreeable to such a messy tribute in memory of the AEF. Soil was valuable to the French peasants for growing crops. Moreover, France's landscape ·was her own. Pershing saw eye to eye with the French government in its conclusion that it could not continue to allow an unlimited spread of American monuments which gave the impression that Americans had done most of the fighting on the western front.

Congress confirmed the appointment of the Battle Monuments Commission under Pershing which should have full authority. The bodies of our soldiers who fell in France— those whom their relatives did not want brought home— were to be gathered in cemeteries on the sites of the main battlefields. In characteristic deliberate care and thoroughness he sought designs suitable for monuments in the spirit of the whole which should rise above the fields of white crosses in a worthy landscape setting.

In summer he went to France to watch over the progress of the construction. Any visitor would always be shown by an attendant the location of the grave of son, husband, brother or father who had paid war's final price as a soldier. France in its pride of its art and taste would have a permanent reminder for future generations that we were "over there" in 1917-18.

Meanwhile Pershing was writing his memoirs. There were many suggestions that others with the writing gift should save him labor. But he would have no ghosting, though he consulted those who had been close to him in command and submitted parts of the manuscript to them, and in some instances the whole. He was writing all himself, writing and rewriting slowly. It was to be his account. He was commander-in-chief. Friends wondered if he would ever have that book finished. "I am getting on with it," he would say.

Time was friendly, no driver to make him its slave, as it was in the days when he was driving his army. He could afford to be late without Colonel Boyd, eye on that confounded clock in his office at Chaumont, trying to maneuver him away from finishing the problem in hand.

Colonel Adamson, his veteran confidential secretary, who had gone to France with the rank of a field clerk, was a fixture at a desk in the reception room of the Washington office. Adamson could hold out no assurance that the General would be in time for an appointment which was a social call. He knew the General was coming over that morning, but he was not quite certain as to the hour.

J.J.P. lived at his club. He went out so rarely to large dinners that lion hunting hostesses gave him up as a dead loss. He avoided all formal functions except those at which he thought it was his duty to appear. He chose to be with friends. His fondness for dancing still held, and he liked to think he would never be too old for that. He was not displeased that a charming young woman should find him welcome as a partner, especially if she danced well.

Out of that cruel tragedy of the fire at the Presidio his son Warren had survived. It had been a gracious thought of Secretary Baker when he sent Warren, then a boy, with an army sergeant after the Armistice, on a visit to his father in France.

Later, when father called on Warren at his preparatory school, father's was an understanding smile upon learning that son did not want to walk across the campus with him,

as that was putting on just too much side. And then Warren
was in college. Father was most gratified with his son's progress, though he never told son so in flattering terms.

"He is a good, straight boy, and getting on well in his
studies. What's more, he is well liked." (Father's judgment
of son was correct. Warren was to be voted the most popular
man in his class on graduation.)

Sometimes J.J.P. telephoned that he would not be at
the office at all, but wouldn't you come to lunch. On one
occasion he said, "I hope you don't mind my inviting S——
to sit with us. He always seems so lonely about the club."

S—— had done important service at home in the war,
but it had not been much recognized. He had become somewhat prolix in his technical enthusiasm as a scientist, and
therefore a bit of a bore whom others were inclined to pass
by with a pleasant greeting without inviting further conversation.

Inevitably, in the course of the luncheon, some persons
in the dining-room came over to the General's table to
greet him or recall themselves to him. This day one was a
Franco-American of considerable wealth who entertained
a good deal in Paris.

"General," he said, "I am hoping that when you come
to Paris next summer you will dine with me to meet
Marshal Foch, whom I know quite well."

Pershing replied that he lived very quietly in France,
was much preoccupied with overseeing the progress of the
battle memorials, and rarely went out to dinner. After the
prospective host had withdrawn, he said, "As if I hadn't
met Foch!" Of course the invitation to Marshal Foch would
have been to meet General Pershing.

This recalls J.J.P.'s reference to a visit to Foch. An invalided French soldier as chauffeur met the former commander of two millions of American soldiers in France at
the station and drove him in an antiquated automobile to
the little chateau where the Generalissimo of the Allied

armies spent his declining years. The two had a delightful talk in the glow of the bright side of their mutual reminiscenses.

The years passed. J.J.P. had turned the three score and ten mark before the publication of his *My Experiences in the World War*. This is great history, for all time the faithful, indispensable textbook of the command of the AEF which no American can know too well. Naturally there was much it would not occur to him to say about himself. The close-knit narrative in the logical processes of his mind sometimes takes too much knowledge for granted on the part of the lay reader.

The completed manuscript for the printer, after the many copyings, bore many corrections and interlineations in his own hand. He noted that a representative of his publisher had the Distinguished Service Cross in his buttonhole.

"How did you get that?" J.J.P. asked.

"Oh, I was lucky," was the reply. "Some one was kind."

"No one got that in the AEF," said J.J.P. emphatically, "unless he deserved it."

He had established a routine of life. In summer he would be in France overseeing the work on the war memorials; in the fall and spring in Washington; in winter in Arizona. Harbord frequently joined him in Arizona. On the way to and from Arizona he would stop over in Laclede. As he once said, his eyes sparkling, "Why, I can just smell I am near Missouri as I approach the border." His sister, Miss May Pershing, lived quietly in Laclede, not inclined to go far afield to bask in the "reflected glory" of her famous brother. His mother had lived to see him a marked man in the Army and content he had not studied law.

In his office in Washington, as in France, he would rise

and turn away from his desk to look out of the window in thought when some idea or problem gripped his attention, and, one judged, sometimes to suppress emotion which would otherwise have brought the brimstone flash into his eyes.

He did this one day when the name of a certain American came up. His eyes were the steel grey. It was still in his mind that this man had favored the French view of the infiltration of our troops into the French army. Such an attitude on the part of a French statesman or general was quite understandable, but J.J.P. could never quite forgive it on the part of a fellow countryman. This was one controversial point of the past which he did not include in his "But that's threshing over old straw."

It was said of him that he had mellowed with age. He was happy that his soldiers with the passing of time had come to appreciate the object of his discipline.

In mind is a reserve officer in whom some example of it, of which he was a victim, had aroused a bitter personal animosity. He had longed for the chance to tell the cold, heartless brute just what he thought of him.

"Come on and meet him," was the suggestion one day when this veteran of tough drill, marches and battle was in Washington.

"Alright, I'll try to be polite, but I'll not promise, now I am no longer under his orders, but a free citizen, not to get in a thrust for the sake of auld lang syne."

Any thrust was parried by the handshake and the greeting he received. The impression left on him was that of a delightful veteran reunion. He had met the Pershing with blue lights in his eyes whom others had known when he was off duty before his stern consecration to his task in France.

A memorable occasion for those present was the anniversary dinner of the sailing of the pioneer staff to France when he was the host to the Baltic Society formed from its members. As J.J.P. came into the room, and Harbord greeted him, someone remarked, "You seem to know each other already." There was no rank, no medals worn at the dinner. Privates, field clerks and generals—"we" of the Society—were enjoying a family reunion. There were a few speeches, but none by J.J.P. When one speaker remarked that, after all, the Commander-in-Chief really loved his soldiers, Harbord responded that he did not always take care to let them know it. And J.J.P. smiled.

Another year and another year passed. Clemenceau and Joffre were long since dead. Taps had also been sounded for Foch, Haig and Mangin. Lloyd George survived as a lonely free lance without a following in the Commons. But Pétain still lived to welcome J.J.P. back to France. The monument on the Romagne heights of the Meuse-Argonne had been dedicated—the task of the battle memorials practically finished.

Then came the word that General Pershing was near death in Arizona. Throughout the land there was instant response. People of all classes were intent for the latest bulletins. It seemed today and then tomorrow that he could last only a few hours longer. The funeral train was being prepared ready to bring him to Washington. We pioneers of the Baltic Society were included among those who received notes of inquiry as to who would be present so he might be assigned places in the funeral procession. But J.J.P. won this battle, too.

The following summer, rather against his doctor's advice, he went to France. There were still some details about the battle memorials which required his attention as a reason for going. He returned looking better than when he went.

The War Department had been moved from the old State, War and Navy Building, leaving it entirely to the State Department. But ambassador emeritus Pershing's office was undisturbed with the faithful Adamson still on duty. The General of the Armies came to his office occasionally from the Walter Reed Hospital where the doctors held him in a suite to correct "a little rheumatic complication." He had daily rides and walks, but cavalryman Pershing had had to give up horseback riding.

Another European war had come. He followed it closely. General George C. Marshall, the Chief of Staff, brought him the latest information and maps. He asked questions as incisive as those in GHQ days.

There is a memory of a talk at the Walter Reed Hospital which ran back to the days of Caesar's commentaries, Caesar's bridge over the Rhine and Roman wars and dealings with the Germanic tribes. Again they had to be beaten by force of arms. There was reference to the controversies among the Allies with which he had been so familiar in 1917-18. "Probably they're having their troubles now, but they will stick together," he said.

A reference to the Armistice terms and the Versailles Treaty with relation to the present situation brought this response: "You know what my views were,"—which have been already given.

Colonel Charles A. Lindbergh had just made a speech which had drawn not only controversial fire but even extremist charges that he was pro-Nazi.

"It's too bad. A fine boy, a great flyer. But he has got mixed up in politics, which he knew nothing about," said the canny son of Laclede who always drew the line between what was the soldier's and the statesman's business.

"Well, General, this is reminder that you are the only hero we have left and we hope you will take care."

He threw back his head in a burst of relishing laughter, with the reassurance that he did not think there was much danger now of his getting off the reservation. And "There's the record," as he was given to saying about the AEF. January 10, 1940.

42

Over There In Spirit

"BUT STILL I DO NOT UNDERSTAND," said J.J.P. when I rose to go in my call on him after my return from the battle in northern France which followed the German invasion of May 10, 1940. "Please sit down. Go on! I want to hear more."

Now all the battlefields his army had won in 1917-18 were in the possession of the enemy whom it had fought. The Germans held Paris, they were over the Loire. Their swift onrush had completed the military downfall of France in thirty-seven days. The survivors of the British army had escaped from Dunkerque to an all but defenceless homeland.

General Pershing, back in his little sitting room in the hotel apartment, looked in better health than when I had seen him while he was having a "check up" in the Walter Reed Hospital, before I went to Europe. Yet I had a singularly good reason for keeping faith with the established habit of his friends not to overtax his strength by over-arousing his interest in any subject, which was

365

becoming more high pitched on that of the French disaster with his "But still I do not understand" as the prelude to more penetrating questions.

Early in the war he had expressed his firm confidence in the French army. His view of it, however, in his latest visit to France after his partial convalescence from his illness, had been subject to the honors and courtesies paid to his prestige, rank and age by high French officers and officials. He was under the reminiscent spell of the French army of Joffre, Foch, Pétain, Mangin and Gouraud, of the British army of Haig and Rawlinson, of the French army of the Marne and Verdun, and of the British army of Mons, Ypres, the Somme and its mighty concluding drive from Roye in 1918. His loyalty to old friends and his faith in them extended to old brothers in arms.

It was hard to explain the contrast in the French army when it was at its best in the first world war with that in the "phony" period of the second while the German army was massing and training in the winter of 1939-40 on the Franco-Dutch-Belgian frontier. Soldiers and people had trusted to the Maginot Line to lock the door against invasion. French soldier morale slipped into indifference in its inactive defensive role for six months before the launching, May 10, of the German martial avalanche for which this softening process had prepared the way.

Having emphasized this contrast, I told J.J.P. of the journey I had made late in April from the Meuse River in the region north of the Marne, south to the Belgian frontier and on to the Atlantic coast, which had little secondary defense back of the front line.

French and British divisions were in a position along the Belgian frontier to rush to the support of Belgium and Holland immediately they were attacked. The object of this was political rather than military in the long range aim, in which Paris and London were really united, to bring the United States into the war. Not to go to the aid of the little low countries would estrange American sympathy.

But the Belgian and Dutch army staffs had refused any confidential conference with the Anglo-French staffs to plan for coöperation in such an emergency. This foreboded a further complication against the timing and unity in the integration of German air power, armor and infantry when the Anglo-French armies, in spite of their supposed unified command, were without cohesion as a whole or within themselves.

The Germans released actually not one but two coordinate avalanches. That through the low countries, after quickly crushing Dutch resistance, drove the disjointed French, British and Belgian forces before it. Then, after the surrender of the Belgian army, it drove on to Dunkerque.

At the same time the other avalanche, having broken through French resistance on the Meuse, had wide-open opportunity in the practically defenseless area to which I have referred. It had little difficulty in protecting is flanks to drive on to the Atlantic Coast. Thus the French army in northern France was cut in two parts, preparatory to the envelopment of both, and driving the British army into the sea. Then the southward German movement sped past the rear of the Maginot line, leaving its useless guns pointing in the opposite direction.

Such in its rough outline, as I knew it and told it to J.J.P., was the German plan, which was as classic in its simplicity in making the most of skillful execution as the triumph of Miltiades at Marathon, Hannibal at Cannae, or Napoleon at Austerlitz with the latest weapons of their times.

When I resumed my seat, in response to what was literally an order from my old commander, I continued to do my best clumsily out of my limited observation and information in further analysis. But still he said that he could not understand.

What he did not understand, and I venture to say possibly no military historian will ever quite understand, is how such errors could ever have been committed on the Allied side in sacrifice of the unchanging principles of war. How could it ever have happened that a French army, with its immortal traditions, which boasted a total of five millions of men, including its trained reserves, could have been so quickly driven in rout across France?

When finally I rose to go J.J.P. was standing as erect and resolute as in dark hours in France. The steely flash was in his blue-gray eyes as he said:

"I wish I had been over there with my GHQ and the divisions we had from Cantigny and Château-Thierry to the Meuse-Argonne."

He had deep sympathy for Marshal Pétain, who was caught with the remnants of an exhausted army against overwhelming forces when France turned to the old Marshal too late to save the day. Pétain was all soldier, no politician, to J.J.P., who recalled how in a conference Pétain had said to Foch, "But this is the statesman's business.".

On the field of battle Colonel Pétain had risen in World War I to command of the French army. When he had received its command, after the mutiny following the bloody disaster under Nivelle in the Spring of 1917, he had restored its morale.

Not Foch, but Pétain was the hero of the French soldiers. He had been more than a personal friend to J.J.P. His influence had been back of the American commander's insistence upon time for thorough training and the independence of the American army in a crisis of the fortunes of the first AEF.

And Pétain at eighty-four, older than J.J.P. by four years, was now as good as prisoner of the Nazis, and called pro-Nazi for trying to hold a section of France, from which he could be expelled if Hitler gave the word to two armored divisions. Pershing agreed with Secretary of State Hull and President Roosevelt in their policy in relation to the value of the venerable Marshal's role in the Vichy government for its value as foothold in intelligence and in keeping touch with secret resistance groups. Above all, it was not in J.J.P. to distrust a brother-in-arms whose mettle and honor had stood the test in a common cause.

Not only did J.J.P. say he wished he had been over there, but he changed the tense to say he wished he were over there now with his GHQ. If he could not understand how the downfall of France had happened in such swift, appalling disaster, I understand how his spirit was over there with his pioneer staff in the wish that he could again form an army to help recover the battle fields won from the Kaiser to be lost to Hitler.

Singled out in my recollections of J.J.P. is the shock at the physical change in him when I saw him at the annual dinner of the Baltic Society in May, 1941. It seemed as though suddenly he had become a very old man.

As usual, General Harbord sat on his right, and around the table generals and colonels were mixed with privates. On his left was his former aide, cavalryman George S. Patton Jr. He had given Lieutenant Patton the opportunity to turn to steeds of steel in place of those of flesh in the days of the primitive tanks in 1917-18. Patton now had command of an armored division in our expanding army on the home drill grounds. He gave us a talk in which he stressed the importance of discipline in a way in which the disciple evidently won the approval of the old master. Later Patton showed us some pictures of his division at

work with characteristic pungent commentary and **pungent** answers to our questions.

J.J.P. had excused himself to go home early. We knew that he had come against the advice of his doctor. Before he went he said that he would like to give next year's dinner himself "providing . . ." and the rest was not quite audible to me but intimated it was subject to his realization he was on borrowed time and to the course of world events.

His stoop, his feeble steps, as he withdrew, suggested that whatever the course of events in the warring world he might not be alive on the next anniversary of the day of his departure in 1917 for Europe on the steamer Baltic. But his resilient vitality had fooled doctors too many times for them to make any prophecies about how long it would hold out.

Because J.J.P. walked with a cane did not limit his keeping touch with the progress of the war, and particularly the forming of our army under General Marshall, Chief of Staff. Captain Marshall, one of his finds in France, rising to be a Brigadier-General, had been second to Brigadier-General Hugh Drum in the planning and operations of the Battle of the Meuse-Argonne.

When the choice was between the two as to which one should become Chief of Staff and thus become the wartime Chief in our greatest war, the nod of Pershing in Marshall's favor in addition to Marshall's more agreeable appeal to President Roosevelt is generally accepted as having been decisive. Drum's friends and admirers thought he was the stronger and sounder man of the two. In the gamble of war, which excites the gamble for personal power and promotion in the armed services, it was Drum's lot, after his service in training and command, to be classed as too old for field command and retired as a lieutenant general.

Those close to J.J.P. were given to saying that Pearl Harbor had extended his borrowed time. Now that the war had become our war his interest in it was accordingly intensified. His spirit would triumph over the weakening flesh to see it through to victory. In following its progress he had not only France mapped in his mind from personal service but also Manchuria and Japan and the Philippines as familiar backgrounds in which to watch the moves.

By his wish there should not be another dinner of the Baltic Society until the war was won. Anniversary dinners were not in order for the Spartan iron commander when all energies should be centered on winning the war. His shoulders were less bent, his steps not so feeble as they had been. If he could not be in the war, the son who had survived the fire, which caused the death of his wife and his other two children, would be fighting in the father's place.

The General's eyes would twinkle and his face light with pride as he told again how Warren had called him up early in the war preparations. Warren was hesitant, confused and diffident about what he had to say. It was the same Warren who when J.J.P. visited him at school said, "Father, I hope you will not mind if I don't walk back across the campus with you. It's too much swank."

J.J.P. had not pressed his desire that Warren should go to West Point. The choice was with the son who chose a civil career. When Warren was at Yale the father said, "He's a fine boy. I'm proud of him and it's good to hear that he is well liked." When Warren was told of this remark he observed, "Father never said that much to me." Later Warren was voted the most popular man of his class at Yale.

"Come on! What's all this about?" the father said while Warren groped for words over the telephone.

When Private Pershing reported to four-star General Pershing that he had enlisted in the Army J.J.P. was as pleased as though he himself had received another star. Son wanted father not to use any influence on his behalf and it took no further argument to get the assurance he need not worry on that score. Escaping publicity Warren worked his way up until he was a major, after having been with the First Army from Normandy to the Elbe.

"He doesn't say much about himself," Father would remark, "but I think he is making a good soldier."

43

Seeing It Through Again

In WORKING OUT THE CONSPIRACY of friends, experts and in the army itself, in guarding Pershing's health to enable him to live to see the war through, the doctors thought this could best be done by his return where he could be under their intimate attention to Walter Reed Hospital, set in its spacious grounds with all its facilities. A little apartment of a small sitting room, entry hall and bedroom was specially prepared at the hospital. He became concerned about his being the subject of such favoritism as a spectator in the rear in wartime. So the thing to do was for the caller to express the common view of the veterans who had served under him that he should have these quarters, always stressing how little room he really occupied.

Here there was no sound except the fountain outside his window in the grounds. Here in his easy chair he could read the communiqués from the fronts, and the letters which Colonel Adamson brought to him and the answers

373

to letters which he still signed in the same clear hand, if not as firm as when he was ten years younger. From time to time letters summoned distant memories of his long career. One day he had one enclosing a clipping about his Indian fighting days. He lived with that as a young cavalryman.

It was in the Fall of 1942, when I mentioned the huge army we already had under arms, he exclaimed in the change of subject from the West in the eighteen-eighties to France in 1942, "Where is that huge army?"

He put the question in a flash of impatience, closing the subject as I rose to go. After the huge army had been in training for two years, longer than it took in 1917-18 to form and send an army of two millions to France to end that war, army battle action overseas had so far been limited to the Bataan defense and MacArthur's small forces in later counter offensive action in the Southwest Pacific.

Our landing in North Africa was the answer to his impatience and to Eisenhower's. He did not know Eisenhower well. Eisenhower had never directly served under him. His own choice for the European command would have been General Lesley McNair, who had won his laurels as a tactician in the first AEF. I know that McNair, who had been the home drillmaster-in-chief of our huge army at home, was also Marshall's choice. In the Army many would have favored Krueger, who later became MacArthur's right hand. Eisenhower, too, had a German name, but Krueger had been born in Germany and come with his parents as a boy to the United States. All three, McNair, Krueger and Eisenhower, had proved themselves to be masters in war planning. Eisenhower was President Roosevelt's choice, one agreeable to Prime Minister Churchill, one who was both diplomat and tactician, the popular "Ike."

Once Eisenhower was chosen, J.J.P., as one who himself had borne the burden of the day as commander-in-chief, understood how Eisenhower in turn alone knew the problems with which he had to deal as the arbiter of controversies in responsibility for the final decisions. My impression was that, as J.J.P. saw it, he favored by-passing Italy with the closed ports, once she had yielded, instead of undertaking the laborious and costly land campaign up the peninsula; and also that he favored striking directly across the English channel. But again any such opinion would be subject to the qualification that General Eisenhower knew the military situation, his was the task and he was subject to over-all political influences. It was not in J.J.P. to turn arm-chair critic when remote from the scene of action.

Pershing's support of the schools to inculcate the handling of "large formations" never minimized to him the importance of service with troops. He put a world of meaning into his "He knows troops." In his judgment of an officer this was a prime essential, which no academic training could replace, whether in command of a hundred or a million men.

When the name of one of the commanders in World War II who had served as a youngster under him, was mentioned, he might nod or say, "He's a fine officer." Higher praise from him was "He's a fighter," which he paid in forecast in the training period to some of his disciples of the first AEF. Still higher praise was in "He's a fighter—a fighter," which I knew meant, with the progress of action, more than that the man was a gallant soldier, more than that he was an aggressive leader in the field. It meant that he had a combination of the all around qualities of initiative, training, judgment and experience in knowing how to strike and when to strike and strike hard, which fitted him for battle command.

Higher praise yet, the highest in the Pershing lexicon was "He's a fighter—a fighter—a fighter." There was a pause of reflection before the first repetition of the word and a longer one before its second repetition. That reflection seemed to sum up his knowledge and analysis of the man's record and potentialities in that economy of words which became more characteristic of the silent commander-in-chief in his later aging years. I recall that among those who received the triple tribute were MacArthur and Patton, as though their successes were in line with what he had expected of them. Mention of Marshall, his choice, brought the simple, conclusive "He's a great Chief of Staff."

With every passing month in the war one more for him beyond the eightieth birthday, he remained on, summer and winter, in his apartment at the hospital. A soldier who had obeyed orders, and demanded his own should be obeyed as a commander, he was a patient who obeyed the orders of the doctors who understood, however, the psychological value in the therapy in his case of letting him have his way about certain things. Smoking was out, but he was not denied a little Bourbon, with which his friends saw to it he was well supplied.

He had paid his last brief call to his office. The time came when he was no longer able to take a brief ride in his car in fair weather. He received fewer of his friends, those personally close to him or his career as a soldier, and these on his "good days." In the double sense General Harbord, his great right hand in France, was doubtless closest to him. His friendship with Charles M. Dawes antedated Dawes' service under him in France. Dawes, five years his junior, made trips to Washington to see him.

Age inclined Dawes more and more to exercise his conversational gift. Dawes saved J.J.P. from having to do much talking himself and entertained him. His fondness for Charlie included a sense of Charlie's histrionics, which he expressed when he remarked that Charlie's upside down pipe was all right, but he was carrying it a little far when he took it out of his tail pocket at a full dress dinner party.

The report got around that J.J.P. had become senile, or say "gaga" or "balmy." For example, when General de Gaulle called on him, he was said to have asked de Gaulle when he had last seen Pétain. That was not quite the way the question was put, but it was put in a way that had a subtle edge to it of which J.J.P. had always been quite capable. It was reminding de Gaule that Pétain of Verdun was also a French soldier and had been Pershing's brother-in-arms, who had stuck it in France in her disaster and done his service to his country as he saw it. And maybe J.J.P. did not like de Gaulle, whom President Roosevelt had found very "difficult," and of whom Churchill once said that he found the Cross of Lorraine the hardest cross he had to bear.

J.J.P. had his prejudices, but how far he was from senility appeared in such flashes as his remark in August 1944. It was then that the triple tribute was in order both for MacArthur in his making good on "I will be back" in the Philippines and for Patton in his lightning campaign in France. J.J.P. had lived to see our old battle fields in France and cemeteries of our dead who fell under him being recovered.

I called on him after having been to the Pentagon, flush with elation while the Anglo-Canadian armies were sweeping up the French coast, Hodge's First Army was driving toward the West Wall and Patton's on past Paris to the Meuse. High and lower officers at the Pentagon were saying the war would be over any day. The planning body was being rushed with a "must" to have its re-

377

deployment point system ready for application not later than October 1.

But Patton was being stopped, whether or not from faulty support, in front of Metz on ground which J.J.P. knew from his own experience. J.J.P. said that he hoped in the hard fighting to come General Eisenhower would not be handicapped by lack of supplies as he had been in his own final drive. Very hard fighting, including that of the Bulge, was to come before the unconditional surrender ten months later, fulfilled his wish to live until the hour of victory.

But what about the other wish, as the corollary of victory for him, which had also been said to share in keeping him alive: the wish that he might be flown abroad to see the sons of the first victors which had won the second in their triumph. He would like to salute the new veterans marching past in review, when he was not equal to leading them as he led his own.

One care of his friends had been to cheer him on in this illusion through the war. Would he now insist upon going against the doctors' advice, as he had upon his trip to France after the all but mortal stroke of illness in Arizona? What if he said he was a soldier and used to taking a soldier's chances, and if he never arrived, or arriving he never returned, that would be a fitting end for him?

Nature, however, had answered the question in the helplessness of his flagging strength, which his will could not combat. One side of his body was paralyzed. It was no longer a cane for him, but he had to be lifted in and out of bed. Surely it was only a matter of hours, if not days, before his death. But again he fooled the doctors. The heartbeats which had become very faint became stronger.

His sister, Miss May Pershing, came from Missouri to remain near him. His happiness was in her devotion and in Warren who had enough points for discharge and came often from New York to see him. General Pershing now was taking his orders from the doctor, from his sister, from Major Pershing and Colonel Adamson.

Until, in spite of strong sentimental protests, his office with all its personal mementos was moved by arbitrary official order two years after the end of World War II to the Pentagon, it remained as it was the last time he visited his last official headquarters.

Colonel Adamson, veteran secretary and confidant through more than three decades, occupied the unchanged outer room, saying "Good morning, General" when J. J. P. opened the door under "The General of the Armies."

Under that title J.J.P. of the old war outranked all the five-star generals of the new war. Marshall, MacArthur, or Eisenhower with his five stars, was not General of the Armies but General of the Army. It was not their desire or in the mood of Congress to create the rank of Field Marshal in the Army of the United States when Washington, Grant, Lee and Pershing had never been so named. It had been long since Pershing had been in uniform, but were he to choose it was in his discretion to add another star to his constellation. In time, though Army circles will still have the fact in mind, the public will be no more concerned about how many stars Pershing had than Washington or Grant or Lee; or MacArthur, Eisenhower than Paul Jones, MacDonough, Perry, Farragut, Dewey or Nimitz.

Colonel Adamson kept in touch with the care of the cemeteries of the dead of the first AEF in France by the Battle Monuments Commission. He reported the substance of messages and letters which would interest J.J.P., who liked to hear that the veterans who had served under

379

him and old friends and associates had not forgotten him.

His sister read the news to him. Having lived to see the war with Japan won, he was still interested to know the progress of events in a post-war world more troubled than after that of World War I. On his good days his mind was clear and active. But the silences of the silent commander grew longer, on the shortening borrowed time, as he waited for the long silence.

After the stroke which paralyzed one side of his body his still observant eyes, in the consciousness of his frailty, could not fail to note the shock which his friends could not always conceal at the sight of his crippled state. I preferred not to submit him or myself to the strain, but to remember him as the athletic Captain Pershing with whom I had tramped over the Manchurian hills and as he grew to his task in France in his strength, and in his limitations which were frequently a source of strength. It was good to know that he suffered no pain as he slipped away to the last second of his borrowed time.